BOATMAN'S
HANDBOOK

THE NEW LOOK-IT-UP BOOK

BOATMAN'S HANDBOOK

by Tom Bottomley

Hearst Marine Books/New York

EMERGENCIES ▶

SAFETY ▶

SEAMANSHIP ▶

PILOTING ▶

WEATHER ▶

ELECTRONICS ▶

RACING ▶

AMENITIES ▶

SOURCES ▶

GOVERNMENT ▶

TABLES ▶

MAINTENANCE ▶

CONTENTS

FOLLOW THE ARROWS ▶

To find desired information quickly, place your thumb at the arrow for the appropriate section, and flip through the pages to the matching tabbed page edges in the book.

EMERGENCIES ▶

SAFETY ▶

SEAMANSHIP ▶

PILOTING ▶

WEATHER ▶

ELECTRONICS ▶

RACING ▶

AMENITIES ▶

SOURCES ▶

GOVERNMENT ▶

TABLES ▶

MAINTENANCE ▶

Library of Congress Catalog Card Number: 84-81082

ISBN 0-688-03925-1

Printed in the United States of America

First Edition

1   2   3   4   5   6   7   8   9   10

BOOK DESIGN BY ARLENE GOLDBERG

INTRODUCTION

Ten years ago Tom Bottomley and I started talking about a tight little book full of necessary boating facts—some that weren't vital, but good to know about.

If you love boats and the water, you acquire knowledge about them. Some of it is practical information, some of it is lore—facts to yarn about on a rainy weekend. Some of the information may come in useful someday. Some of it you work with all the time, and some is in the back of your head, waiting to be recalled when needed.

So we talked about it, and Tom started putting it together, and when it came out people said, "It's a natural." You can tell how good a book is by the letters you get—people saying "You ought to put this and this in the next edition," or "Are you sure about that?" or "I remember one time when . . ." That's what they always say about *Boatman's Handbook.*

The first time Tom and I went cruising together, for a long weekend aboard the little sloop *Merrywend,* was a cruise just made for this little book. We had an emergency: One of our friends aboard got so seasick you could have named a new color, dismal green, after his face. (See page 15 for this book's notes on seasickness.) A couple of the crew started singing folksongs that evening. Well, Tom didn't include a tape with this new edition, but the idea for the Amenities chapter probably came out of that songfest.

In the intervening decade *Boatman's Handbook* has gone through three editions and the government has started changing all the black buoys to green (and changed a lot of other rules, mainly by international agreement and mainly for the better). Technical safety standards have improved—which reminds me: If you are really serious about your boating, it's a good idea to join the American Boat and Yacht Council. That's the outfit (see page 198) which sets the standards for boats and equipment. Each new *Boatman's Handbook* keeps up with the changes. Like good cognac, it just keeps improving.

Some things stay the same, of course. The weather seems to change but the patterns are the same, the signs are the same, and your ability to predict it may improve at times or take a setback. A great short course in weather—and easy to read—is Tom Bottomley's chapter in this very book. It's good middle-of-the-week reading—and makes for a sort of weekend insurance policy. Not that Tom tells you how to guarantee the weather—just how to know enough about it in advance to enjoy it or avoid it.

If I was sitting in the lee of the longboat and you asked me "What books should be in that tiny little bookshelf aboard *Wumpus*?" my answer would be, "First, *Chapman's*, and second, *The Boatman's Handbook*." And I would add, "Of course, Tom has been working on all the recent editions of *Chapman's Piloting, Seamanship & Small Boat Handling*, enjoying boats, running powerboat races, and playing the bagpipes, so no wonder *Boatman's Handbook* has class!"

—JOHN R. WHITING

1.

EMERGENCIES

Safe boating practices minimize the danger of accidents afloat; indeed, recreational boating is one of the safest of all participant sports. However, the prudent skipper should know what to do in an emergency. Study this section; have your spouse or other regular crew members study it so the right steps will be taken if you are not present or are incapacitated. Make regular "man overboard" and "fire"drills a part of your safety routine.

MAN OVERBOARD

Here are steps to follow if someone falls out of, or off, your boat:

1. *Post a lookout.* It is imperative that the person in the water be kept in sight at all times, or at least the spot where he was last seen. Designate a specific crewman to do nothing but act as this lookout. At night, keep a search- or flashlight on the person.

2. *Throw over a life preserver.* Throw the man overboard a life ring, buoyant cushion, or other buoyant device, even though he may be a strong swimmer. A water-activated strobe light attached to a life ring is extremely effective at night.

3. *Don't let anyone jump in the water to help,* except in the case of a small child or elderly or handicapped adult. In such a case, be sure the rescuer takes a life ring or other buoyant device with him.

4. *Maneuver to return* to the spot where the person fell overboard. Determine *in advance* whether turning to port or starboard is fastest. Stopping and backing down may be the fastest for some boats, but this should be done *only* in daylight, and *only* when the person in the water can be seen clearly. *Never* back down over the spot where a person went down! If you are alone, note your compass heading, and turn back 180 degrees on the reciprocal heading. Otherwise, follow the signals of your lookout. Sailboat operators should carry out man overboard drills from a variety of headings in respect to the wind, in order to minimize confusion and loss of time in a real emergency.

5. *Use additional markers.* In some circumstances, particularly at night, it may be helpful to throw over additional buoyant objects to ensure that the path back to the victim can be traced.

6. *Maneuver for the pick up.* In some cases, you can approach from windward of the victim, and let the boat drift down toward him, providing a lee. In most cases, however, it is best to approach from leeward in order to avoid having your boat blow right over the victim. Just slight amounts of power will be needed to keep your boat under control. A sailboat should approach nearly on the wind so that it can luff up to stop headway when the victim is reached. In any case, stop the boat a short distance from the victim, and throw him a light line, such as a ski tow rope, that floats. It is less hazardous than trying to maneuver your boat right up to him.

7. *Get the victim on board.* If necessary, have a man who is physically able ready to go into the water to assist the victim. This crewman should take a light safety line with him. A transom-boarding platform is a help in getting the victim aboard, or a boarding ladder can be rigged. A line with a large loop, tied with a bowline, may be hung over

the side to provide a foothold or handhold. Be sure the propeller is stopped whenever there is a person in the water near the stern of the boat.

8. *Call for help if necessary.* If the victim is not rescued immediately, get on the radio with the urgent communications signal Pan to summon assistance from the Coast Guard, marine police, and nearby boats. Continue the search until the victim is located or you are released by a competent authority.

EXPLOSIONS AND FIRES

Fires on a boat are serious, but usually they can be brought under control if you act quickly and your boat is properly equipped with the required portable or fixed extinguisher systems.

Explosions

1. In the case of an explosion, be ready to go over the side. Grab a life preserver, if possible.

2. When clear of danger, check about and account for all those who were aboard. Render such assistance as you can to anyone burned, injured, or without a buoyant device. Keep everyone together to facilitate rescue.

Fires

1. If possible, apply the extinguishing agent by:
   a. Using a fire extinguisher,
   b. Discharging a fixed smothering system, or
   c. Applying water to wood or materials of that type.

2. If practical, jettison burning materials.

3. Reduce the air supply to the fire by:
   a. Maneuvering the vessel to reduce the effect of wind. It is generally recommended that the boat be turned into the wind, as the fire is usually aft; this allows persons on board not needed for fighting the fire to assemble on the bow.

    b. Closing hatches, ports, vents, doors, etc., if the fire is in an area where this action will be effective.

4. Make preparations for abandoning your boat:
    a. Put on lifesaving devices, and
    b. Signal for assistance by radio or any other means available.

LEAKS AND DAMAGE CONTROL

The circumstances of suddenly taking on water are so varied as to permit only the most generalized advance planning, but in most cases, the following steps to be taken by the skipper may be effective:

1. Immediately switch on all bilge pumps. The risk of harm to the pumps by running them dry is far less than that of having water in the bilge get a head start. Turn them off as soon as you are sure they are not needed.

2. Assign members of the crew to operate manual bilge pumps, if necessary.

3. Assign a member of the crew to inspect for leaks, to pull up floor boards and check the bilges, if necessary.

4. If the boat is taking on water, turn helm over to another crew member, and take charge of the damage-control actions. In most cases, the boat should be slowed or stopped to minimize inflow of water; in some cases, a hole may be kept above water by remaining on plane.

5. If regular pumps, manual and electric, do not handle influx of water, stop your engine, shut the water intake seacock, transfer the water intake to the bilge and restart the engine so its water pump is also drawing water from the bilge. Note: There must be enough water flowing in the bilge to meet the engine's cooling needs, and caution must be exercised to prevent debris from being sucked into the cooling system.

6. If possible, cover the hole from the outside with canvas, bunk sheets, towels, or any other material available. Lash

or nail it in place. It may be possible to nail boards over the hole, or a piece of tin from a can, to reduce leakage. On fiberglass or aluminum hulls, clinch the nails over from the inside to prevent the patch from falling away from the hull. The object is to restrict water flow to an amount that can be handled by your pumps.

7. Call the Coast Guard for assistance if you have a radiotelephone, or display one or more of the distress signals described in Figure 1.1.

DISTRESS SIGNALS

Accepted forms of distress signals have been written into the various Rules of the Road or related Pilot Rules. They are illustrated in Figure 1.1.

RADIOTELEPHONE DISTRESS PROCEDURE

1. If a radio is so equipped, activate the Radiotelephone Alarm Signal.

2. Give the distress signal Mayday three times.

3. Give your boat's name and call sign three times.

4. Give particulars of your boat's position (latitude and longitude, if in the open sea, or true bearing and distance in miles from a known geographical position).

5. Give the nature of the distress, the kind of assistance required, the number of persons aboard, and any other information that would facilitate rescue.

FIRST AID

Injury or Ailment	Treatment
Burns	Treat for shock. Relieve pain and prevent contamination. Avoid greasy ointments.

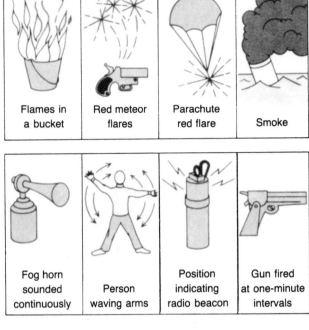

Figure 1.1

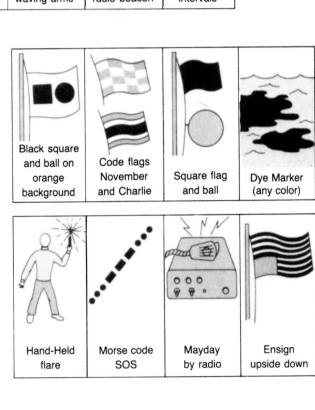

Convulsions Seek medical aid. Restrain patient from self-injury.

Cuts Place a thick gauze pad over the wound, bandage snugly with adhesive strips. Minor cuts—wash with soap and water, dry, and dress as above.

Electrocution Apply mouth-to-mouth resuscitation. Treat for shock.

Fainting Lower the patient's head, loosen the clothing and sprinkle the face lightly with cold water. If the patient does not respond, summon medical aid immediately. Keep the person warm.

Fever Apply cold head compresses. Rub the body with a mixture of 50 percent alcohol and water. Keep the patient in a bunk or bed and have him take aspirin or hot tea.

Fractures Seek medical aid. Keep the patient lying down and warm. Do not move him if spine or skull fractures are suspected. If the patient must be moved, immobilize any broken limbs with splints.

Heat Exhaustion Shade the patient; have him lie down with his head low. Wrap him in a blanket; give him a cup of strong coffee or tea. Seek medical aid.

Jellyfish, Man-of-war, etc., Stings Rinse the area with fresh water, wash with soap (green germicidal soap if possible) and apply a household ammonia.

Seasickness Stay in fresh air if possible and breathe deeply. Move, stay busy. If vomiting, take liquids as soon as possible afterward.

Shock The patient should lie down and remain quiet. Keep him warm, but not perspiring. Raise his feet if he feels faint; raise his chest and head slightly if breathing is difficult.

◀ **Figure 1.1** Distress signals are contained in both the Inland and International Rules. These are the ones that are officially recognized, but in an emergency a skipper can use any means possible to summon help. In the United States this includes flying the national ensign upside down.

Figure 1.2
ARTIFICIAL RESPIRATION

Every boatman should have a working knowledge of the principles of artificial respiration. When the need for it arises, there is no time to search for instructions or to study each step while at the same time attempting to apply the treatment. A boatman who has familiarized himself in advance with one of the accepted methods is more likely to work with calm assurance, saving precious minutes that could mean the difference between success and failure.

Through the courtesy of The American National Red Cross,

we reproduce below the simplified illustrated methods they advocate. In recent years, the mouth-to-mouth method, illustrated in steps 1 to 5, has come into widespread use. Recognizing, however, that some rescuers cannot or will not apply this method, the Red Cross includes instructions for the older manual chest pressure—arm lift (Silvester) and back pressure—arm lift (Holger Nielsen) methods. Study carefully the additional instructions at the bottom of the page applicable to all methods.

If victim is not breathing, begin some form of artificial respiration at once. Wipe out quickly any foreign matter visible in the mouth, using your fingers or a cloth wrapped around your fingers.

MOUTH-TO-MOUTH (MOUTH-TO-NOSE) METHOD

Tilt victim's head back (1). Pull or push the jaw into a jutting-out position (2).

If victim is a small child, place your mouth tightly over his mouth and nose and blow gently into his lungs about twenty times a minute. If victim is an adult (3), cover the mouth with your mouth, pinch his nostrils shut, and blow vigorously about twelve times a minute.

If unable to get air into lungs of victim, and if head and jaw positions are correct, suspect foreign matter in throat. To remove it, suspend a small child momentarily by the ankles or place child in position shown in 4, and slap sharply between shoulder blades.

If the victim is adult, place in position shown in 5, and use same procedure.

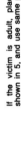

MANUAL METHODS OF ARTIFICIAL RESPIRATION

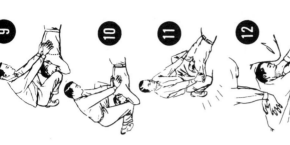

Rescuers who cannot, or will not, use mouth-to-mouth or mouth-to-nose technique should use a manual method.

THE CHEST PRESSURE-ARM LIFT (SILVESTER) METHOD

Place the victim in a face-up position and put something under his shoulders to raise them and allow the head to drop backward.

Kneel at the victim's head, grasp his wrists, cross them, and press them over the lower chest (6). This should cause air to flow out.

Immediately release this pressure and pull the arms outward and upward over his head and backward as far as possible (7). This should cause air to rush in.

Repeat this cycle about twelve times per minute, checking the mouth frequently for obstructions.

If a second rescuer is available, have him hold the victim's head so that the jaw is jutting out (8). The helper should be alert to detect the presence of any stomach contents in the mouth and keep the mouth as clean as possible at all times.

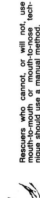

THE BACK PRESSURE-ARM LIFT (HOLGER NIELSEN) METHOD

Place the victim facedown, bend his elbows, and place his hands one upon the other, turn his head slightly to one side and extend it as far as possible, making sure that the chin is jutting out. Kneel at the head of the victim. Place your hands on the flat of the victim's back so that the palms lie just below an imaginary line running between the armpits (9).

Rock forward until the arms are approximately vertical and allow the weight of the upper part of your body to exert steady, even pressure downward upon the hands (10).

Immediately draw his arms upward and toward you, applying enough lift to feel resistance and tension at his shoulders (11). Then lower the arms to the ground. Repeat this cycle about twelve times per minute, checking the mouth frequently for obstruction.

If a second rescuer is available, have him hold the victim's head so that the jaw continues to jut out (12). The helper should be alert to detect any stomach contents in the mouth and keep the mouth as clean as possible at all times.

RELATED INFORMATION FOR ALL METHODS

If vomiting occurs, quickly turn the victim on his side, wipe out the mouth, and then reposition him.

When a victim is revived, keep him as quiet as possible until he is breathing regularly. Keep him from becoming chilled and otherwise treat him for shock. Continue artificial respiration until the victim begins to breathe for himself or a physician pronounces him dead or he appears to be dead beyond any doubt.

Because respiratory and other disturbances may develop as an aftermath, a doctor's care is necessary during the recovery period.

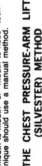

Sunburn Relieve discomfort from a mild burn with olive oil or petroleum jelly. If the burn is severe or the victim feels sick, seek medical aid and treat as for a regular burn.

Sunstroke Have the person lie down with his head elevated. Loosen the clothing and keep the victim in shade. Give no stimulants and seek medical aid.

Based on Chris-Craft Boatman's Guide: First Aid
See the "Boating Safety" section for information on first-aid kits and their contents.

ACCIDENTS

In case of collision, accident, or other casualty involving a boat subject to federal law, the law requires the operator, if and so far as he can do so without serious danger to his own vessel or persons aboard, to render such assistance as may be necessary and practicable to other persons affected by the incident in order to save them from any danger that results. The operator must also give his name and address and the identification of his vessel to any person injured and to the owner of any property damaged.

A written report of the accident is required if the incident results in death or an injury that requires medical treatment beyond first aid, the disappearance from a vessel under circumstances that indicate death or injury, or if there is property damage totaling more than two hundred dollars. If death occurs within twenty-four hours of the accident, or a person has a reportable injury or disappears from a boat, the report must be made within forty-eight hours; otherwise, it must be made within ten days of the accident.

Most state boating laws require that these reports be made to a designated state office or official. In the absence of such a state provision, the report should go to the Coast Guard officer in charge, marine inspection, at the Coast Guard office nearest the site of the accident.

Written accident reports should contain the following:

1. The numbers and/or names of the vessels involved.

2. The locality where the accident occurred.

3. The time and date when the accident occurred.

4. The weather and sea conditions at the time of the accident.

5. The name, address, age, and boat-operating experience of the operator of the reporting vessel.

6. The names and addresses of the operators of the other vessels involved.

7. The names and addresses of the owners of the vessels or property involved.

8. The names and addresses of any person or persons injured or killed.

9. The nature and extent of injury to any person or persons.

10. A description of damage to the property (including vessels) and the estimated cost of repairs.

11. A description of the accident (including opinions as to the causes).

12. The length, propulsion, horsepower, fuel, and construction of the reporting vessel.

13. Names and addresses of known witnesses.

2.

SAFETY

Boating safety requires carrying equipment to be used in an emergency, as well as operating precautions to prevent emergencies. Here are your basic requirements:

TOOLS AND PARTS

1. **Tools for on-board repairs should include:**
   Set of combination open-end/box wrenches in $\frac{7}{16}$, $\frac{1}{2}$, $\frac{9}{16}$, $\frac{5}{8}$, $\frac{11}{16}$, and $\frac{3}{4}$ inch sizes.
   10-inch open-end adjustable wrench.
   Screwdriver assortment, including one for Phillips heads.
   Pair of slip-joint (ordinary) pliers.
   Pair of sharp diagonal-cutting pliers.
   Vise grip or locking plier-wrench.

1. **On-board spare parts:**
   Vee belt for each size used on engine(s), matched-belt pairs, if such are used.
   Water-pump impeller (for inboard engines).
   Set of spark plugs (for gasoline engines).
   Fuel pump and strainer, fuel filter elements if separate filters are installed.
   Distributor cap, rotor arm, condenser, breaker-point set.

At least two spares for each type fuse used aboard the boat.

FIRST-AID KIT

The container for your first-aid kit should be plastic; avoid a metal that could rust, or cardboard that could soak up moisture. Seal it with tape to keep it moisture-tight, but do not lock it. The kit should contain both the following simple instruments, and consumable supplies:

1. **Instruments:**
   Scissors, small and sharp. If there is room for two pairs, one should be of the blunt-end surgical type.
   Tweezers, small, pointed. Tips must meet exactly to pick up small objects.
   Safety pins, assorted sizes.
   Thermometer, inexpensive oral-rectal type, in a case.
   Tourniquet. Use only on major bleeding that cannot be controlled by pressure; follow instructions *exactly.*
   Eye-washing cup, small, metal.
   Cross Venti-breather device to aid in mouth-to-mouth resuscitation.
   Hot water bottle.
   Ice bag.

2. **Supplies:**
   Within reasonable limits, substitutions can be made to reflect local availability or personal preferences.
   Bandages, 1-, 2-, and 4-inch sterile gauze squares, individually wrapped. Bandage rolls, 1 inch and 2 inch. Band-Aids or equivalent, assorted size, plus butterfly closures.
   Triangular bandage, 40 inches, for use as sling or major compress.
   Elastic bandage, 3-inch width, for sprains or splints.
   Adhesive tape, waterproof, 1 inch and 2 inch by 5 or 10 yards.
   Absorbent cotton, standard size roll.
   Applicators, cotton-tipped individual swabs, such as Q-tips.

Antiseptic liquid, such as tincture of iodine or Merthiolate.

Petroleum jelly, small jar.

Antiseptic ointment, 1-ounce tube of Bacitracin or Polysporin, or as recommended by your doctor.

Antiseptic-anesthetic first-aid spray, such as Medi-quik or Bactine.

Nupercainal ointment, 1-ounce tube.

Pain killer, aspirin or related compounds.

Sleeping pills, Seconal or equivalent as prescribed by your doctor.

Antibiotics, for use *only* if there will be a delay in reaching a doctor and infection appears serious. Use ampicillin, cephalosporin, or similar drug as prescribed by your doctor.

Ophthalmic (eye) ointment, small tube of Butyn sulphate with Metaphen.

Antihistamine, Pyrabenzamine tablets, or as prescribed by your doctor.

Ammonia inhalants.

Seasickness remedy, Dramamine, Marezine, Bonamine, or Bonine tablets or suppositories.

Anti-acid preparation, liquid or tablet.

Laxative.

Antidiarrhea drug, 3-ounce bottle of Paregoric (prescription required) or 8-ounce bottle of Kaopectate.

First aid manual.

FIRE EXTINGUISHERS

The type and number of fire extinguishers required for boats of each class are shown in Table 10.2. (See "Government Requirements" section). In choosing those for your boat, you will find the following information valuable:

Classes of Fires

Fires are classified into three categories:

Class A—fires in ordinary combustible materials such as wood, paper, cloth, etc., where the "quenching-cooling" effect of quantities of water or solutions containing large percentages of water is most effective in reducing the temperature of the burning material below the ignition temperature.

Class B—fires in flammable petroleum products or other flammable liquids, greases, etc., where the "blanketing-smothering" effect of oxygen-excluding media is most effective.

Class C—fires involving electrical equipment where the electrical conductivity of the extinguishing media is of first importance.

Fire Extinguishers

Fire extinguishers are classified on the same A, B, and C systems as are fires. Some types of extinguishers, however, have a suitability greater than their basic classification. Extinguishers required by law on boats are in the B category, but a carbon-dioxide or dry-chemical extinguisher will also have value in fighting an electrical (C) fire. On the other hand, a foam-type B extinguisher is effective on ordinary Class A fires but is *not* safe on Class C electrical fires. Boatmen should remember that for typical Class A fires in wood, paper, or bedding, the popular dry-chemical extinguishers are *not* as suitable as an ordinary bucket of water.

Fire extinguishers should be distributed around the boat in relation to potential hazards. One should also be near the boat's control station where it can be grabbed quickly by the helmsman. Another should be mounted near the skipper's bunk so that he can roll out at night with it in his hand. Other locations include the galley *(but remember that water is best on a stove alcohol fire)* and any other compartment at some distance from the location of other extinguishers. Fire extinguishers should be mounted where they are clearly visible to all on board as they move about the boat.

It is important to keep in mind that the small extinguishers usually carried on boats normally discharge the extinguishing agent for only *eight to twelve seconds,* and then are empty.

BILGE VENTILATION

All boats, including auxiliary sailboats that use gasoline as a fuel for propulsion, generating electricity, or mechanical power, must have proper ventilation for every engine and fuel compartment, unless the boat is of "open construction." To qualify as a boat of open construction, a vessel must meet all of the following requirements:

1. As a minimum, engine- and fuel-tank compartments must have fifteen square inches of open area directly exposed to the atmosphere for each cubic foot of *net* compartment volume. (Net volume is found by determining total volume and then subtracting the volume occupied by the engine, tank, and other accessories.)

2. There must be no long or narrow unventilated spaces accessible from the engine- or fuel-tank compartments into which fire could spread.

3. Long, narrow compartments, such as side panels, if joining engine- or fuel-tank compartments and not serving as ducts, must have at least fifteen square inches of open area per cubic foot through frequent openings along the compartment's full length.

Boats not of open construction built prior to July 31, 1980, must have at least two ventilation ducts fitted with cowls at their openings to the atmosphere for each engine and tank compartment. An exception is made for fuel-tank compartments if each electrical component in the compartment is "ignition protected," in accordance with Coast Guard standards, and fuel tanks are vented to the outside of the boat.

The ventilators, ducts, and cowls must be installed so that they provide efficient removal of explosive or flammable gases from bilges of *each* engine and fuel-tank compartment. Intake ducting must be installed to extend from the cowls to at least midway to the bilge or at least below the level of the carburetor air intake. Exhaust ducting must be installed to extend from the lower portion of the bilge to the cowls in the open atmosphere. Ducts should not be installed so low that they could become obstructed by a normal accumulation of bilge water. See Figure 2.1.

To create a flow through the ducting system, at least when under way or when there is a wind, cowls (scoops) or other fittings of equal effectiveness are needed on all ducts. A wind-actuated rotary exhauster or mechanical blower is equivalent to a cowl on an exhaust duct.

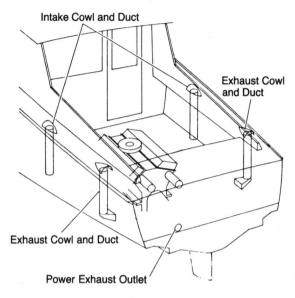

Intake Cowl and Duct

Exhaust Cowl
and Duct

Exhaust Cowl and Duct

Power Exhaust Outlet

Figure 2.1 Natural ventilation system used on some older boats has two intake and two exhaust ducts with cowls. Exhaust ducts lead low, where fumes tend to sink.

Lack of adequate bilge ventilation can result in an order from a Coast Guard boarding officer for "termination of unsafe use" of the boat.

Ducts Required

Ducts are a necessary part of a ventilation system. A mere hole in the hull won't do; that's a vent, not a ventilator. "Vents," the Coast Guard explains, "are openings that permit venting, or escape of gases due to pressure differential. Ventilators are openings that are fitted with *cowls* to direct the flow of air and vapors in or out of *ducts* that channel movement of air for the actual displacement of fumes from the space being ventilated."

Size of Ducts

Ventilation must be adequate for the size and design of the boat. There should be no construction in the ducting system that is smaller than the minimum cross-sectional area required for reasonable efficiency. Where a stated size of duct is not available, the next *larger* size should be used.

Small Motorboats.   To determine the minimum cross-sectional area of the cowls and ducts of motorboats having small-engine and/or fuel-tank compartments, see Table 2.1, which is based on *net* compartment volume (as previously defined).

Cruisers and Larger Boats.   For most cruisers and other large motorboats, Table 2.2, which is based on the craft's beam, is a practical guide for determination of the minimum size of ducts and cowls.

Ducting Materials

For safety and long life, ducts should be made of nonferrous,

Table 2.1
Ventilation Requirements for Small Powerboats

NET VOLUME CUBIC FEET	TOTAL COWL AREA SQUARE INCHES	ONE-INTAKE AND ONE-EXHAUST SYSTEM MINIMUM INSIDE DIAMETER FOR EACH DUCT (INCHES)	TWO-INTAKE AND TWO-EXHAUST SYSTEM MINIMUM INSIDE DIAMETER FOR EACH DUCT (INCHES)
Up to 8	3	2	
10	4	2¼	—
12	5	2½	—
14	6	2¾	—
17	7	3	—
20	8	3¼	2½
23	10	3½	2½
27	11	3¾	3
30	13	4	3
35	14	4¼	3
39	16	4½	3
43	19	4¾	3
48	20	5	3

Note: 1 cu. ft. = 0.028 cu. m; 1 inch = 2.54 cm; 1 cu. in. = 6.45 cu. cm

Table 2.2

Ventilation Requirements for Large Powerboats

TWO-INTAKE AND TWO-EXHAUST SYSTEM

VESSEL BEAM (FEET)	MINIMUM INSIDE DIAMETER FOR EACH DUCT (INCHES)	COWL AREA (SQUARE INCHES)
7	3	7.0
8	3¼	8.0
9	3½	9.6
10	3½	9.6
11	3¾	11.0
12	4	12.5
13	4¼	14.2
14	4¼	14.2
15	4½	15.9
16	4½	15.9
17	4½	17.7
18	5	19.6
19	5	19.6

Note: 1 foot = 0.305 m; 1 inch = 2.54 cm; 1 sq. in. = 6.45 sq. cm.

galvanized ferrous, or sturdy high-temperature-resistant nonmetallic materials. Ducts should be routed clear of, and protected from, contact with hot engine surfaces.

Positioning of Cowls

Normally, the intake cowl will face forward in an area of free airflow under way, and the exhaust cowl will face aft where a suction effect can be expected.

The two cowls, or sets of cowls, should be located with respect to each other, horizontally and/or vertically, so as to prevent return of fumes removed from any space to the same or any other space. Intake cowls should be positioned to avoid pick-up vapors from fueling operations.

Air for Carburetors

Openings into the engine compartments for entry of air to the carburetor are in addition to requirements of the ventilation system.

Requirements for Newer Boats

On boats built after July 31, 1980, each compartment having a permanently installed gasoline engine must be ventilated by a powered-exhaust blower system unless it is open construction as defined before. Each exhaust blower, or combination of blowers, must be rated at an airflow capacity not less than a value computed by formulas based on the net volume of the engine compartment plus other compartments open thereto. The installed blower or blowers must be tested to prove that they actually do move air at a rate determined by other formulas also based on compartment volume. See Figure 2.2.

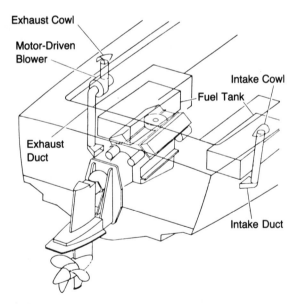

Figure 2.2 Blowers are required equipment on new boats and must be operated before the engine is started. If, in an exhaust duct as shown, they should not interfere with the functioning of the duct as a natural ventilator.

The engine compartment, and other compartments open to it where the aggregate area of openings exceeds 2 percent of the area between the compartments, must *also* have a *natural* ventilation system.

There must be a warning label as close as practicable to the ignition switch that advises of the danger of gasoline vapors and the need to run the exhaust blower for at least *four minutes* and then check the engine compartment for fuel vapors *before* starting the engine.

Natural ventilation systems are also required for any compartment containing both a permanently installed fuel tank and any electrical component that is not ignition protected in accordance with existing Coast Guard electrical standards for boats; or a compartment that contains a fuel tank that vents into that compartment (highly unlikely); or one having a nonmetallic fuel tank that exceeds a specified permeability rate. The new regulations specify the required cross-sectional area of ducts for natural ventilation based on compartment net volume and how ducts shall be installed.

The regulations above concern the manufacturer of the boat, but there is also a requirement placed on the operator that these ventilation systems be operable anytime the boat is in use. Because such systems are so desirable, it is recommended that they be installed on *any* gasoline-powered motorboat or auxiliary.

GENERAL SAFETY PRECAUTIONS

Ventilation systems are *not* designed to remove vapors in large quantities such as might be caused by breaks in fuel lines, leaking tanks, or dripping carburetors. If gas odors are detected, repairs are generally needed.

Before starting the engine, especially on calm days and on boats without a power ventilation system, the engine compartment should be opened to dissipate any vapors that might be present. The smaller the compartment, the quicker an explosive mixture of gasoline vapors can develop.

Regardless of the ventilation system installed, always open hatches and use your nose to detect any gasoline odors. Even the slightest trace should warn you to search for the cause and to ventilate the compartment thoroughly before pressing the starter switch.

FUELING PRECAUTIONS

Certain precautions must be carefully and completely observed every time a boat is fueled with gasoline. Step by step, these are:

Before Fueling

1. Make sure that the boat is securely made fast to the fueling pier. Fuel before darkness, if possible.
2. Stop engines, motors, fans, and other devices capable of producing a spark. Open the master switch if the electrical system has one. Put out all galley fires and open flames.
3. Close all ports, windows, doors, and hatches so that fumes cannot blow aboard and below.
4. Disembark all passengers and any crew members not needed for the fueling operation.
5. Prohibit all smoking on board and in the vicinity.
6. Have a filled fire extinguisher close at hand.
7. Measure the fuel in the tanks and do not order more than the tank will hold. Allow for expansion.

While Fueling

8. Keep nozzle or can spout in contact with the fill opening to guard against static sparks.
9. Do not spill gasoline.
10. Do not overfill. The practice of filling until fuel flows from the vents is highly dangerous.
11. For outboards, remove portable tanks, and fill on shore.

After Fueling

12. Close fill openings.
13. Wipe up any spilled gasoline; dispose of wipe-up gas ashore.

14. Open all ports, windows, doors, and hatches; turn on bilge power-exhaust blower. Ventilate boat this way at *least* five minutes.

15. Sniff low down in tank and engine compartments. *If any odor of gasoline is present, do not start engines.*

16. Be prepared to cast off lines as soon as engine starts; get clear of pier quickly.

LIGHTNING PROTECTION

One seldom hears of a boat, power or sail, being struck by lightning, yet cases have been reported. A skipper can add to both his physical safety and his peace of mind by obtaining some basic information and taking a few precautionary actions.

Protective Principles

A grounded conductor, or lightning protective mast, will generally divert to itself direct lightning strokes that might otherwise fall within a cone-shaped space, the apex of which is the top of the conductor or mast and the base a circle at the water's surface having a radius approximately twice the conductor's height. Probability of protection is considered to be 99 percent within this 60-degree angle as shown in Figure 2.3. Probability of protection can be increased to 99.9 percent if mast height is raised so that the cone-apex angle is reduced to 45 degrees.

To provide an adequately grounded conductor or protective mast, the entire circuit from the masthead to the ground (water) connection should have a conductivity equivalent to a Number 8 gauge wire. The path to ground followed by the conductor should be essentially straight, with no sharp bends.

If there are metal objects of considerable size within a few feet of the grounding conductor, there will be a strong tendency for sparks or side flashes to jump from the grounding conductor to the metal object at the nearest point. To prevent such possibly damaging flashes, an interconnecting conductor should be provided at all likely places.

Large metallic objects within the hull or superstructure of a boat

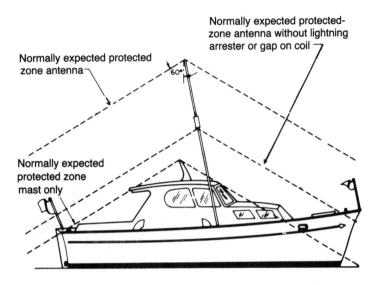

Figure 2.3 Under certain conditions, a grounded radio antenna can provide a cone of protection from lightning strikes for a boat and its occupants. (A.B.Y.C. Safety Standards)

should be interconnected with the lightning protective system to prevent a dangerous rise of voltage due to a lightning flash.

Protective Measures

For powerboats, a radio antenna may serve as a lightning or protective mast provided it is equipped with a transmitting-type lightning arrester or means for grounding during electrical storms and that the antenna height is sufficient to provide an adequate cone of protection for the length of the craft. Antennas with loading coils are considered to end at a point immediately *below the coil* unless the coil has a suitable gap for bypassing lightning current. The size of the grounding conductor, interconnection, and grounding of metallic masses should be in accordance with principles noted earlier.

Sailboats with metallic standing rigging will be adequately protected provided that all rigging is grounded and a proper cone of protection exists. Interconnection and grounding of metallic masses should be done as on powerboats.

SAFETY

Metal objects situated wholly on a boat's exterior should be connected to the grounding conductor at their upper or nearest end. Metal objects within the boat may be connected to the lightning protective system directly or through the bonding system that grounds underwater metal parts.

Metal objects that project through cabintops, decks, etc., should be bonded to the nearest lightning conductor at the point where the object emerges from the boat and again at its lowest extreme end within the boat. Spotlights and other objects projecting through cabintops should be solidly grounded regardless of the cone of protection.

A ground connection for lightning protection may consist of any metal surface, normally submerged, which has an area of at least one square foot. Propellers and metallic rudder surfaces may be used for this purpose; the radio ground plate is more than adequate. A steel hull itself constitutes a good ground connection.

Protection for Personnel

As the basic purpose of lightning protection is safety of personnel, the following precautions should be taken by the crew and guests.

Individuals should remain inside a closed boat as much as practicable during an electrical storm.

Persons should avoid making contact with any items connected to a lightning protective conductor, and especially in such a way as to bridge between two parts of the grounding system.

No one should be in the water during a lightning storm.

WATER-SKIING SAFETY

Water skiing, one of the most popular sports related to boating, does present problems in safety afloat. The following guides should do much to reduce hazards:

1. Allow no one who is not qualified as a basic swimmer to engage in water skiing. A ski belt or vest is intended to keep a stunned or unconscious skier afloat.

2. Ski only in safe areas, out of channels, and away from

Figure 2.4 This simple set of hand signals will allow adequate communication from the skier to the operator or observer on the towing boat. All must be thoroughly familiar with the full set of signals if maximum safety is to be achieved.

(USCG Recreational Boating Guide)

other boats. Some bodies of water will have areas designated for this sport, with skiing prohibited elsewhere.

3. Install a wide-angle rear-view mirror, or take along a second person to act as lookout. This will permit watching the skier *and* the waters ahead. Some state laws require this mirror, or a second person in the boat, or both.

4. Make sure the skier wears the proper lifesaving device.

5. If the skier falls, approach him from the lee side; stop your motor before taking him aboard.

6. In taking the skier on board, be careful not to swamp the boat. On smaller boats, it is usually safer to take a person aboard at the stern.

Skiing Signals

The following set of signals is recommended by the American Water Ski Association; see Figure 2.4. Make sure that the skier, boat operator, and safety observer all know and understand these signals:

Faster—Palm of one hand pointing upward.

Slower—Palm pointing downward.

Speed Okay—Arm upraised with thumb and finger joined to form a circle.

Right Turn—Arm outstretched pointing to the right.

Left Turn—Arm outstretched pointing to the left.

Return to Drop-off Area—Arm at 45 degrees from body pointing down to water and swinging.

Cut Motor—Finger drawn across throat.

Stop—Hand up, palm forward, policeman style.

Skier Okay after Fall—Hands clenched together overhead.

Pick Me Up, or Fallen Skier, Watch Out—One ski extended vertically out of water.

3.

SEAMANSHIP

Obviously, it takes more than a study of these pages to become a seasoned skipper. Given here are the things you *should* know, the minimum arts of good seamanship. Here are the most common and useful knots and splices, basic anchoring techniques, docking techniques, and lock-and-bridge procedures.

To supplement this information, every boatman—whether new to the sport or with years of experience—can benefit from classes in piloting and seamanship given free by the U.S. Power Squadrons, the U.S. Coast Guard Auxiliary, and the American Red Cross. (Addresses are given in the "Organizations" section of the *Boatman's Handbook.*)

KNOTS AND SPLICES

Illustrated here are eight knots that every boatman should know. They represent just a few of the many that were developed for shipboard use during the age of the square-riggers, but they are all that are needed on the average pleasure boat.

Also presented are the eye splice, short splice, and long splice. Because the eye splice is used for so many applications, it is shown as made with double-braided nylon line as well as standard three-strand rope. The method illustrated is that developed by Samson Cordage Works.

Figure 3.1 Overhand knot is used to keep the end of a line from unlaying. This knot jams and may become almost impossible to untie.

Figure 3.2 The figure eight knot can be used as a "stopper" to prevent a line from running through a sheave. It does not jam and can be untied easily.

Figure 3.3 The square or reef knot is used for tying light lines of the same size together, for tying awning stops, reef points, and similar uses. It can jam after being stressed heavily and become difficult to untie.

Figure 3.4 The bowline will not slip, does not pinch or kink the rope as much as some other knots, and it does not jam or become difficult to untie. By tying a bowline with a small loop, and passing the line through the loop, a running bowline is obtained. This is an excellent form of running noose. Bowlines are used wherever a secure loop or running noose is needed in the end of a line, such as one to be secured

to a bollard. They also may be used in securing lines to anchors.

Figure 3.5 The clove hitch is used for making a line fast temporarily to a pile or bollard.

Figure 3.6 Two half hitches are used for making a line fast to a bollard, pile, timber, or stanchion. Note that the knot consists of a turn around the fixed object, and a clove hitch around the standing part of the line.

Figure 3.7 Fisherman's bend, or anchor bend, is handy for making fast to a buoy or spar, or to the ring of an anchor.

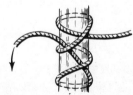

Figure 3.8 Use a rolling hitch to bend a line to a spar or rope. Close the turns up tight and take the strain on the arrow-tipped end.

Figure 3.9 Correct method of making fast to a cleat: the half hitch that completes the fastening is taken with the free part of the line. The line then can be freed without taking up slack in the standing part.

Figure 3.10 Common incorrect method of making fast to a cleat: The half hitch is taken with the standing part of the line, and the line cannot be freed unless it is possible to take up slack on the standing part.

Eye Splice

1. Start by unlaying the strands about six inches to one foot or more, or six to ten turns of lay, depending on rope size. Whip the ends of each strand. With synthetic line, it's helpful to use masking or friction tape around the unlaid strands every four inches to six inches, to help hold the "turn" in the strand.

2. Form a loop in the rope by laying the end back along the standing part. Hold the standing part away from you in the left hand, loop toward you. The stranded end can be worked with the right hand.

3. The size of loop is determined by Point X, Figure 3.11, where the opened strands are first tucked under the standing part of the rope. If splice is to go around a thimble, the rope is laid snugly in the thimble groove and Point X will be at the tapered end of the thimble. The thimble may be taped or tied in place until the splice is finished.

4. Lay the three opened strands across the standing part as shown in Figure 3.11 so the center strand B lies over and directly along the standing part. Left-hand strand A leads off to the left; right-hand strand C to the right of the standing part.

5. Tuck ends of strands A, B, and C under the strands of the standing part; see Figure 3.12. Start with center strand B. Select the topmost strand 2 of the standing part near Point X, and tuck B under it. Haul it up snug, but not so tight as

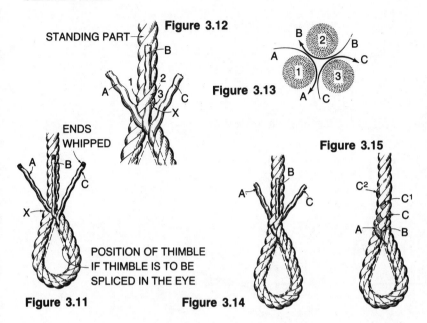

Figure 3.12

STANDING PART

Figure 3.13

ENDS WHIPPED

Figure 3.15

POSITION OF THIMBLE IF THIMBLE IS TO BE SPLICED IN THE EYE

Figure 3.11   **Figure 3.14**

to distort the natural lay of all strands. Tuck is made from right to left, against the lay of the standing part.

6. Tuck strand A under strand 1, which lies to the left of strand 2. Tuck strand C under strand 3, which lies to the right of strand 2. Tuck from right to left in every case. The greatest risk of a wrong start is in the first tuck of strand C. It must go under 3 from right to left; refer to Figure 3.13. If the first three tucks are correct, splice will look as shown in Figure 3.14.

7. Complete splice by making at least two additional tucks with each strand, in rotation, in manila line, and at least four additional tucks in synthetic line. As each tuck is made, be sure it passes from right to left under one strand of the standing part, then over the next one above it. This is shown in Figure 3.15. Note C, C^1, and C^2, the same strand as it appears after successive tucks.

The eye splice with double-braided synthetic line is illustrated and described in Figures 3.16–3.23 and their captions.

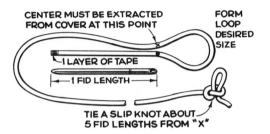

Figure 3.16 Tightly tape end with one layer of tape. Mark a big dot one fid length from end of line. From the dot, form a loop the size of the eye you want and mark with an *X* as shown.

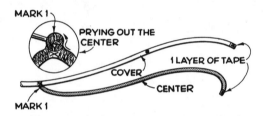

Figure 3.17 Bend line sharply at X and spread strands apart firmly to make opening so center can be pried out. Mark one big line on center where it comes out (this is Mark #1), and use your fingers to pull all the center out of the cover from X to the end. Pull on paper tape inside center until it breaks back at slip knot; you need to get rid of it so you can splice. Put a layer of tape on end of center.

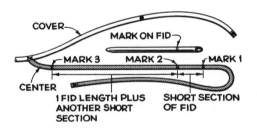

Figure 3.18 Pull out more of the center. From Mark #1, measure a distance equal to the short section of the fid, and mark two heavy lines (this is Mark #2). Mark #3 is three heavy lines at a distance of one fid length plus one short section of fid from Mark #2.

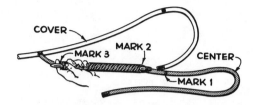

Figure 3.19 Insert fid into center at Mark #2, and slide it lengthwise through "tunnel" until point sticks out at mark #3.

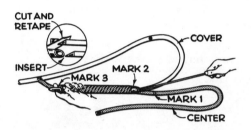

Figure 3.20 Cut across taped end of cover to form a point and retape tightly with one layer of tape. Jam this point into open end of the fid. Jam pusher into fid behind the tape. Hold center gently at Mark #3, and push both fid and cover through the center until dot almost disappears at Mark #2.

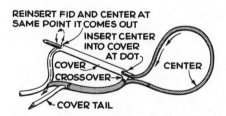

Figure 3.21 Note how center tail must travel through cover. It must go in close to dot and come out through opening at X. On large eyes, several passes may be necessary for fid to reach X. When this occurs simply reinsert fid at exact place it comes out and continue to X. To start, insert fid in cover at dot and slide it through tunnel to X. Form tapered point on center tail, jam it into open end of fid, and push fid and center through the cover. After fid comes out at X, pull all center tail through cover until tight, then pull cover tail tight.

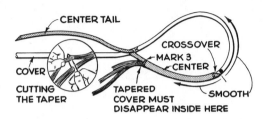

Figure 3.22 Unravel cover tail braid all the way to Mark #3 and cut off groups of strands at staggered intervals to form a tapered end. Hold loop at crossover in one hand and firmly smooth both sides of loop away from crossover. Do this until the tapered tail section completely disappears inside Mark #3.

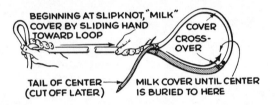

Figure 3.23 Hold rope at slipknot and gently begin to "milk" or slide the cover slack toward the loop. You'll see the center begin to disappear into the cover. Go back to the knot and continue sliding cover more and more firmly until all center and the crossover are buried inside the cover.

Short Splice

A short splice is used where two ropes are to be permanently joined, provided they do not have to pass through the sheave hole, swallow, or throat of a block. When a rope must pass through a block, a long splice must be made.

> **1.** Unlay the strands of both rope ends for a short distance, as described for the eye splice. Whip the ends, or fuse them if synthetic line is used, and seize the ropes to prevent the strands from unlaying too far.

> **2.** Bring the ends of the ropes together so that the strands of one lie alternately between the strands of the other, as shown in Figure 3.24. Tie all the strands of one rope tem-

Figure 3.24

Figure 3.25

porarily to the other; see Figure 3.25 (some boatmen elim-inate this step, as it is not essential).

3. Remove the seizing from one rope, and tuck in the strands from the other, just as if it were an eye splice, working from right to left with each strand passing over and under the strands of the other rope.

4. Remove the temporary seizing from the other rope, and repeat the above process with the other strands. Splice should appear as shown in Figure 3.26.

5. Short splice, and eye splice, can be tapered by cutting out yarns from the strands after the necessary full tucks have been made. Never cut end strands off too close to the standing part of the rope; a heavy strain may allow them to work out.

Figure 3.26

Figure 3.27

6. A second method of making the splice is to start as in Figure 3.24, and then tie pairs of strands from opposite ends in an overhand knot; see Figure 3.27. This, in effect, makes the first tuck.

ANCHOR TYPES

Danforth

This is a lightweight anchor with long, sharp flukes designed so that heavy strains bury the anchor completely. It tends to work down through soft bottoms to firmer holding ground below, burying part of the anchor line (rode) as well as the anchor itself. Anchor

has a round rod at the crown end to prevent the anchor from rolling or rotating. See Figure 3.28.

Plow (CQR)

This is another anchor that tends to bury itself completely, and in form resembles the farmer's plowshare. When lowered, it first lies on its side on the bottom. When a pull is put on the rode, it rights itself, driving the point of the plow into the bottom; additional strain on the rode buries the anchor completely. Because the shank pivots, this anchor tends to remain buried even when the angle of pull is changed by wind or current, but it breaks out easily with a vertical pull.

Kedges

A kedge is the traditional anchor, with arms, flukes, and stocks as distinguished from modern stockless types. Holding power depends more on anchor weight than design. Shoulders on the flukes are

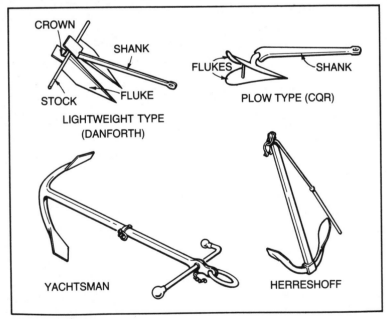

Figure 3.28

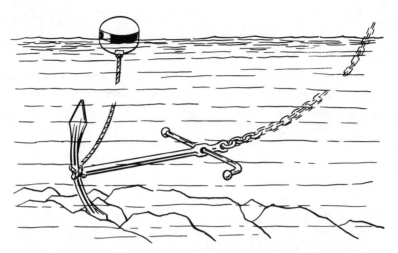

SEAMANSHIP

Figure 3.29 A buoyed trip line to the crown will permit an anchor fouled in rocky bottom to be hauled up fluke first.

nearly square and invite fouling the rode as a vessel swings. Dull bills make it difficult to bite in hard bottoms.

Yachtsman and Herreshoff

These evolved from the kedges and feature changes in the size and shape of fluke relative to the arm. Flukes are diamond-shaped to reduce risk of fouling, and sharpened bills permit better penetration of the bottom. These are not burying-type anchors and serve best on rocky bottoms. Retrieval, using a trip line (see Figure 3.29), is not too difficult if the anchor is snagged.

Grapnels

These are stockless anchors with five curved, sharp-billed clawlike prongs at the crown end of the shank. They are not used to anchor a boat in position. By dragging one back and forth over the bottom, the boatman can grapple for a piece of equipment lost overboard.

BASIC ANCHORING TECHNIQUES

1. Enough rode for the selected anchorage should be coiled on forward deck so as to run freely and without kinking or fouling. Make sure it is properly secured to the anchor, and that the bitter end is secured.

2. Having selected a suitable spot, run in slowly. Use ranges ashore, buoys, or landmarks; later these will aid in determining if you are holding or dragging, especially if the marks are visible at night.

3. Give rocks, shoals, reefs, or other boats as wide a berth as possible. Your boat may swing in a full circle while at anchor.

4. As you approach spot where anchor is to be lowered, head up against wind or current, as needed, to hold your boat on the heading it will assume when anchored. Check other boats of your type that are at anchor in the area.

5. In a motorboat or auxiliary under power, bring the bow up slowly to the point where the anchor is to be lowered. Check the headway by putting the boat into reverse, if necessary. Just as the boat gathers sternway, lower—do not drop—the anchor until it hits bottom, crown first. *Do not stand in the coils of the anchor line on deck.*

6. With the anchor on the bottom and the boat reversing slowly, pay out the rode, preferably with a turn around a bitt, as the boat takes it. When a scope (see Figure 3.30) of 7:1 or 8:1 is reached, snub the line by holding it on the

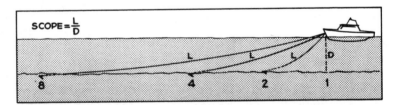

Figure 3.30 Scope is the ratio of length of rode (L) to depth of water (D), plus allowance for height of bow above water. At (1) length of rode equals the depth. At (2) rode length is twice the depth; at (4) four times the depth. Note how the angle between rode and bottom decreases. At (8) the scope is 8:1 and the short length of chain at the anchor lies flat on the bottom.

bitt: The anchor should take a quick, sure bite into the bottom. Snubbing too soon may cause the anchor to drag. Once the anchor is set, the line can be shortened somewhat if the anchorage is crowded and such a scope would be excessive.

7. In setting a lightweight burial-type anchor, particularly on soft mud bottoms where the anchor can sink and skid, snub the rode briefly when a scope of 2:1 is reached to start the points to dig in properly, then back down until full scope has been paid out.

8. When the proper scope has been attained, apply a back-down load in excess of any that may be anticipated from wind or current. Check your ranges to see if the anchor is dragging.

9. Make the anchor rode fast and shut off the boat's engine(s).

Anchoring Without Power

1. When under sail, approach your anchorage with the wind abeam so you can spill the wind from your sail to slow the boat down, or trim in to gain more headway. Make the approach under mainsail only.

2. When you reach the point where the anchor is to be lowered, you should just have steerageway, but no more. Shoot the bow directly into the wind, let the sheet run, and drop the sail. As the boat loses headway, her bow will fall off and the boat will begin to drift to leeward. Now lower your anchor.

3. As the boat drifts back, pay out scope. Occasionally give a few jerks on the line; this helps to set the anchor. Hand test the line by pulling it. Your anchor will be holding when the boat is drawn toward it as you pull on the line. Pay out the usual scope of 7:1 or 8:1.

Rocky Bottoms

If the bottom is foul or rocky in the area where you must anchor, it is advisable to rig a buoyed trip line, as shown in Figure 3.29. Make a light line fast to the crown; the line should be long enough to reach the surface, where it is buoyed with any convenient float. Be sure to allow for rise in tide. If the anchor does not come free with a normal pull on the rode, haul in on the trip line, and the anchor will be freed, crown first.

Anchor Dragging

1. If it appears that your anchor is dragging, pay out more scope with an occasional sharp pull to help give the anchor a new bite. If you are dragging badly, take a turn around a bitt and snub the line occasionally. If the anchor is not holding by the time you have paid out a scope of 10:1, haul it back aboard and try again—preferably with a larger anchor.

2. If you do not have a larger (storm) anchor, you can add a sentinel to the anchor line (Figure 3.31). This is simply a weight sent more than halfway down the rode. It lowers the angle of pull on the anchor and puts a sag in the line that must be straightened out before a load is thrown on the anchor. Some authorities advise use of a sentinel only to curtail swing room in a crowded, but calm and protected, anchorage. They note that in a seaway, in a mod-

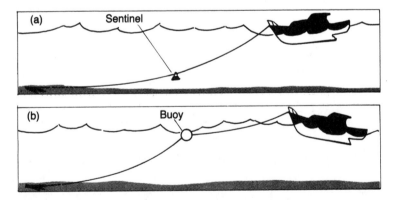

Figure 3.31 Two methods of increasing anchor efficiency in rough weather. See text for advantages and disadvantages of each.

erate chop, the sentinel can reach a point of resonance and actually cut through the rode.

3. An alternative to the sentinel is a buoy on the anchor line. This carries the vertical hold in the anchoring system and limits the basic load on the boat to that required to hold the boat in position. The buoy permits the boat's bow to rise up easily over wave crests, rather than being pulled down into them, increasing the loads on both anchor and rode.

GETTING UNDER WAY

When you are ready to *weigh anchor* and get under way, run up to the anchor slowly under power, so that the line can be taken in easily without hauling the boat up to it. Ordinarily the anchor will break out readily when the line stands vertically.

As the line comes in, it can be whipped up and down to free it of any grass or weed it may have picked up. This clears the line before it comes on deck. If the anchor is not too heavy, mud can be washed off by swinging it back and forth near the surface as it leaves the water. With care, the line can be snubbed around a bit and the anchor allowed to wash off as the boat gathers way, preferably astern. Two things must be watched: Don't allow the flukes to hit the topsides and be careful that water flowing past the anchor doesn't get too good a hold and take it out of your hands.

Manila, if used, must be coiled loosely on deck and allowed to dry thoroughly before stowing below. When the anchor is on deck, the stock (if there is one) can be folded and the anchor lashed down securely in its chocks.

PERMANENT MOORINGS

Permanent moorings, as distinguished from ordinary ground tackle in daily use, consist of the gear used when boats are to be left unattended for long periods, at yacht-club anchorages, for example. The traditional system has often consisted of a mushroom anchor, chain from the anchor to a buoy, and a pennant of stainless steel or nylon from the buoy to a light pick-up float at the pennant's end. See Figure 3.32.

Mushroom anchors, especially the type with a heavy bulb cast in the shank, have been able through suction to develop great holding power under ideal conditions if they are allowed time enough to bury deep in bottoms that will permit such burying.

Ideally, scope for the mooring anchor should be five to seven times the depth of the water, but this often means a swinging radius of several hundred feet. In crowded anchorages, this is impossible. The recommended standards shown in Table 3.1 were prepared by

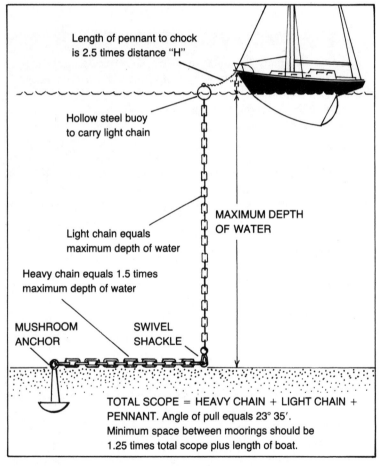

Length of pennant to chock is 2.5 times distance "H"

Hollow steel buoy to carry light chain

MAXIMUM DEPTH OF WATER

Light chain equals maximum depth of water

Heavy chain equals 1.5 times maximum depth of water

MUSHROOM ANCHOR

SWIVEL SHACKLE

TOTAL SCOPE = HEAVY CHAIN + LIGHT CHAIN + PENNANT. Angle of pull equals 23° 35'. Minimum space between moorings should be 1.25 times total scope plus length of boat.

Figure 3.32

Table 3.1

ANCHOR WEIGHT* (pounds)

BOAT LENGTH (Maximum)	Lunch hook	Working anchor	Storm anchor
20'	4 (10)	5 (20)	12 (40)
30'	5 (15)	12 (30)	18 (60)
40'	12 (20)	18 (40)	28 (80)

*Bold-face figures based on modern lightweight burial-type anchors of efficient design. Figures in parentheses show how weights would be increased, using a formula of ½, 1 pound and 2 pounds per foot for certain kedges.

the Manhasset Bay Yacht Club of Port Washington, N.Y., to meet average conditions.

Mooring Buoys

To comply with nationwide uniform state waterway regulations (applicable on waters under state control), mooring buoys should be white with a horizontal blue band. Buoys used in any mooring system should be of a type that transmits strain directly through chain or rod. See Figure 3.33. Buoys perform a useful function in removing much of the vertical load: The pennant is under a more nearly horizontal load, and the boat's bow is freer to lift to heavy seas.

Figure 3.33 A plastic foam buoy. Note how the strain is transmitted by a solid rod that runs through the buoy.

Table 3.2

SUGGESTED RODE AND ANCHOR SIZES*

For Storm Anchor (Winds up to 60 knots)

L.O.A.	BEAM		RODE		ANCHOR		
	SAIL	POWER	NYLON	CHAIN	NORTHILL	STANDARD	HI-TENSILE
10'	4'	4'	100'-¼"	3'-³⁄₁₆"	12 lb. (6-R)	8-S	5-H
15'	5'	5'	125'-¼"	3'-³⁄₁₆"	12 lb. (6-R)	8-S	5-H
20'	6'	7'	150'-⅜"	4'-¼"	27 lb. (12-R)	13-S	12-H
25'	6'	8'	200'-⅜"	4'-¼"	27 lb. (12-R)	22-S	12-H
30'	7'	10'	250'-⁷⁄₁₆"	5'-⁵⁄₁₆"	46 lb. (20-R)	22-S	20-H
35'	8'	12'	300'-½"	6'-⅜"	46 lb. (20-R)	40-S	35-H
40'	10'	14'	400'-⅝"	8'-⁷⁄₁₆"	80 lb. (30-R)	65-S	60-H
50'	12'	16'	500'-⅝"	8'-⁷⁄₁₆"	105 lb. (50-R)	130-S	60-H
60'	14'	19'	500'-¾"	8'-½"	105 lb. (50-R)	180-S	90-H

For Working Anchor (Winds up to 30 knots)

L.O.A.	BEAM		RODE		ANCHOR		
	SAIL	POWER	NYLON	CHAIN	NORTHILL	STANDARD	HI-TENSILE
10'	4'	4'	80'-¼"	3'-³⁄₁₆"	6 lb. (3-R)	4-S	5-H
15'	5'	5'	100'-¼"	3'-³⁄₁₆"	6 lb. (3-R)	8-S	5-H
20'	6'	7'	120'-¼"	3'-³⁄₁₆"	12 lb. (6-R)	8-S	5-H
25'	6'	8'	150'-⅜"	3'-³⁄₁₆"	12 lb. (6-R)	8-S	5-H
30'	7'	10'	180'-⅜"	4'-¼"	27 lb. (12-R)	13-S	12-H
35'	8'	12'	200'-⅜"	4'-¼"	27 lb. (12-R)	22-S	12-H
40'	10'	14'	250'-⁷⁄₁₆"	5'-⁵⁄₁₆"	46 lb. (20-R)	22-S	20-H
50'	12'	16'	300'-½"	6'-⅜"	46 lb. (20-R)	40-S	35-H
60'	14'	19'	300'-½"	6'-⅜"	80 lb. (30-R)	65-S	35-H

For Lunch Hook

L.O.A.	BEAM		RODE		ANCHOR		
	SAIL	POWER	NYLON	CHAIN	NORTHILL	STANDARD	HI-TENSILE
10'	4'	4'	70'-¼"	3'-³⁄₁₆"	6 lb. (3-R)	2½-S	5-H
15'	5'	5'	80'-¼"	3'-³⁄₁₆"	6 lb. (3-R)	2½-S	5-H
20'	6'	7'	90'-¼"	3'-³⁄₁₆"	6 lb. (3-R)	2½-S	5-H
25'	6'	8'	100'-¼"	3'-³⁄₁₆"	6 lb. (3-R)	4-S	5-H
30'	7'	10'	125'-¼"	3'-³⁄₁₆"	6 lb. (3-R)	4-S	5-H
35'	8'	12'	150'-¼"	3'-³⁄₁₆"	12 lb. (6-R)	4-S	5-H
40'	10'	14'	175'-⅜"	4'-¼"	12 lb. (6-R)	8-S	5-H
50'	12'	16'	200'-⅜"	4'-¼"	12 lb. (6-R)	8-S	12-H
60'	14'	19'	200'-⅜"	4'-¼"	27 lb. (12-R)	13-S	12-H

*Suggested sizes assume fair holding ground, scope of at least 7:1 and moderate shelter from heavy seas.

PLOW ANCHORS—Woolsey, manufacturer of the Plowright anchor, makes the following recommendations for winds up to 30 knots; for *working anchors*, 10'-21', 6 lbs.—22'-32', 12 lbs.—32'-36', 3 lbs.—36'-39', 22 lbs.—39'-44', 35 lbs. For *lunch hooks*, they advise stepping down one size. For *storm anchors*, up one size.

KEDGES—Holding powers vary widely with the type. Best to consult manufacturer for individual recommendations.

Table 3.3

SUGGESTIONS FOR PERMANENT YACHT MOORINGS
For Wind Velocities Up to 75 M.P.H.

Boat Length Overall	Mushroom Anchor (Min. Wt.)	Heavy Chain		Light Chain		Length (Minim.) (Feet)	Pennant Diameter (Inches)			Total Scope (Chocks to Mushroom) (Feet)
		Length (Feet)	Diameter (Inches)	Length (Feet)	Diameter (Inches)		Manila	Nylon	Stainless Steel	
—FOR MOTOR BOATS—										
25	225	30	⅞	20	⅜	20	1	⅞	⁹⁄₃₂	70
35	300	35	1	20	⁷⁄₁₆	20	1¼	1	¹¹⁄₃₂	75
45	400	40	1	20	½	20	1½	1¼	⅜	80
55	500	50	1	20	⁹⁄₁₆	20	2	1½	⁷⁄₁₆	90
—FOR RACING TYPE SAILBOATS—										
25	125	30	⅝	20	⁵⁄₁₆	20	1	⅞	⁹⁄₃₂	70
35	200	30	¾	20	⅜	20	1¼	1	¹¹⁄₃₂	70
45	325	35	1	20	⁷⁄₁₆	20	1½	1¼	⅜	75
55	450	45	1	20	⁹⁄₁₆	20	2	1½	⁷⁄₁₆	85
—FOR CRUISING TYPE SAILBOATS—										
25	175	30	¾	20	⁵⁄₁₆	20	1	⅞	⁹⁄₃₂	70
35	250	30	1	20	⅜	20	1¼	1	¹¹⁄₃₂	70
45	400	40	1	20	⁷⁄₁₆	20	1½	1¼	⅜	80
55	550	55	1	20	⁹⁄₁₆	20	2	1½	⁷⁄₁₆	95

DOCKING

To handle a boat, or a ship, you must first *know* it. Know *what it will do, how fast it will do it,* and *in what space.* No article or text can give you this knowledge—it can come only from actual experience and practice. But attention can be drawn to certain basics that will enable you to get much more from experience. Some of the more important of these are:

1. *The propeller controls the direction of a boat when docking, almost as much as the rudder.*
   A vessel with a propeller that turns in a clockwise direction when viewed from astern with the engine turning ahead (called a right-handed vessel) is the most common. This vessel's bow will usually swing to port slowly when going ahead, even with the rudder amidships, *but* the stern will swing rather sharply to port when the vessel is

going astern, often regardless of where the rudder is. For left-handed vessels the effects are reversed.

2. *This "turning effect" of the propeller is much more pronounced when going astern.*
   Since much of a rudder's effect comes from the wash of the propeller rushing past it, if the engine is reversed, this wash will be directed in a direction *away* from the rudder and much of the effect of the helm is lost. The propeller takes over in a pronounced fashion.

3. *Brief spurts of engine power may be used to turn the bow or stern of the vessel as desired, without getting the boat under way.*
   With the rudder to starboard, a brief spurt of the engine (throttle is opened momentarily) will swing the bow to starboard *but,* if the engine is cut off before the vessel gathers way, most of the power of the engine will have gone into turning the vessel rather than getting it moving through the water. The heavier the boat, the more this is so. Don't be afraid to gun your engine briefly to gain maneuverability. A boat's pretty heavy and won't shoot ahead the moment power is applied.

4. *The wind, tide, and current can often be as much help in docking as the engines and helm.*
   Nature will often dock your boat for you, if given half a chance. Why waste gas and temper fighting her? A good policy many times is: Ride with the current.

Now to the actual processes of docking. These are presented in outline form to make it easier to grasp details without wading through a lot of text. The word "wind" will be used to cover whichever factor has the most effect on the vessel at the moment, whether it is actually the wind, or whether it may be tide or current. In calm or still water almost any of the methods outlined will work equally well. Boats are shown port side to the docks; for the reverse condition, simply reverse the rudder orders but maintain the same engine speeds and directions.

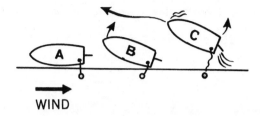

WIND

Figure 3.34 *Leaving a dock, boat alongside dock, wind ahead:* A. Single up to one stern line, no power, no rudder. B. Let wind swing bow out, or push bow out with boat hook. C. With bow out 15 or 20 degrees, swing stern clear by using hard left rudder (right rudder if dock is to starboard) and brief spurts of power. Let stern line go when boat is a few feet from the dock and go ahead slowly. Steer away from the dock with slight rudder.

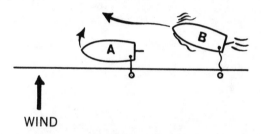

WIND

Figure 3.35 *Leaving a dock, boat alongside dock, wind off the dock:* A. Single up to one stern line and let the wind swing the bow out. B. Ease off on the stern line until clear of the dock. Let go the line and go ahead slowly. Steer away from the dock with slight rudder.

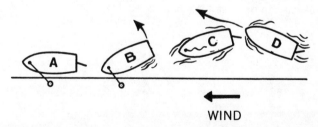

WIND

Figure 3.36 *Leaving a dock, boat alongside dock, wind astern:* A. Single up to bow spring line. B. Let wind swing the stern out or use the engine in brief spurts with hard left rudder (right rudder if moored starboard side to dock). C. Reverse engine and back off slowly; cast off line. D. When well clear of dock, go ahead slowly and use slight rudder to steer away from the dock.

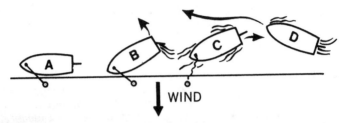

Figure 3.37 *Leaving a dock, boat alongside dock, wind on the dock:* A. Single up to bow spring line led well aft. B. Use spurts of power ahead to bring stern out, using hard left rudder (right rudder if dock is to starboard). C. Use engine in reverse to back away from dock, cast off bow spring. D. When well clear, go ahead with engine and steer clear of the dock.

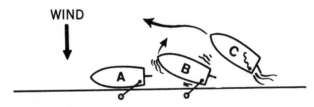

Figure 3.38 *Leaving a dock, boat alongside dock, wind on the dock:* A. Single up to single stern spring line. B. Use half to full power astern to swing bow out, no rudder. C. Use rudder half left (half right if dock is to starboard) and engine slow ahead to bring stern out. Cast off line and go ahead slowly using slight rudder to steer clear of dock.

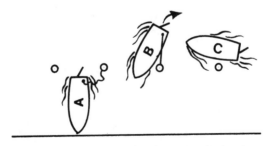

Figure 3.39 *Leaving a slip:* A. Single up to single stern line, long

enough to reach from stern cleat to a point forward about two thirds the length of the boat. Make outboard end of line fast to outer end of the slip. B. Go astern slowly until line is taut, then swing rudder hard left. Boat's stern will swing to port under full control. C. Cast off when clear, go ahead, give a slight kick of left rudder to swing stern out, then use slight right rudder to steer clear.

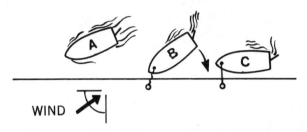

WIND

Figure 3.40 *Docking, wind off the dock or ahead:* A. Approach slowly at an angle of 30 to 40 degrees to the dock. B. Put engine in reverse to halt boat with bow about one foot from dock, get bowline ashore. C. With hard right rudder, use spurts of power ahead to bring stern in to dock. Tie up.

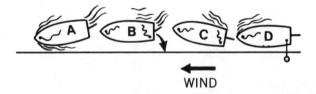

WIND

Figure 3.41 *Docking, wind astern:* A. Approach closely to dock, at an angle of 10 to 15 degrees. B. When one or two feet from dock, use right rudder and brief spurt of power to start stern swinging toward dock. C. As soon as stern starts to swing in (boat parallel to dock), reverse engine to stop boat. D. Get stern line ashore and let wind bring bow in to dock. Tie up.

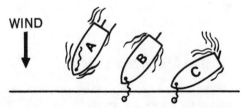

WIND

Figure 3.42 *Docking, wind on the dock:* A. Approach at a steep angle of about 60 to 80 degrees. B. Reverse engine to stop boat about a foot from dock; ease boat off with boathook if possible; get bowline ashore. C. Let wind bring stern in, using engine in reverse and hard right rudder for braking action. Tie up.

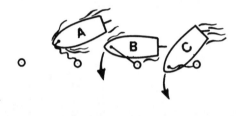

Figure 3.43 *Entering a slip, wind anywhere but astern:* A. Approach slowly, roughly parallel to end of slip. Pass a line to the pile or cleat nearest your approach. B. Reverse engine to slow the approach and stop the boat just short of the far piling, with the line taut. C. Put rudder hard left and use spurt of power to swing boat into slip, using the pile as a pivot. Ease into slip and tie up.

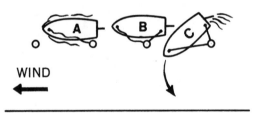

WIND

Figure 3.44 *Entering a slip, wind astern:* Approach as in Figure 3.43, but use enough power to stop boat completely after passing the bowline. B. Pass a stern line to the same pile or cleat. C. Haul both lines taut and use engine, wind, and rudder to ease boat around and into the slip. Tie up.

DAMS AND LOCKS

Dams on our inland waterways, without locks, would restrict river cruising to the individual pools and prevent through navigation except to small vessels light enough to be portaged around the dams.

Locks, in conjunction with the dams, provide the means for boats to move from level to level. Locks vary in size but since they must invariably handle commercial traffic, their limiting dimensions offer no restriction to the movement of pleasure craft.

Locks are practically watertight chambers with gates at each end. Valves are provided to admit water as required. When a vessel is about to be locked upstream to a higher level, the upstream gate is closed, the downstream gate opened, and the water stands at the lower level. The vessel enters the lock through the open gates at the lower end, the gates close behind her, and water is valved in until the chamber is full to the upstream level. Now the upstream gate is opened, and the boat is free to resume her course upstream. Locking down is naturally the reverse of this procedure.

Signals are provided for vessels approaching a lock (commonly a long and a short blast) answered by signals from the lock tender. The river boatman should familiarize himself with the special signals applicable to the particular waterway he is using.

On the Ohio, vessels sound a long and a short blast on the whistle from a distance of not more than one mile from the lock. On the New York State Barge Canal, they signal with three distinct blasts. When approaching a lock, boats must wait for the lockmaster's signal before entering. When bound downstream, stay in the clear at least four hundred feet upstream from the end of the guide wall leading along the bank into the lock. Approach through the buoyed channel directly toward the lock and keep clear of spillway sections of the dam. Be particularly careful not to obstruct the movement of any large commercial craft that may be leaving the lock. When bound upstream, keep well clear of the turbulent water invariably found below a dam.

On the Mississippi, signs are painted on the river face of the guide wall warning small craft not to pass a given point until signaled by the lock attendant. Near this sign a signal cord is placed. Small craft may use this to alert lock attendants, in lieu of signals used on other waters.

Traffic signal lights at the Ohio locks resemble those you find on the highway—red, amber, and green, arranged vertically. Flashing red warns: Do not enter, stand clear. Flashing amber signifies: Approach, but under full control. Flashing green gives you the all-clear signal to enter. (On N.Y. State canals, a fixed green light gives clearance to enter; fixed red requires the vessel to wait. United States and commercial vessels take precedence; pleasure boats may be locked through with commercial craft if a safe distance may be maintained between them.)

Where locks are in pairs (landward and riverward), the lockmaster on the Ohio may also use an air horn, the significance of his blasts as following: one long, enter landward lock; two long, enter riverward lock; one short, leave landward lock; two short, leave riverward lock.

The Secretary of the Army has established an order of priority with respect to the handling of traffic at locks, giving precedence in this order: 1, U.S. military craft; 2, mail boats; 3, commercial passenger craft; 4, commercial tows; 5, commercial fishermen; and 6, pleasure boats. This means that small pleasure craft may sometimes have to wait to be locked through with other vessels. In deciding on an order of precedence, the lockmaster also takes into account whether vessels of the same class are arriving at landward or riverward locks, and whether they are bound upstream or downstream.

The concrete walls of locks are usually rough and dirty. Consequently a boat will need adequate fender protection. Ordinary cylindrical fenders will pick up dirt and roll on the wall to smear the topsides. Fender boards, consisting of a plank (2 by 6 perhaps, several feet long) suspended horizontally outside the usual fenders, work well amidships or aft where sides are reasonably straight. Bags of hay have the same objection as cylindrical fenders, except on heavily flared bows at the edge of deck where they flatten down and work pretty well. Auto tires wrapped with burlap would be ideal except that their use is illegal in some canals. As you can't be sure which side of a lock you'll be using, it's wise to fender both sides.

Another essential in locking is adequate line. How heavy it is to be depends on the size of boat; how long depends on the depth of the locks. Good ⅜-inch nylon or Dacron is generally adequate for average size cruisers. In general, each line (bow and stern) will have to be at least twice as long as the depth of the lock. The object of this is to permit your running the bight of a line around a bollard on the top of the lock wall, using it double. Then, on the lower level, when you're ready to cast off, you can haul the line in without assistance from above. At Little Falls, N.Y., the drop is roughly forty feet, so one hundred feet is not too much for the length of each of the two lock lines in such cases.

Ladders are often recessed into lock walls and on some canals small boats can follow the ladder up, rung by rung, with boat hook or lock lines. On the Ohio, boats are requested not to use the ladders. In addition to big bollards along the top of the lock walls, some locks have other recessed posts at intervals in the walls in vertical line. Locking up, lines can be cleared successively from lower posts and transferred to higher ones within reach. In other locks, floating mooring hooks move up and down to follow the pool levels.

Rising or falling, stand by your lock lines at all times and tend them carefully. This requires a hand forward and another aft, though with only two aboard the helmsman could handle the after line. One of the most dangerous practices is to make fast to a bollard above and then secure to a bitt or cleat on deck. If the level drops, your boat is "hung," with risk of serious damage.

Entering and leaving locks, it's always imperative to throttle down and keep the boat under complete control. This is especially true when locking through with other boats. Sometimes, on fleet cruises, it will be necessary to tie up two abreast at each lock wall. This is entirely feasible as long as all boats are intelligently handled.

Occasionally one hears cautions concerning the possibility of a boat's being tossed about as water boils into locks from the open valves. Actually, lock tenders on our inland waters are careful to control this flow, and there is little cause for apprehension on this score. With a light boat, however, some thought should be given to placement in a lock when passing through with large commercial craft. A light hull, directly astern of a powerful tug, can take quite a tossing around when her big wheel starts to throw the water astern.

There are various kinds of locks, all of which accomplish the same end of effecting a change of level. Gates may swing or roll back and in cases are hoisted in vertical lift, permitting traffic to pass through under the gate. On the Trent Waterway in Canada, a hydraulic lock lifts the boat in a water-filled chamber and in another instance a marine railway actually hauls the boat out to get her up over a hill. Through passage on a waterway like the Trent, then, is obviously limited to vessels within the capacity of the ways to haul. At Troy, N.Y., a federally operated time lock opens only at slated intervals— on the hour—occasionally causing a slight delay in lockage.

Lock permits, once necessary for pleasure boats, are no longer required to navigate the New York State Barge Canal. On western

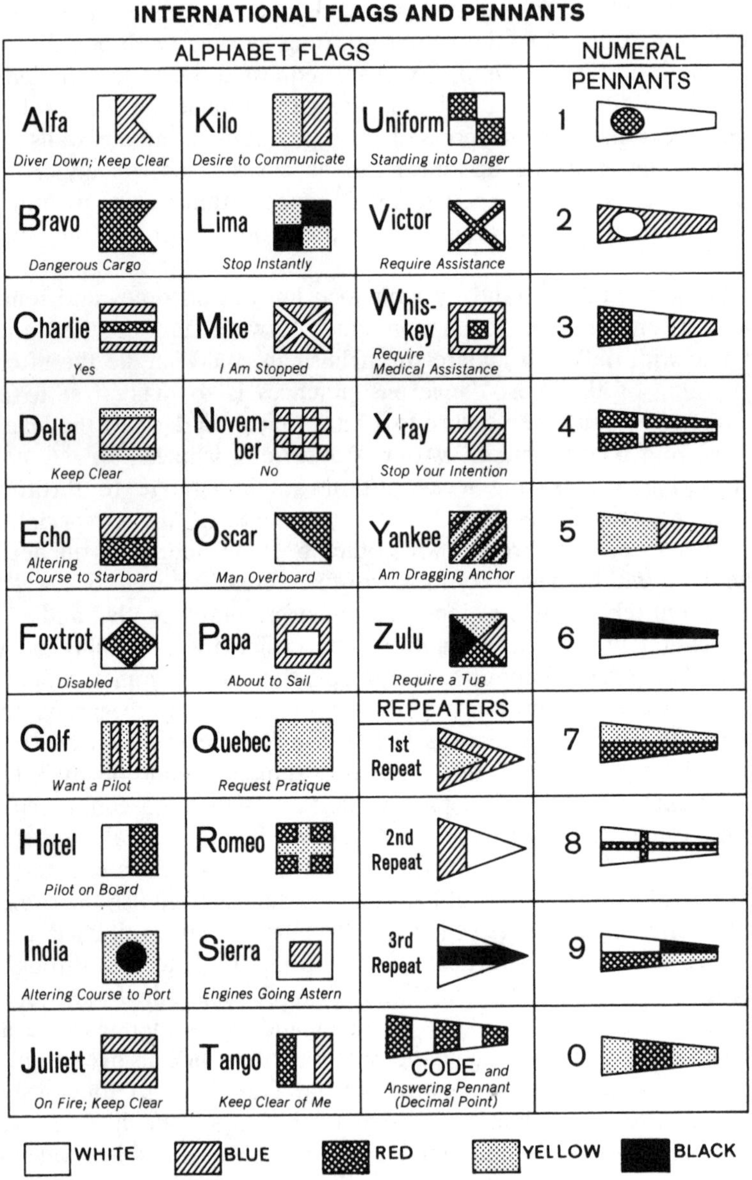

INTERNATIONAL FLAGS AND PENNANTS

ALPHABET FLAGS			NUMERAL PENNANTS
Alfa Diver Down; Keep Clear	**Kilo** Desire to Communicate	**Uniform** Standing into Danger	1
Bravo Dangerous Cargo	**Lima** Stop Instantly	**Victor** Require Assistance	2
Charlie Yes	**Mike** I Am Stopped	**Whis-key** Require Medical Assistance	3
Delta Keep Clear	**Novem-ber** No	**X'ray** Stop Your Intention	4
Echo Altering Course to Starboard	**Oscar** Man Overboard	**Yankee** Am Dragging Anchor	5
Foxtrot Disabled	**Papa** About to Sail	**Zulu** Require a Tug	6
		REPEATERS	
Golf Want a Pilot	**Quebec** Request Pratique	**1st Repeat**	7
Hotel Pilot on Board	**Romeo**	**2nd Repeat**	8
India Altering Course to Port	**Sierra** Engines Going Astern	**3rd Repeat**	9
Juliett On Fire; Keep Clear	**Tango** Keep Clear of Me	**CODE** and Answering Pennant (Decimal Point)	0

WHITE   BLUE   RED   YELLOW   BLACK

Figure 3.45 International Flags and Pennants.

rivers, no special permission or clearance is required for passage through the locks. There are regulations to be observed, however, and copies of these should be obtained from Army Engineer Offices at Chicago or St. Louis.

INTERNATIONAL FLAGS AND PENNANTS

Alphabet and numeral pennants are illustrated in Figure 3.45 and the manner in which they should be used is shown in figure 3.46. Note the meanings given to the individual flags; learn to recognize at least those that convey an emergency message, such as *V* and *W*. You should also know the multiple-flag emergency signals, and if you race a sailboat, you'll need to know the signals used in races and regattas.

Emergency Signals

In addition to the single-flag emergency signals, the following multiple-flag emergency messages may be displayed:

A E   I must abandon my vessel.
A N   I need a doctor.

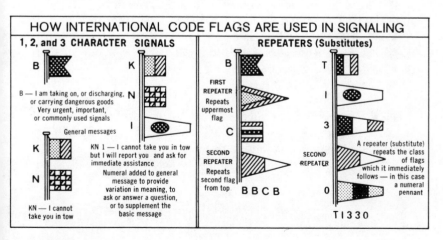

Figure 3.46

CB4   I require immediate assistance; I am aground.
CB5   I require immediate assistance; I am drifting.
CB6   I require immediate assistance; I am on fire.
CB7   I require immediate assistance; I have sprung a leak.
KQ1   I am ready to be taken in tow.
N C   I am in distress and require immediate assistance.
Z L   Your signal has been received but not understood.

Racing Signals

D   Do you assent to postponing the race until later in the day?
E   Do you assent to calling the race off for the day?
T   Send club launch.
W   Permission to leave squadron is requested.
X   Permission to proceed at will is requested.
Y   Leave all marks to starboard.
Z   Leave all marks to port.
A I   Finish—This yacht will take time at finish.
A J   Finish—Will you take time at finish?
A K   Finish—Yachts will take their own time at finish.
A N   Race Committee—Is committee on board committee boat?
A O   Race Committee—Report is ready.
A P   Race Committee—Report on board this vessel at . . .
A Q   Race Committee—Do you agree to race tomorrow?
A V   Start—Race will be sailed on . . .
A W   Start—Race will be sailed today at . . .
A X   Start—Race will be sailed tomorrow at . . .
A Y   Start—When will race be started?

Naval Oceanographic Office Publication 102 lists meanings for all standard flag signals. Also given are specific rules for signaling by flag, flashing light, sound, and radio.

4.

PILOTING AND NAVIGATION

RULES OF THE ROAD

There are two sets of rules of the road of concern to boaters in the United States: the International Rules for use offshore, and the Inland Rules that must be followed on all waters within the demarcation lines that separate U.S. from International Rules waters. Since the requirements of both sets of rules are almost identical for recreational craft, it is not difficult to learn the actions to be taken, signals to be sounded, and lights to be carried when operating offshore or on inland waters.

The wise boatman will have a thorough knowledge of the rules that apply to all types of boats and ships that operate in his home waters. These are detailed in Chapters 4 and 5 of *Chapman's Piloting, Seamanship and Small Boat Handling,* published by Hearst Marine Books, as well as in the Coast Guard publication *Navigation Rules, International-Inland,* which is available at most chart outlets. The major requirements that apply to recreational boats are listed briefly here.

Whistle Signals

The U.S. Inland Rules call for whistle signals to be given in certain situations, as discussed below. The skipper who signals first signifies his intent to take a specific action; the other skipper responds with the *same signal* to indicate that this intent is understood and that the action will cause no problem. If the action to be taken may lead to a problem, or the first skipper's signal is not understood, the second skipper responds with the *danger signal* of five or more short blasts.

Under International Rules, a whistle signal indicates that a specific action will be taken. They are often called rudder signals for this reason, and they are not answered, although in some cases, such as a meeting situation as described below, the second vessel may sound the same signal and take the same action as the first.

Meeting Head-on

When meeting a boat head-on, keep to the right. Show that you intend to do so by swinging the bow of your boat in that direction, even more than necessary. The proper signal is one short blast from either boat, to be answered by one blast from the other. A short blast is one second.

If a boat is coming toward you head-on, but is so far to your right that the boats will pass at a safe distance, both can maintain course. One boat may signal his intention to do so with two blasts of his horn; the other boat should answer with the same signal.

Danger Zone

Your boat's danger zone is the area from dead ahead to 112.5 degrees abaft the starboard beam. A boat in your danger zone has the right of way, if coming toward you. Your boat is the burdened vessel and must alter course, slow down, or stop if necessary, to avoid collision. The privileged vessel may sound one blast of his horn; if so, you must answer with one blast.

Overtaking

The boat being overtaken is the privileged vessel and should hold course and speed. The overtaking boat is the burdened vessel and must keep clear until it is well forward of the privileged vessel and no danger of collision exists. A boat is overtaking another when it is approaching a point more than 112.5 degrees abaft the beam of the privileged vessel on either side.

If the overtaking boat plans to pass to the left of the privileged vessel (leaving it to starboard), a signal of two blasts is given, and is answered by the same signal. If the overtaking vessel plans to leave the privileged vessel to port, a signal of one blast is given, and is answered by the same signal.

Crossed Signals

In head-on meeting situations, either vessel can signal first; in overtaking situations, the burdened vessel signals first, to indicate on which side she desires to pass. In crossing situations, the privileged vessel signals first. In any case, the second vessel answers with the *same* signal to show that the intent of the first boat is understood. If the skipper of the second vessel believes the action signaled by the first boat will lead to a collision, or is in any other way dangerous, he should sound the *danger* signal of four or more short blasts. *Never* answer a two-blast signal with one blast, or a one-blast signal with two blasts.

General Prudential Rule

Each set of rules has its General Prudential Rule or equivalent that makes it mandatory for the *privileged* vessel to alter course, slow down, stop, or take such other action as may be necessary to avoid a collision, if a collision might result should she hold her course and speed.

LIGHTED BUOYS

The United States has what is called a lateral system of buoyage, in which buoy shapes, colors, numbers, and light characteristics indicate the side on which the buoy is to be passed. The United States is making some changes, as noted below, to conform to the buoyage system of the International Association of Lighthouse Authorities (IALA). The changes are scheduled for completion by 1989.

Symbols and Meaning

Illustration	Lights which do not change color	Lights which show color variations	Phase description
	F. = Fixed	Alt. = Alternating	A continuous light. (Steady)
	F. Fl. = Fixed and flashing	Alt. F. Fl. = Alternating fixed and flashing	A fixed light varied at regular intervals by a flash of greater brilliance.
	F. Gp. Fl. = Fixed and group flashing	Alt. F. Gp. Fl. = Alternating fixed and group flashing	A fixed light varied at regular intervals by groups of two or more flashes of greater brilliance.
	Fl. = Flashing	Alt. Fl. = Alternating flashing	Showing a single flash at regular intervals, the duration of light always being less than the duration of darkness.
	Gp. Fl. = Group flashing	Alt. Gp. Fl. = Alternating group flashing	Showing at regular intervals groups of two or more flashes.
	Gp. Fl. (2+1) = Composite group flashing	. . . .	Light flashes are combined in alternate groups of different numbers.

	code		description
			...of different duration are grouped in such a manner as to produce a Morse character or characters.
	Qk. Fl. = Quick flashing	. . . .	Shows not fewer than sixty flashes per minute.
	I. Qk. Fl. = Interrupted quick flashing	. . . .	Shows quick flashes for about four seconds, followed by a dark period of about four seconds.
	E. Int. = Equal interval. (Isophase)	. . . .	Light with all durations of light and darkness equal.
	Occ. = Occulting	Alt. Occ. = Alternating occulting	A light totally eclipsed at regular intervals, the duration of light always greater than the duration of darkness.
	Gp. Occ. = Group occulting	. . . .	A light with a group of two or more eclipses at regular intervals.
	Gp. Occ. (2+3) = Composite group occulting	. . . .	A light in which the occultations are combined in alternate groups of different numbers.

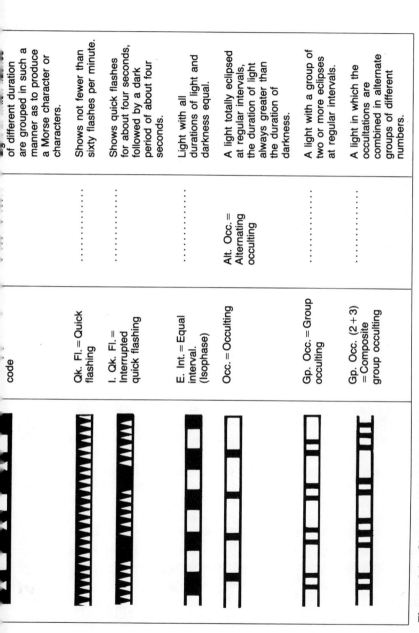

Figure 4.1 Characteristic Light Phases.

Color of Lights

For all lighted buoys in the lateral system, the following system of colors is used:

Green lights on buoys mark the left-hand side of a channel returning from seaward (black, green, odd-numbered buoys) or red-and-black (red-and-green) horizontally banded buoys with a black topmost band.

Red lights on buoys mark the right-hand side of a channel when entering from sea (red, even-numbered buoys) or red-and-black horizontally banded buoys with a red topmost band.

White lights on buoys may mark either side of channels in lieu of red or green. White lights are often used to increase the range of visibility, perhaps at a change in the channel's direction. White will no longer be used on buoys marking the sides of channels under the IALA-B system.

Light Phase Characteristics

Flashing lights (flashing at a rate of not more than thirty flashes per minute) are placed only on black or red buoys, or on special-purpose buoys.

Quick flashing lights (not fewer than sixty flashes each minute) are placed only on channel-edge–marking black-and-red buoys; these are used to indicate that *special caution* in piloting is required, as at sharp turns or changes in the width of the waterway, or to mark hazards that must be passed only on one side.

Interrupted quick flashing lights are used only on buoys painted with red-and-black horizontal bands. These are the buoys at channel junctions and obstructions that can be passed on either side. In the IALA-B system, these will be red-and-green horizontally banded buoys with a white composite group flashing light (2 + 1)—two flashes followed by a single flash, repeated.

Morse code "A" flashing white lights are placed only on black-and-white vertically striped buoys that mark a fairway or midchannel; these are passed close to on either side.

PRIMARY SEACOAST LIGHTS

If you do any extended cruising, you should know how to identify

(1)	(2)	(3)		(4)	(5)	(6)		(7)
No.	Name Character and period of light (Duration in italics)	Location Latitude, N. Deg. Min.	Longitude, W. Deg. Min.	Light or daybeacon above water Feet	Candlepower Miles seen in italics	Structure, vessel, or buoy top of lantern above ground Feet	Established, Moved or rebuilt Year	Radiobeacon, fog signal, sectors and remarks

EIGHTH DISTRICT

7482 6466 J4O34	GALVESTON JETTY LIGHT On south jetty, near east end. Alt. Fl. W. & R., 10^S *0.4^{S}Wfl. 4.6^{S}ec.* *0.4^{S}Rfl. 4.6^{S}ec.* *Resident Personnel.*	29 19.7	94 41.5	91	W. 250,000 R. 140,000 *15*	Cream-colored cylindrical brick tower with black pilasters, on skeleton structure.	1916	RADIOBEACON: Antenna 70 feet 278° from light tower. See p. XVII for method of operation. HORN: diaphragm; 1 blast ev 20^S(fl(2^{S}bl). Special Radio Direction Finder Calibration Service, see p. XIX.

Figure 4.2 Excerpt from the Light List Vol. II (Atlantic and Gulf coasts) describes Galveston Jetty Light illustrated in Figure 4.3.

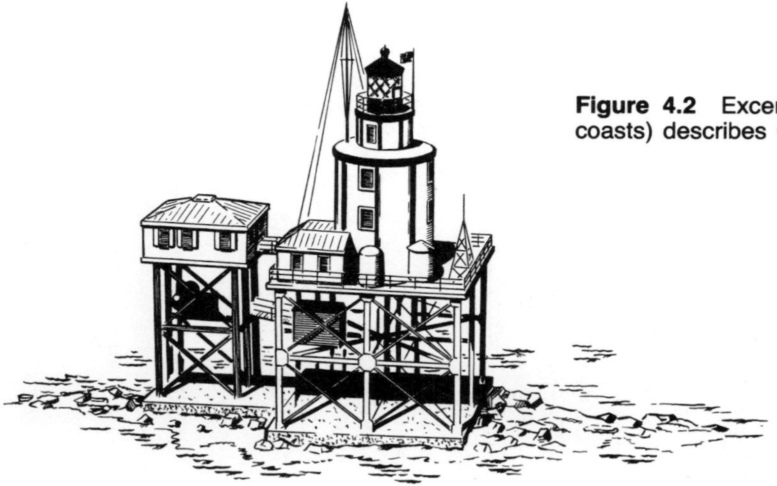

Figure 4.3 Galveston Jetty Light.

all major and secondary light structures (or ships) in your cruising area. Light lists published by the Coast Guard are available that give the following information for each light: name, character and period of light; location; height of structure above water; description of structure, vessel, or buoy; and special characteristics. (See the Government Publications listing, Section IX).

The excerpt and drawing, Figures 4.2 and 4.3, illustrate a typical major light and its description. The light number in this case is of little significance. The structure is identified as Galveston Jetty Light, with a light that flashes alternately white and red on a ten-second cycle: a four-tenths second white flash, four and six-tenths second interval, four-tenths second red flash, and four and six-tenths second interval. It is located on the south jetty at latitude 29°19.7 and longitude 94°41.5 and its light is ninety-one feet above sea level. The white light is of 250,000 candlepower; the red light is 140,000 candlepower, and in normal visibility it can be seen from a distance of fifteen miles. The description is self-explanatory. It has a radio beacon, with antenna located seventy feet away from the light tower at a true bearing of 278°; a description of its use by boatmen is given on page 283 of the *Light List.* The fog signal is generated by a diaphragm horn, and it is a single two-second blast given every twenty seconds. A special direction finder calibration service is available, and a description of its operation is given on page 344 of the *Light List.*

DEMARCATION LINES

The following information on demarcation lines is taken from the Coast Guard publication *Navigation Rules, International-Inland.* Note that these demarcation lines are printed on the appropriate charts and labeled as such.

§80.01 General basis and purpose of demarcation lines.

(a) The regulations in this part establish the lines of demarcation delineating those waters upon which mariners shall comply with the International Regulations for Preventing Collisions at Sea, 1972 (72 COLREGS) and those waters upon which mariners shall comply with the Inland Navigation Rules.

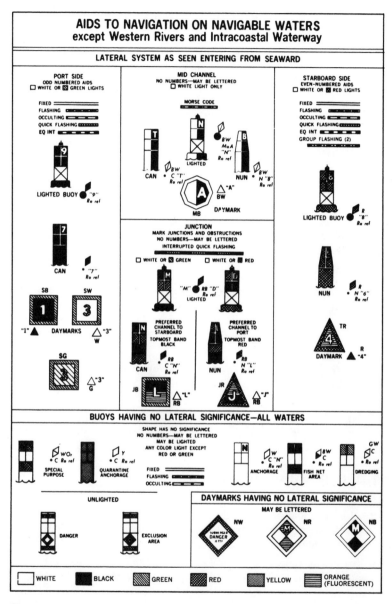

Figure 4.4

PILOTING

(b) The waters inside of the lines are Inland Rules Waters. The waters outside the lines are COLREGS Waters.

(c) The regulations in this part do not apply to the Great Lakes or their connecting and tributary waters as described in Part 97 of this chapter.

ATLANTIC COAST

First District

§80.105 Calais, ME, to Cape Small, ME.

The 72 COLREGS shall apply on the harbors, bays, and inlets on the east coast of Maine from International Bridge at Calais, ME, to the southwesternmost extremity of Bald Head at Cape Small.

§80.110 Casco Bay, ME.

(a) A line drawn from the southwesternmost extremity of Bald Head at Cape Small to the southeasternmost extremity of Ragged Island; thence to the southern tangent of Jaquish Island thence to Little Mark Island Monument Light; thence to the northernmost extremity of Jewell Island.

(b) A line drawn from the tower on Jewell Island charted in approximate position latitude 43°40.6'N. longitude 70°05.9'W. to the northeasternmost extremity of Outer Green Island.

(c) A line drawn from the southwesternmost extremity of Outer Green Island to Ram Island Ledge Light; thence to Portland Head Light.

§80.115 Portland Head, ME, to Cape Ann, MA.

(a) Except inside lines specifically described in this section, the 72 COLREGS shall apply on the harbors, bays, and inlets on the east coast of Maine, New Hampshire, and Massachusetts from Portland Head to Halibut Point at Cape Ann.

(b) A line drawn from the southernmost tower on Gerrish Island charted in approximate position latitude 43°04.0'N., longitude 70°41.2'W. to Whaleback Light; thence to Jeffrey Point Light; thence to the northeasternmost extremity of Frost Point.

(c) A line drawn from the northernmost extremity of Farm Point to Annisquam Harbor Light.

§80.120 Cape Ann, MA, to Marblehead Neck, MA.

(a) Except inside lines specifically described in this section, the 72 COLREGS shall apply on the harbors, bays, and inlets on the east coast of Massachusetts from Halibut Point at Cape Ann to Marblehead Neck.

(b) A line drawn from Gloucester Harbor Breakwater Light to the twin towers charted in approximate position latitude 42°35.1'N., longitude 70°41.6'W.

(c) A line drawn from the westernmost extremity of Gales Point to the easternmost extremity of House Island; thence to Bakers Island Light; thence to Marblehead Light.

[CGD 81-017, 46 FR 28154, May 26, 1981]

§80.125 Marblehead Neck, MA, to Nahant, MA.

The 72 COLREGS apply on the harbors, bays, and inlets on the east coast of Massachusetts from Marblehead Neck to the easternmost tower at Nahant, charted in approximate position latitude 42°25.4'N., longitude 70°54.6'W.

[CGD 81-017, 46 FR 28154, May 26, 1981]

§80.130 Boston Harbor entrance.

A line drawn from easternmost tower at Nahant, charted in approximate position latitude 42°25.4'N., longitude 70°54.6'W., to Boston Lighted Horn Buoy "B"; thence to the easternmost radio tower at Hull, charted in approximate position latitude 42°16.7'N., longitude 70°52.6'W.

[CGD 80-017, 46 FR 28154, May 26, 1981]

§80.135 Hull, MA, to Race Point, MA.

(a) Except inside lines described in this section, the 72 COLREGS apply on the harbors, bays, and inlets on the east coast of Massachusetts from the easternmost radio tower at Hull, charted in approximate position latitude 42°16.7'N., longitude 70°52.6'W., to Race Point on Cape Cod.

(b) A line drawn from Cape Cod Canal Breakwater Light 4 south to the shoreline.

[CGD 80-017, 46 FR 28154, May 26, 1981]

§80.145 Race Point, MA, to Watch Hill, RI.

(a) Except inside lines specifically described in this section, the 72 COLREGS shall apply on the sounds, bays, harbors, and inlets along the coast of Cape Cod and the southern coasts of Massachusetts and Rhode Island from Race Point to Watch Hill.

(b) A line drawn from Nobska Point Light to Tarpaulin Cove Light on the southeastern side of Naushon Island; thence from the southernmost tangent of Naushon Island to the easternmost extremity of Nashawena Island; thence from the southwesternmost extremity of Nashawena Island to the easternmost extremity of Cuttyhunk Island; thence from the southwestern tangent of Cuttyhunk Island to the tower on Gooseberry Neck charted in approximate position latitude 41°29.1′N., longitude 71°02.3′W.

(c) A line drawn from Sakonnet Breakwater Light 2 to the silo on Sacnuest Point charted in approximate position latitude 41°28.5′N., longitude 71°09.8′W.

(d) An east-west line drawn through Beavertail Light between Brenton Point and the Boston Neck shoreline.

[CGD 81-017, 46 FR 28154, May 26, 1981]

§80.150 Block Island, RI.

The 72 COLREGS shall apply on the harbors of Block Island.

Third District

§80.305 Watch Hill, RI to Montauk Point, NY.

(a) A line drawn from Watch Hill Light to East Point on Fishers Island.

(b) A line drawn from Race Point to Race Rock Light; thence to Little Gull Island Light; thence to East Point on Plum Island.

(c) A line drawn from Plum Island Harbor East Dolphin Light to Plum Island Harbor West Dolphin Light.

(d) A line drawn from Plum Island Light to Orient Point Light; thence to Orient Point.

(e) A line drawn from the lighthouse ruins at the southwestern end of Long Beach Point to Cornelius Point.

(f) A line drawn from Coecles Harbor Entrance Light to Sungic Point.

PILOTING

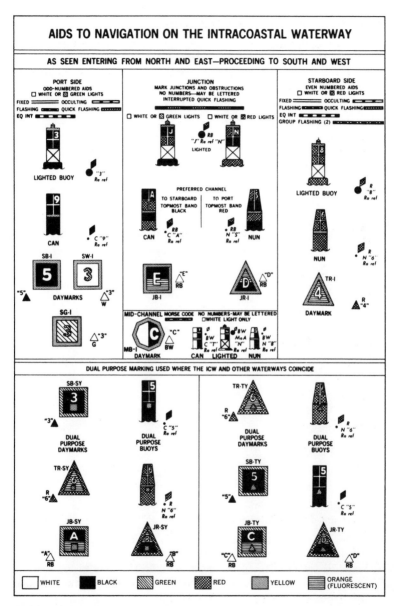

Figure 4.5

(g) A line drawn from Nichols Point to Cedar Island Light.

(h) A line drawn from Three Mile Harbor West Breakwater Light to Three Mile Harbor East Breakwater Light.

(i) A line drawn from Montauk West Jetty Light 2 to Montauk East Jetty Light 1.

[CGD 81-017, 46 FR 28154, May 26, 1981]

§80.310 Montauk Point, NY, to Atlantic Beach, NY.

(a) A line drawn from Shinnecock Inlet East Breakwater Light to Shinnecock Inlet West Breakwater Light.

(b) A line drawn from Moriches Inlet East Breakwater Light to Moriches Inlet West Breakwater Light.

(c) A line drawn from Fire Island Inlet Breakwater Light 348° true to the southernmost extremity of the spit of land at the western end of Oak Beach.

(d) A line drawn from Jones Inlet Light 322° true across the southwest tangent of the island on the north side of Jones Inlet to the shoreline.

[CGD 81-017, 46 FR 28154, May 26, 1981]

§80.315 New York Harbor.

A line drawn from East Rockaway Inlet Breakwater Light to Sandy Hook Light.

§80.320 Sandy Hook, NJ, to Cape May, NJ.

(a) A line drawn from Shark River Inlet North Breakwater Light 2 to Shark River Inlet South Breakwater Light 1.

(b) A line drawn from Manasquan Inlet North Breakwater Light to Manasquan Inlet South Breakwater Light.

(c) A line drawn from Barnegat Inlet North Breakwater Light 2 to Barnegat Inlet South Breakwater Light 5 continues along the lines formed by the submerged Barnegat Inlet Breakwaters to the shoreline.

(d) A line drawn from the seaward tangent of Long Beach Island to the seaward tangent to Pullen Island across Beach Haven and Little Egg Inlets.

(e) A line drawn from the seaward tangent of Pullen Island to the seaward tangent of Brigantine Island across Brigantine Inlet.

(f) A line drawn from the seaward extremity of Absecon Inlet North Jetty to Atlantic City Light.

(g) A line drawn from the southernmost point of Longport at latitude 39°18.2′N., longitude 74°32.2′W. to the northeasternmost point of Ocean City at latitude 39°17.6′N., longitude 74°33.1′W. across Great Egg Harbor Inlet.

(h) A line drawn parallel with the general trend of highwater shoreline across Corson Inlet.

(i) A line formed by the centerline of the Townsend Inlet Highway Bridge.

(j) A line formed by the shoreline of Seven Mile Beach and Hereford Inlet Light.

(k) A line drawn from Cape May Inlet East Jetty Light to Cape May Inlet West Jetty Light.

§80.325 Delaware Bay.

A line drawn from Cape May Light to Harbor of Refuge Light; thence to the northernmost extremity of Cape Henlopen.

Fifth District

§80.505 Cape Henlopen, DE, to Cape Charles, VA.

(a) A line drawn from Indian River Inlet North Jetty Light to Indian River Inlet South Jetty Light.

(b) A line drawn from Ocean City Inlet Light 6 234° true across Ocean City Inlet to the submerged south breakwater.

(c) A line drawn from Assateague Beach Tower Light to the tower charted at latitude 37°52.6′N., longitude 75°26.7′W.

(d) A line formed by the range of Wachapreague Inlet Light 3 and Parramore Beach Lookout Tower drawn across Wachapreague Inlet.

(e) A line drawn from the lookout tower charted on the northern end of Hog Island to the seaward tangent of Parramore Beach.

(f) A line drawn 207° true from the lookout tower charted on the southern end of Hog Island across Great Machipongo Inlet.

(g) A line formed by the range of the two cupolas charted on the southern end of Cobb Island drawn across Sand Shoal Inlet.

(h) Except as provided elsewhere in this section from Cape Henlopen to Cape Charles, lines drawn parallel with the general trend of the highwater shoreline across the entrances to small bays and inlets.

§80.510 Chesapeake Bay Entrance, VA.

A line drawn from Cape Charles Light to Cape Henry Light.

§80.515 Cape Henry, VA, to Cape Hatteras, NC.

(a) A line drawn from Rudee Inlet Jetty Light 2 to Rudee Inlet Jetty Light 1.

(b) A line formed by the centerline of the highway bridge across Oregon Inlet.

§80.520 Cape Hatteras, NC, to Cape Lookout, NC.

(a) A line drawn from Hatteras Inlet Light 255° true to the eastern end of Ocracoke Island.

(b) A line drawn from the westernmost extremity of Ocracoke Island at latitude 35°04.0'N., longitude 76°00.8'W. to the northeastern extremity of Portsmouth Island at latitude 35°03.7'N., longitude 76°02.3'W.

(c) A line drawn across Drum Inlet parallel with the general trend of the highwater shoreline.

§80.525 Cape Lookout, NC, to Cape Fear, NC.

(a) A line drawn from Cape Lookout Light to the seaward tangent of the southeastern end of Shackleford Banks.

(b) A line drawn from Morehead City Channel Range Front Light to the seaward extremity of the Beaufort Inlet west jetty.

(c) A line drawn from the southernmost extremity of Bogue Banks at latitude 34°38.7'N., longitude 77°06.0'W. across Bogue Inlet to the northernmost extremity of Bear Beach at latitude 34°38.5'N., longitude 77°07.1'W.

(d) A line drawn from the tower charted in approximate position latitude 34°31.5'N., longitude 77°20.8'W. to the seaward tangent of the shoreline on the northeast side of New River Inlet.

(e) A line drawn across New Topsail Inlet between the closest extremities of the shore on either side of the inlet from latitude 34°20.8'N., longitude 77°39.2'W. to latitude 34°20.6'N., longitude 77°39.6'W.

(f) A line drawn from the seaward extremity of the jetty on the northeast side of Masonboro Inlet west to the shoreline approximately 0.6 mile southwest of the inlet.

(g) Except as provided elsewhere in this section from Cape Lookout to Cape Fear, lines drawn parallel with the general trend of the highwater shoreline across the entrance of small bays and inlets.

§80.530 Cape Fear, NC, to Little River Inlet, NC.

(a) A line drawn from the abandoned lighthouse charted in approximate position latitude 33°52.4'N., longitude 78°00.1'W. across the Cape Fear River Entrance to Oak Island Light.

(b) Except as provided elsewhere in this section from Cape Fear to Little River Inlet, lines drawn parallel with the general trend of the highwater shoreline across the entrance to small inlets.

Seventh District

§80.703 Little River Inlet, SC, to Cape Romain, SC.

(a) A line drawn from the westernmost extremity of the sand spit on Bird Island to the easternmost extremity of Waties Island across Little River Inlet.

(b) Lines drawn parallel with the general trend of the highwater shoreline across Hog Inlet, Murrels Inlet, Midway Inlet, Pawleys Inlet, and North Inlet.

(c) A line drawn from the charted position of Winyah Bay North Jetty End Buoy 2N south to the Winyah Bay South Jetty.

(d) A line drawn from Santee Point to the seaward tangent of Cedar Island.

(e) A line drawn from Cedar Island Point west to Murphy Island.

(f) A north-south line (longitude 79°20.3'W.) drawn from Murphy Island to the northernmost extremity of Cape Island Point.

§80.707 Cape Romain, SC, to Sullivans Island, SC.

(a) A line drawn from the western extremity of Cape Romain 292° true to Racoon Key on the west side of Racoon Creek.

(b) A line drawn from the westernmost extremity of Sandy Point across Bull Bay to the northernmost extremity of Northeast Point.

(c) A line drawn from the southernmost extremity of Bull Island to the easternmost extremity of Capers Island.

(d) A line formed by the overhead power cable from Capers Island to Dewees Island.

(e) A line formed by the overhead power cable from Dewees Island to Isle of Palms.

(f) A line formed by the centerline of the highway bridge between Isle of Palms and Sullivans Island over Breach Inlet.

§80.710 Charleston Harbor, SC.

(a) A line formed by the submerged north jetty from the shore to the west end of the north jetty.

(b) A line drawn from across the seaward extremity of the Charleston Harbor Jetties.

(c) A line drawn from the west end of the South Jetty across the South Entrance to Charleston Harbor to shore on a line formed by the submerged south jetty.

§80.712 Morris Island, SC, to Hilton Head Island, SC.

(a) A line drawn from the Folly Island Loran Tower charted in approximate position latitude 32°41.0′W., longitude 79°53.2′W. to the abandoned lighthouse tower on the northside of Lighthouse Inlet; thence west to the shoreline of Morris Island.

(b) A straight line drawn from the seaward tangent of Folly Island through Folly River Daybeacon 10 across Stono River to the shoreline of Sandy Point.

(c) A line drawn from the southernmost extremity of Seabrook Island 257° true across the North Edisto River Entrance to the shore of Botany Bay Island.

(d) A line drawn from the microwave antenna tower on Edisto Beach charted in approximate position latitude 32°29.3′N., longitude 80°19.2′W. across St. Helena Sound to the abandoned lighthouse tower on Hunting Island.

(e) A line formed by the centerline of the highway bridge between Hunting Island and Fripp Island.

(f) A line drawn from the westernmost extremity of Bull Point on Capers Island to Port Royal Sound Channel Rear Range Light;

thence 245° true to the easternmost extremity of Hilton Head at latitude 32°13.2'N., longitude 80°40.1'W.

§80.715 Savannah River.

A line drawn from the southernmost tank on Hilton Head Island charted in approximate position latitude 32°06.7'N., longitude 80°49.3'W. to Bloody Point Range Rear Light; thence to Tybee (Range Rear) Light.

§80.717 Tybee Island, GA, to St. Simons Island, GA.

(a) A line drawn from the southernmost extremity of Savannah Beach on Tybee Island 255° true across Tybee Inlet to the shore of Little Tybee Island south of the entrance to Buck Hammock Creek.

(b) A straight line drawn from the northernmost extremity of Wassaw Island 031° true through Tybee River Daybeacon 1 to the shore of Little Tybee Island.

(c) A line drawn approximately parallel with the general trend of the highwater shorelines from the seaward tangent of Wassau Island to the seaward tangent of Bradley Point on Ossabaw Island.

(d) A north-south line (longitude 80°08.4'W.) drawn from the southernmost extremity of Ossabaw Island to St. Catherines Island.

(e) A north-south line (longitude 80°10.6'W.) drawn from the southernmost extremity of St. Catherines Island to Northeast Point on Blackbeard Island.

(f) A line following the general trend of the seaward highwater shoreline across Cabretta inlet.

(g) A north-south line (longitude 81°16.9'W.) drawn from the southwesternmost point on Sapelo Island to Wolf Island.

(h) A north-south line (longitude 81°17.1'W.) drawn from the southeasternmost point of Wolf Island to the northeasternmost point on Little St. Simons Island.

(i) A line drawn from the northeasternmost extremity of Sea Island 045° true to Little St. Simons Island.

(j) An east-west line from the southernmost extremity of Sea Island across Goulds Inlet to St. Simons Island.

§80.720 St. Simons Island, GA, to Amelia Island, FL.

(a) A line drawn from St. Simons Light to the northernmost tank on Jekyll Island charted in approximate position latitude 31°05.9′N., longitude 81°24.5′W.

(b) A line drawn from the southernmost tank on Jekyll Island charted in approximate position latitude 31°01.6′N., longitude 81°25.2′W. to coordinate latitude 30°59.4′N., longitude 81°23.7′W. (0.5 nautical mile east of the charted position of St. Andrew Sound Lighted Buoy 32); thence to the abandoned lighthouse tower on the north end of Little Cumberland Island charted in approximate position latitude 30°58.5′N., longitude 81°24.8′W.

(c) A line drawn across the seaward extremity of the St. Marys Entrance Jetties.

§80.723 Amelia Island, FL, to Cape Canaveral, FL.

(a) A line drawn from the southernmost extremity of Amelia Island to the northeasternmost extremity of Little Talbot Island.

(b) A line formed by the centerline of the highway bridge from Little Talbot Island to Fort George Island.

(c) A line drawn across the seaward extremity of the St. Johns River Entrance Jetties.

(d) A line drawn across the seaward extremity of the St. Augustine Inlet Jetties.

(e) A line formed by the centerline of the highway bridge over Matanzas Inlet.

(f) A line drawn across the seaward extremity of the Ponce de Leon Inlet Jetties.

§80.727 Cape Canaveral, FL, to Miami Beach, FL.

(a) A line drawn across the seaward extremity of the Port Canaveral Entrance Channel Jetties.

(b) A line drawn across the seaward extremity of the Sebastian Inlet Jetties.

(c) A line drawn across the seaward extremity of the Fort Pierce Inlet Jetties.

(d) A north-south line (longitude 80°09.8′W.) drawn across St. Lucie Inlet through St. Lucie Inlet Entrance Range Front Daybeacon.

(e) A line drawn from the seaward extremity of Jupiter Inlet North Jetty to the northeast extremity of the concrete apron on the south side of Jupiter inlet.

(f) A line drawn across the seaward extremity of the Lake Worth Inlet Jetties.

(g) A line drawn across the seaward extremity of the South Lake Worth Inlet Jetties.

(h) A line drawn from Boca Raton Inlet North Jetty Light 2 to Boca Raton Inlet South Jetty Light 1.

(i) A line drawn from Hillsboro Inlet Light to Hillsboro Inlet Entrance Light 2; thence to Hillsboro Inlet Entrance Light 1; thence west to the shoreline.

(j) A line drawn across the seaward extremity of the Port Everglades Entrance Jetties.

(k) A line formed by the centerline of the highway bridge over Bakers Haulover Inlet.

§80.730 Miami Harbor, FL.

A line drawn across the seaward extremity of the Miami Harbor Government Cut Jetties.

§80.735 Miami, FL, to Long Key, FL.

(a) A line drawn from the southernmost extremity of Fisher Island 211° true to the point latitude 25°45.1′N., longitude 80°08.6′W. on Virginia Key.

(b) A line formed by the centerline of the highway bridge between Virginia Key and Key Biscayne.

(c) A line drawn from the abandoned lighthouse tower on Cape Florida to Biscayne Channel Light 8; thence to the northernmost extremity on Soldier Key.

(d) A line drawn from the southernmost extremity on Soldier Key to the northernmost extremity of the Ragged Keys.

(e) A line drawn from the Ragged Keys to the southernmost extremity of Angelfish Key following the general trend of the seaward shoreline.

(f) A line drawn on the centerline of the Overseas Highway (U.S. 1) and bridges from latitude 25°19.3′N., longitude 80°16.0′W. at Little Angelfish Creek to the radar dome charted on Long Key at approximate position latitude 24°49.32N., longitude 80°49.2′W.

[CGD 81-017, 46 FR 28154, May 26, 1981]

PUERTO RICO AND VIRGIN ISLANDS

Seventh District

§80.738 Puerto Rico and Virgin Islands

(a) Except inside lines specifically described in this section, the 72 COLREGS shall apply on all other bays, harbors, and lagoons of Puerto Rico and the U.S. Virgin Islands.

(b) A line drawn from Puerto San Juan Light to Cabras Light across the entrance of San Juan Harbor.

GULF COAST

Seventh District

§80.740 Long Key, FL, to Cape Sable, FL.

A line drawn from the radar dome charted on Long Key at approximate position latitude 24°49.3′N., longitude 80°49.2′W. to Long Key Light 1; thence to Arsenic Bank Light 1; thence to Arsenic Bank Light 2; thence to Sprigger Bank Light 5; thence to Schooner Bank Light 6; thence to Oxfoot Bank Light 10; thence to East Cape Light 2; thence through East Cape Daybeacon 1A to the shoreline at East Cape.

§80.745 Cape Sable, FL, to Cape Romano, FL.

(a) A line drawn following the general trend of the mainland, highwater shoreline from Cape Sable at East Cape to Little Shark River Light 1; thence to westernmost extremity of Shark Point; thence following the general trend of the mainland, highwater shoreline crossing the entrances of Harney River, Broad Creek, Broad River, Rodgers River First Bay, Chatham River, Huston River, to the shoreline at coordinate latitude 25°41.8′N., longitude 18°17.9′W.

(b) The 72 COLREGS shall apply to the waters surrounding the Ten Thousand Islands and the bays, creeks, inlets, and rivers between Chatham Bend and Marco Island except inside lines specifically described in this part.

(c) A north-south line drawn at longitude 18°20.2′W. across the entrance to Lopez River.

(d) A line drawn across the entrance to Turner River parallel to the general trend of the shoreline.

(e) A line formed by the centerline of Highway 92 Bridge at Goodland.

§80.748 Cape Romano, FL, to Sanibel Island, FL.

(a) A line drawn across Big Marco Pass parallel to the general trend of the seaward, highwater shoreline.

(b) A line drawn from the northwesternmost extremity of Coconut Island 000°T across Capri Pass.

(c) Lines drawn across Hurricane and Little Marco Passes parallel to the general trend of the seaward, highwater shoreline.

(d) A straight line drawn from Gordon Pass Light 4 through Daybeacon 5 to the shore.

(e) A line drawn across the seaward extremity of Doctors Pass Jetties.

(f) Lines drawn across Wiggins, Big Hickory, New, and Big Carlos Passes parallel to the general trend of the seaward highwater shoreland.

(g) A straight line drawn from Sanibel Island Light through Matanzas Pass Channel Light 2 to the shore of Estero Island.

[CGD 80-017, 46 FR 28154, May 26, 1981]

§80.750 Sanibel Island, FL, to St. Petersburg, FL.

(a) Lines drawn across Redfish and Captiva Passes parallel to the general trend of the seaward, highwater shorelines.

(b) A line drawn from La Costa Test Pile North Light to Port Boca Grande Light.

(c) Lines drawn across Gasparilla and Stump Passes parallel to the general trend of the seaward, highwater shorelines.

(d) A line across the seaward extremity of Venice Inlet Jetties.

(e) A line drawn across Midnight Pass parallel to the general trend of the seaward, highwater shoreline.

(f) A line drawn from Big Sarasota Pass Light 14 to the southernmost extremity of Lido Key.

(g) A line drawn across New Pass tangent to the seaward, highwater shoreline of Longboat Key.

(h) A line drawn across Longboat Pass parallel to the seaward, highwater shoreline.

(i) A line drawn from the northwesternmost extremity of Bean Point to the southeasternmost extremity of Egmont Key.

(j) A straight line drawn from Egmont Key Light through Egmont Channel Range Rear Light to the shoreline on Mullet Key.

(k) A line drawn from the northernmost extremity of Mullet Key across Bunces Pass and South Channel to Pass-a-Grille Light 8; thence to Pass-a-Grille Daybeacon 9; thence to the southwesternmost extremity of Long Key.

[CGD 80-017, 46 FR 28154, May 26, 1981]

§80.753 St. Petersburg, FL, to the Anclote, FL.

(a) A line drawn across Blind Pass parallel with the general trend of the seaward, highwater shoreline.

(b) Lines formed by the centerline of the highway bridges over Johns and Clearwater Passes.

(c) A line drawn across Dunedin and Hurricane Passes parallel with the general trend of the seaward, highwater shoreline.

(d) A line drawn from the northernmost extremity of Honeymoon Island to Anclote Anchorage South Entrance Light 7; thence to Anclote Keys Light; thence a straight line through Anclote River Cut B Range Rear Light to the shoreline.

§80.755 Anclote, FL, to the Suncoast Keys, FL.

(a) Except inside lines specifically described in this section, the 72 COLREGS shall apply on the bays, bayous, creeks, marinas, and rivers from Anclote to the Suncoast Keys.

(b) A north-south line drawn at longitude 82°38.3′W. across the Chassahowitzka River Entrance.

§80.757 Suncoast Keys, FL, to Horseshoe Point, FL.

(a) Except inside lines specifically described in this section, the 72 COLREGS shall apply on the bays, bayous, creeks, and marinas from the Suncoast Keys to Horseshoe Point.

(b) A line formed by the centerline of Highway 44 Bridge over the Salt River.

(c) ·A north-south line drawn through Crystal River Entrance Daybeacon 25 across the river entrance.

(d) A north-south line drawn through the Cross Florida Barge Canal Daybeacon 38 across the canal.

(e) A north-south line drawn through Withlacoochee River Daybeacon 40 across the river.

(f) A line drawn from the westernmost extremity of South Point north to the shoreline across the Waccasassa River Entrance.

(g) A line drawn from position latitude 29°16.6'N., longitude 83°06.7'W. 300° true to the shoreline of Hog Island.

(h) A north-south line drawn through Suwannee River Wadley Pass Channel Daybeacons 30 and 31 across the Suwannee River.

§80.760 Horseshoe Point, FL, to Rock Islands, FL.

(a) Except inside lines specifically described provided in this section, the 72 COLREGS shall apply on the bays, bayous, creeks, marinas, and rivers from Horseshoe Point to the Rock Islands.

(b) A north-south line drawn through Steinhatchee River Light 21.

(c) A line drawn from Fenholloway River Approach Light FR east across the entrance to Fenholloway River.

Eighth District

§80.805 Rock Island, FL, to Cape San Blas, FL.

(a) A north-south line drawn from the Econfina River Light to the opposite shore.

(b) A line drawn from Gamble Point Light to the southernmost extremity of Cabell Point.

(c) A line drawn from St. Marks (Range Rear) Light to St. Marks Channel Light 11; thence to the southernmost extremity of Live Oak Point; thence through Shell Point Light to the southernmost extremity of Ochlockonee Point; thence to Bald Point.

(d) A line drawn from the south shore of Southwest Cape at longitude 84°22.7'W. to Dog Island Reef East Light 1; thence to Turkey Point Light 2; thence to the easternmost extremity of Dog Island.

(e) A line drawn from the westernmost extremity of Dog Island to the easternmost extremity of St. George Island.

(f) A line drawn across the seaward extremity of the St. George Island Channel Jetties.

(g) A line drawn from the northwesternmost extremity of Sand Island to West Pass Light 7.

(h) A line drawn from the westernmost extremity of St. Vincent Island to the southeast, highwater shoreline of Indian Peninsula at longitude 85°13.5′W.

§80.810 Cape San Blas, FL, to Perdido Bay, FL.

(a) A line drawn from St. Joseph Range A Rear Light through St. Joseph Range B Front Light to St. Joseph Point.

(b) A line drawn across the mouth of Salt Creek as an extension of the general trend of the shoreline.

(c) A line drawn from the northernmost extremity of Crooked Island 000°T. to the mainland.

(d) A line drawn from the easternmost extremity of Shell Island 120° true to the shoreline across the east entrance to St. Andrews Bay.

(e) A line drawn between the seaward end of the St. Andrews Bay Entrance Jetties.

(f) A line drawn between the seaward end of the Choctawatchee Bay Entrance Jetties.

(g) A west-east line drawn from Fort McGee Leading Light across the Pensacola Bay Entrance.

(h) A line drawn between the seaward end of the Perdido Pass Jetties.

§80.815 Mobile Bay, AL, to the Chandeleur Islands, LA.

(a) A line drawn across the inlets to Little Lagoon as an extension of the general trend of the shoreline.

(b) A line drawn from Mobile Point Light to Dauphin Island Spit Light to the eastern corner of Fort Gaines at Pelican Point.

(c) A line drawn from the westernmost extremity of Dauphin Island to the easternmost extremity of Petit Bois Island.

(d) A line drawn from Horn Island Pass Entrance Range Front Light on Petit Bois Island to the easternmost extremity of Horn Island.

(e) An east-west line (latitude 30°14.7′N.) drawn between the westernmost extremity of Horn Island to the easternmost extremity of Ship Island.

(f) A curved line drawn following the general trend of the seaward highwater shoreline of Ship Island.

(g) A line drawn from Ship Island Light; thence to Chandeleu Light; thence in a curved line following the general trend of the sea ward, highwater shorelines of the Chandeleur Islands to the island a coordinate latitude 29°31.1'N., longitude 89°05.7'W.; thence to Bren ton Island Light located at latitude 29°29.1'N., longitude 89°09.7'W.

§80.825 Mississippi Passes, LA.

(a) A line drawn from Brenton Island Light to coordinate latitude 29°21.5'N., longitude 89°11.7'W.

(b) A line drawn from coordinate latitude 29°21.5'N., longitude 89°11.7'W. following the general trend of the seaward, highwater shoreline in a southeasterly direction to coordinate latitude 29°12.4'N., longitude 89°06.0'W.; thence following the general trend of the seaward, highwater shoreline in a northeasterly direction to coordinate latitude 29°13.0'N., longitude 89°01.3'W. located on the northwest bank of North Pass.

(c) A line drawn from coordinate latitude 29°13.0'N., longitude 89°01.3'W. to coordinate latitude 29°12.7'N., longitude 89°00.9'W.; thence coordinate latitude 29°10.6'N., longitude 88°59.8'W.; thence coordinate latitude 29°03.5'N., longitude 89°03.7'W., thence Mississippi River South Pass East Jetty Light 4.

(d) A line drawn from Mississippi River South Pass East Jetty Light 4 to Mississippi River South Pass West Jetty Light; thence following the general trend of the seaward highwater shoreline in a northwesterly direction to coordinate latitude 29°03.4'N., longitude 89°13.0'W.; thence west to coordinate latitude 29°03.5'N., longitude 89°15.5'W.; thence following the general trend of the seaward, highwater shoreline in a southwesterly direction to Mississippi River Southwest Pass Entrance Light.

(e) A line drawn from Mississippi River Southwest Pass Entrance Light; thence to the seaward extremity of the Southwest Pass West Jetty located at coordinate latitude 28°54.5'N., longitude 89°26.1'W.

§80.830 Mississippi Passes, LA, to Point Au Fer, LA.

(a) A line drawn from the seaward extremity of the Southwest Pass West Jetty located at coordinate latitude 28°54.5'N., longitude

89°26.1'W.; thence following the general trend of the seaward, high-water jetty and shoreline in a north, northeasterly direction to Old Tower latitude 28°58.8'N., longitude 89°23.3'W.; thence to West Bay Light; thence to coordinate latitude 29°05.2'N., longitude 89°24.3'W.; thence a curved line following the general trend of the highwater shoreline to Point Au Fer Island except as otherwise described in this section.

(b) A line drawn across the seaward extremity of the Empire Waterway (Bayou Fontanelle) entrance jetties.

(c) A line drawn from Barataria Bay Light to the Grand Isle Fishing Jetty Light.

(d) A line drawn between the seaward extremity of the Belle Pass Jetties.

(e) A line drawn from the westernmost extremity of the Timbolies Island to the easternmost extremity of Isles Dernieres.

(f) A north-south line drawn from Caillou Bay Light 13 across Caillou Boca.

(g) A line drawn 107° true from Caillou Bay Boat Landing Light across the entrances to Grand Bayou du Large and Bayou Grand Caillou.

(h) A line drawn on an axis of 103° true through Taylors Bayou Light across the entrances to Jack Stout Bayou, Taylors Bayou, Pelican Pass, and Bayou de West.

§80.835 Point Au Fer, LA, to Calcasieu Pass, LA.

(a) A line drawn from Point Au Fer to Atchafalaya Channel Light 34; thence Point Au Fer Reef Light 33; Atchafalaya Bay Pipeline Light D latitude 29°25.0'N., longitude 91°31.7'W.; thence Atchafalaya Bay Light 1 latitude 29°25.3'N., longitude 91°35.8'W.; thence South Point.

(b) Lines following the general trend of the highwater shoreline drawn across the bayou canal inlet from the Gulf of Mexico between South Point and Calcasieu Pass except as otherwise described in this section.

(c) A line drawn on an axis of 130°T. through Southwest Pass Vermillion Bay Light 4 across Southwest Pass.

(d) A line drawn across the seaward extremity of the Freshwater Bayou Canal Entrance Jetties.

(e) A line drawn from Mermentau Channel East Jetty Light 6 to Mermentau Channel West Jetty Light 7.

(f) A line drawn from the radio tower charted in approximate position latitude 29°45.7'N., longitude 93°06.3'W. 160° true across Mermentau Pass.

(g) A line drawn across the seaward extremity of the Calcasieu Pass Jetties.

§80.840 Sabine Pass, TX, to Galveston, TX.

(a) A line drawn from the Sabine Pass East Jetty Light to the seaward end of the Sabine Pass West Jetty.

(b) A line drawn across the small boat passes through the Sabine Pass East and West Jetties.

(c) A line formed by the centerline of the highway bridge over Rollover Pass at Gilchrist.

§80.845 Galveston, TX, to Freeport, TX.

(a) A line drawn from Galveston North Jetty Light to Galveston South Jetty Light.

(b) A line formed by the centerline of the highway bridge over San Luis Pass.

(c) Lines formed by the centerlines of the highway bridges over the inlets to Christmas Bay (Cedar Cut) and Drum Bay.

(d) A line drawn from the seaward extremity of the Freeport North Jetty to Freeport Entrance Light 6; thence Freeport Entrance Light 7; thence the seaward extremity of Freeport South Jetty.

§80.850 Brazos River, TX, to the Rio Grande, TX.

(a) Except as otherwise described in this section lines drawn continuing the general trend of the seaward, highwater shorelines across the inlets to Brazos River Diversion Channel, San Bernard River, Cedar Lakes, Brown Cedar Cut, Colorado River, Matagorda Bay, Cedar Bayou, Corpus Christi Bay, and Laguna Madre.

(b) A line drawn across the seaward extremity of Matagorda Ship Channel North Jetties.

(c) A line drawn from the seaward tangent of Matagorda Peninsula at Decros Point to Matagorda Bay Buoy 2; thence to Matagorda Light.

(d) A line drawn across the seaward extremity of the Aransas Pass Jetties.

PILOTING

(e) A line drawn across the seaward extremity of the Port Mansfield Entrance Jetties.

(f) A line drawn across the seaward extremity of the Brazos Santiago Pass Jetties.

PACIFIC COAST

Eleventh District

§80.1105 Santa Catalina Island, CA.

The 72 COLREGS shall apply to the harbors on Santa Catalina Island.

§80.1110 San Diego Harbor, CA.

A line drawn from Zunica Jetty Light "V" to Zunica Jetty Light "Z"; thence to Point Loma Light.

§80.1115 Mission Bay, CA.

A line drawn from Mission Bay South Jetty Light 2 to Mission Bay North Jetty Light 1.

§80.1120 Oceanside Harbor, CA.

A line drawn from Oceanside South Jetty Light 4 to Oceanside Breakwater Light 3.

§80.1125 Dana Point Harbor, CA.

A line drawn from Dana Point Jetty Light 6 to Dana Point Breakwater Light 5.

§80.1130 Newport Bay, CA.

A line drawn from Newport Bay East Jetty Light 4 to Newport Bay West Jetty Light 3.

§80.1135 San Pedro Bay—Anaheim Bay, CA.

(a) A line drawn from Anaheim Bay East Jetty Light 6 to Anaheim

Bay West Jetty Light 5; thence to Long Beach Breakwater East End Light 1.

(b) A line drawn from Long Beach Channel Entrance Light 2 to Long Beach Light.

(c) A line drawn from Los Angeles Main Entrance Channel Light 2 to Los Angeles Light.

§80.1140 Redondo Harbor, CA.

A line drawn from Redondo Beach East Jetty Light 2 to Redondo Beach West Jetty Light 3.

§80.1145 Marina Del Rey, CA.

(a) A line drawn from Marina Del Rey Breakwater South Light 1 to Marina Del Rey Light 4.

(b) A line drawn from Marina Del Rey Breakwater North Light 2 to Marina Del Rey Light 3.

(c) A line drawn from Marina Del Rey Light 4 to the seaward extremity of the Ballona Creek South Jetty.

§80.1150 Port Hueneme, CA.

A line drawn from Port Hueneme East Jetty Light 4 to Port Hueneme West Jetty Light 3.

§80.1155 Channel Islands Harbor, CA.

(a) A line drawn from Channel Islands Harbor South Jetty Light 2 to Channel Islands Harbor Breakwater South Light 1.

(b) A line drawn from Channel Islands Harbor Breakwater North Light to Channel Islands Harbor North Jetty Light 5.

§80.1160 Ventura Marina, CA.

A line drawn from Ventura Marina South Jetty Light 6 to Ventura Marina Breakwater South Light 3; thence to Ventura Marina North Jetty Light 7.

§80.1165 Santa Barbara Harbor, CA.

A line drawn from Santa Barbara Harbor Light 4 to Santa Barbara Harbor Breakwater Light.

Twelfth District

§80.1205 San Luis Obispo Bay, CA.

A line drawn from the southernmost extremity of Fossil Point to the seaward extremity of Whaler Island Breakwater.

§80.1210 Estero-Morro Bay, CA.

A line drawn from the seaward extremity of the Morro Bay East Breakwater to the Morro Bay West Breakwater Light.

§80.1215 Monterey Harbor, CA.

A line drawn from Monterey Harbor Light 6 to the northern extremity of Monterey Municipal Wharf 2.

§80.1220 Moss Landing Harbor, CA.

A line drawn from the seaward extremity of the pier located 0.3 mile south of Moss Landing Harbor Entrance to the seaward extremity of the Moss Landing Harbor North Breakwater.

§80.1225 Santa Cruz Harbor, CA.

A line drawn from the seaward extremity of the Santa Cruz Harbor East Breakwater to Santa Cruz Harbor West Breakwater Light; thence to Santa Cruz Light.

§80.1230 Pillar Point Harbor, CA.

A line drawn from Pillar Point Harbor Light 6 to Pillar Point Harbor Light 5.

§80.1250 San Francisco Harbor, CA.

A straight line drawn from Point Bonita Light through Mile Rocks Light to the shore.

§80.1255 Bodega and Tomales Bay, CA.

(a) An east-west line drawn from Sand Point to Avalis Beach.

(b) A line drawn from the seaward extremity of Bodega Harbor North Breakwater to Bodega Harbor Entrance Light 1.

[CGD 81-017, 46 FR 28154, May 26, 1981]

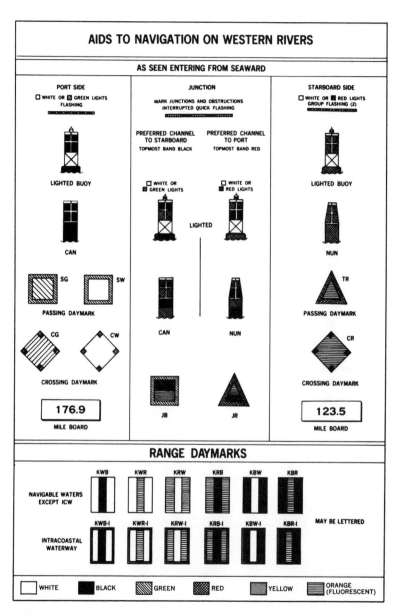

PILOTING

Figure 4.6

§80.1260 Albion River, CA.

A line drawn on an axis of 030° true through Albion River Light 1 across Albion Cove.

§80.1265 Noyo River, CA.

A line drawn from Noyo River Entrance Daybeacon 4 to Noyo River Entrance Light 5.

§80.1270 Arcata-Humboldt Bay, CA.

A line drawn from Humboldt Bay Entrance Light 4 to Humboldt Bay Entrance Light 3.

§80.1275 Crescent City Harbor, CA.

A line drawn from Crescent City Outer Breakwater Light 5 to the southeasternmost extremity of Whaler Island.

Thirteenth District

§80.1305 Chetco River, OR.

A line drawn from the seaward extremity of the Chetco River East Jetty to Chetco River Entrance Light 5.

[CGD 80-017, 46 FR 28154, May 26, 1981]

§80.1310 Rogue River, OR.

A line drawn from the seaward extremity of the Rogue River Entrance South Jetty to Rogue River North Jetty Light 3.

§80.1315 Coquille River, OR.

A line drawn across the seaward extremity of the Coquille River Entrance Jetties.

§80.1320 Coos Bay, OR.

A line drawn across the seaward extremity of the Coos Bay Entrance Jetties.

§80.1325 Umpqua River, OR.

A line drawn across the seaward extremity of the Umpqua River Entrance Jetties.

§80.1330 Siuslaw River, OR.

A line drawn from the seaward extremity of the Siuslaw River Entrance South Jetty to Siuslaw River Light 9.

§80.1335 Alsea Bay, OR.

A line drawn from the seaward shoreline on the north of the Alsea Bay Entrance 165° true across the channel entrance.

§80.1340 Yaquina Bay, OR.

A line drawn from the seaward extremity of Yaquina Bay Entrance South Jetty to the seaward extremity of Yaquina Bay Entrance North Jetty.

§80.1345 Depoe Bay, OR.

A line drawn across the Depoe Bay Channel entrance parallel with the general trend of the highwater shoreline.

§80.1350 Netarts Bay, OR.

A line drawn from the northernmost extremity of the shore on the south side of Netarts Bay north to the opposite shoreline.

§80.1355 Tillamook Bay, OR.

A north-south line drawn from the lookout tower charted on the north side of the entrance to Tillamook Bay south to the Tillamook Bay South Jetty.

§80.1360 Nehalem River, OR.

A line drawn approximately parallel with the general trend of the highwater shoreline across the Nehalem River Entrance.

§80.1365 Columbia River Entrance, OR/WA.

A line drawn from the seaward extremity of the Columbia River

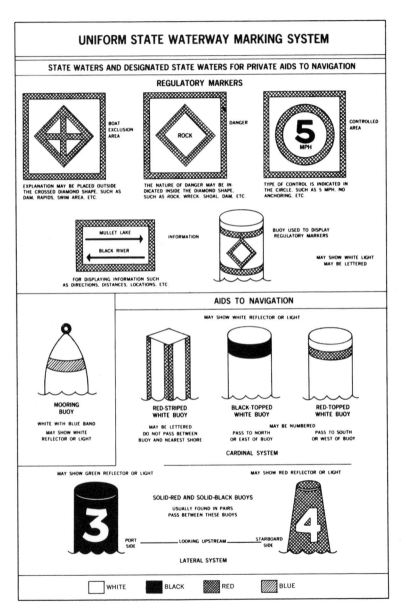

Figure 4.7

North Jetty (above water) 155° true to the seaward extremity of the Columbia River South Jetty (above water).

§80.1370 Willapa Bay, WA.

A line drawn from Willapa Bay Light 171° true to the westernmost tripod charted 1.6 miles south of Leadbetter Point.

§80.1375 Grays Harbor, WA.

A line drawn from across the seaward extremity (above water) of the Grays Harbor Entrance Jetties.

§80.1380 Quillayute River, WA.

A line drawn from the seaward extremity of the Quillayute River Entrance East Jetty to the overhead power cable tower charted on James Island; thence a straight line through Quillayute River Entrance Light 3 to the shoreline.

§80.1385 Strait of Juan de Fuca.

The 72 COLREGS shall apply on all waters of the Strait of Juan de Fuca.

§80.1390 Haro Strait and Strait of Georgia.

The 72 COLREGS shall apply on all waters of the Haro Strait and the Strait of Georgia.

§80.1395 Puget Sound and Adjacent Waters.

The 72 COLREGS shall apply on all waters of Puget Sound and adjacent waters, including Lake Union, Lake Washington, Hood Canal, and all tributaries.

[CGD 81-087, 46 FR 61456, Dec. 17, 1981]

PACIFIC ISLANDS

Fourteenth District

§80.1410 Hawaiian Island Exemption from General Rule

Except as provided elsewhere in this part for Mamala Bay and

Kaneohe Bay on Oahu; Port Allen and Nawiliwili Bay on Kauai; Kahului Harbor on Maui; and Kawailae and Hilo Harbors on Hawaii, the 72 COLREGS shall apply on all other bays, harbors, and lagoons of the Hawaiian Islands (including Midway).

§80.1420 Mamala Bay, Oahu, HI.

A line drawn from Barbers Point Light to Diamond Head Light.

§80.1430 Kaneohe Bay, Oahu, HI.

A straight line drawn from Pyramid Rock Light across Kaneohe Bay through the center of Mokolii Island to the shoreline.

§80.1440 Port Allen, Kauai, HI.

A line drawn from Hanapepe Light to Hanapepe Bay Breakwater Light.

[CGD 80-017, 46 FR 28154, May 26, 1981]

§80.1450 Nawiliwili Harbor, Kauai, HI.

A line drawn from Nawiliwili Harbor Breakwater Light to Kukii Point Light.

§80.1460 Kahului Harbor, Maui, HI.

A line drawn from Kahului Harbor Entrance East Breakwater Light to Kahului Harbor Entrance West Breakwater Light.

§80.1470 Kawaihae Harbor, Hawaii, HI.

A line drawn from Kawaihae Light to the seaward extremity of the Kawaihae South Breakwater.

§80.1480 Hilo Harbor, Hawaii, HI.

A line drawn from the seaward extremity of the Hilo Breakwater 265° true (as an extension of the seaward side of the breakwater) to the shoreline 0.2 nautical mile north of Alealea Point.

§80.1490 Apra Harbor, U.S. Territory of Guam.

A line drawn from the westernmost extremity of Orote Island to the westernmost extremity of Glass Breakwater.

§80.1495 U.S. Pacific Island Possessions

The 72 COLREGS shall apply on the bays, harbors, lagoons, and waters surrounding the U.S. Pacific Island Possessions of American Samoa, Baker, Canton, Howland, Jarvis, Johnson, Palmyra, Swains, and Wake Island. (The Trust Territory of the Pacific Islands is not a U.S. possession, and therefore Part 82 does not apply thereto.)

[CGD 81-017, 46 FR 28154, May 26, 1981]

ALASKA

Seventeenth District

§80.1705 Alaska.

The 72 COLREGS shall apply on all the sounds, bays, harbors, and inlets of Alaska.

[CGD 81-017, 46 FR 28154, May 26, 1981]

TIME AND TIME SIGNALS

Correct time is a necessity to the offshore yachtsman who must use celestial navigation to plot his course and determine his position. For coastal and inland piloting, the time signal given each hour by most normal AM or FM broadcast stations is accurate enough. In most localities ashore, it is possible to dial a time service operated by the phone company for reasonably accurate time information.

The most reliable time signals are those generated by the U.S. Naval Observatory. Signals based on Naval Observatory time are broadcast by the Bureau of Standards stations WWV in Fort Collins, Colo., and WWVH in Hawaii. Details are given in the following excerpts from the General Information section that appears in each *U.S. Coast Pilot.*

In addition to these, reliable signals are broadcast on 3.330, 14.67, and 7.335 MHz by the Dominion Conservatory, Ottawa, Canada. This is a continuous service, with information given in both French and English.

Time Signals

The U.S. system of broadcasting time signals begins at 55 minutes

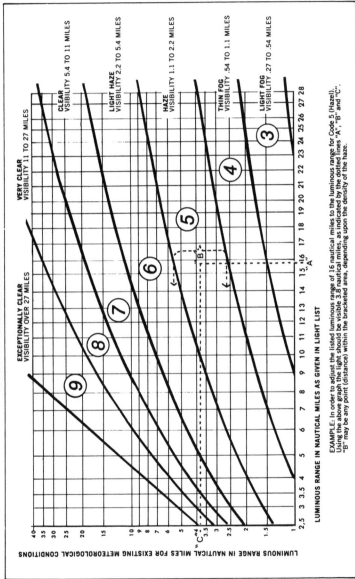

LUMINOUS VISIBILITY DIAGRAM

EXCEPTIONALLY CLEAR
VISIBILITY OVER 27 MILES

VERY CLEAR
VISIBILITY 11 TO 27 MILES

CLEAR
VISIBILITY 5.4 TO 11 MILES

LIGHT HAZE
VISIBILITY 2.2 TO 5.4 MILES

HAZE
VISIBILITY 1.1 TO 2.2 MILES

THIN FOG
VISIBILITY .54 TO 1.1 MILES

LIGHT FOG
VISIBILITY .27 TO .54 MILES

LUMINOUS RANGE IN NAUTICAL MILES FOR EXISTING METEOROLOGICAL CONDITIONS

LUMINOUS RANGE IN NAUTICAL MILES AS GIVEN IN LIGHT LIST

EXAMPLE: In order to adjust the listed luminous range of 16 nautical miles to the luminous range for Code 5 (Haze!).
Using the above graph the light should be visible 3.8 nautical miles, as indicated by the dotted lines "A", "B" and "C".
"B" may be any point (distance) within the bracketed area, depending upon the density of the haze.

Figure 4.8

0 seconds of some hour and continues for 5 minutes. Signals are transmitted on every second of this period except the 29th of each minute, the 51st of the first minute, the 52d of the second minute, the 53d of the third minute, the 54th of the fourth minute, the last 4 seconds of the first 4 minutes, and the last 9 seconds of the last minute. The hour signal is a 1.3-second dash, which is much longer than the others.

In all cases the beginnings of the dashes indicate the beginnings of the seconds, and the ends of the dashes are without significance. The number of dashes sounded in the group at the end of any minute indicates the number of minutes of the signal yet to be sent. In case of signal failure or error, the signal is repeated one hour later.

The United States Naval Observatory in Washington, D.C., is the origin of all government time signals broadcast in the United States and its possessions. The time signals are broadcast by Navy radio station NSS in Washington on the following frequencies: 162 kHz (replaced by 121.95 kHz from 1400 to 2000 on Thursdays), 5870 kHz, 9425 kHz, 13575 kHz, 17050.4 kHz, and 23650 kHz; the hours of transmission are 0155-0200, 0555-0600, 0755-0800, 1155-1200, 1355-1400, 1755-1800, and 2355-0000 Greenwich Mean Time.

The National Bureau of Standards (NBS), in cooperation with the Naval Observatory, broadcasts time signals from its radio station WWV near Fort Collins, Colorado, on radio frequencies of 2.5, 5, 10, 15, and 25 MHz. The service is continuous, day and night. This ensures reliable coverage of the United States and useful coverage of many other parts of the world. The services include standard radio frequencies, standard audio frequencies, standard musical pitch, standard time intervals, time signals, radio propagation forecasts, and geophysical alerts.

Each hour is divided into one-minute slots; each minute (except the first) begins with an 0.8-second tone of 1000 Hz at WWV or 1200 Hz at WWVH. The first minute in each hour begins with an 0.8-second tone of 1500 Hz at both stations. The minute slots are divided into a 45-second segment and two 7.5-second segments: On alternate minutes, the 45-second segment contains either a standard tone or an announcement.

The announcement slots are available to government agencies for their own purposes. Those not used by NBS or other agencies will be filled by another standard tone. To prevent interference in those parts of the world which receive both WWV and WWVH, one sta-

Compass
Deviation Card

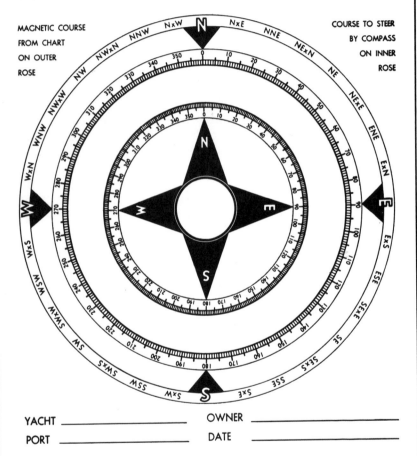

MAGNETIC COURSE
FROM CHART
ON OUTER
ROSE

COURSE TO STEER
BY COMPASS
ON INNER
ROSE

YACHT _____   OWNER _____

PORT _____   DATE _____

Read only MAGNETIC courses on the OUTER rose; only COMPASS courses on the inner one. For each compass heading (inner rose) apply the known deviation and draw a line from that degree or point to the corresponding magnetic heading (outer rose).

TO FIND THE COMPASS COURSE: Locate the magnetic course on the outer rose. Follow the lines to the inner rose and read the compass course.

TO CONVERT COMPASS COURSE TO MAGNETIC COURSE: Locate the compass course on the inner rose. Follow the lines to the outer one and read the magnetic course.

DO NOT CONVERT BEARINGS with this card. To do this find first the deviation for the boat's heading when the bearing was taken. Apply this deviation to the bearing.

Figure 4.9

The Compass

The *compass course* which you must follow in order to maintain a given heading in relation to true north (true course) is determined by correcting the true heading, plotted on a chart, by the amount of variation for the area shown on that chart, to arrive at the *magnetic course*. This in turn is corrected for *deviation* caused by magnetic influences within the boat.

Note that in any given area, the amount and direction of *variation* will not change from that shown on the chart, with any change in the boat's heading. *Deviation*, being the sum of influences of the earth's magnetic field and the boat's magnetic field, will change with every heading.

The amount and direction of variation are shown on the chart. To correct a true course to a magnetic course, *add westerly* variation, *subtract easterly* variation.

Deviation must be determined for each boat, as described below. Again, *add westerly.*

To change a magnetic course to a compass course, *add westerly* deviation, *subtract easterly* deviation. To determine a true heading based on a compass course, reverse the process: *add easterly* deviation and variation, *subtract westerly* deviation and variation.

To prepare a deviation table for your boat, you should

be able to sight over your compass on various headings as you pass a range, and get accurate readings. Use of a pelorus or hand-held compass may be a help, provided that any differences between the boat's compass and hand-held compass readings are taken into account when bearings are recorded.

Two visible objects, preferably ashore or fixed to the bottom, both accurately charted, are selected. From the chart the magnetic range (the magnetic course between the objects) is recorded. A series of runs is made past this range, noting the compass bearing of the two marks on each run when they are in alignment. Each run is made on a new heading, usually in 15 degree increments as shown by the boat's compass. The difference between the plotted magnetic range, and the compass bearing is the deviation for each run. The listing of deviations for each 15 degrees of compass course provides a deviation table for your boat.

Now for each 15 degree compass heading, draw a line from the *inner* compass rose to the *outer* compass rose, applying the deviation as determined above. You can now use the compass deviation card to find a compass course for a given magnetic course, or the reverse, as shown on the card. An example of a deviation table, and the resulting card, is shown below.

Determining the Deviations

Ship's Head Compass	Range bears Compass	Range bears Magnetic	Deviation
000°	082°	087°	5°E
015°	086°	087°	1°E
030°	091°	087°	4°W
045°	096°	087°	9°W
060°	100°	087°	13°W
075°	104°	087°	17°W
090°	106°	087°	19°W
105°	106°	087°	19°W
120°	104°	087°	17°W
135°	101°	087°	14°W
150°	097°	087°	10°W
165°	093°	087°	6°W
180°	089°	087°	2°W
195°	085°	087°	2°E
210°	082°	087°	5°E
225°	079°	087°	8°E
240°	076°	087°	11°E
255°	073°	087°	14°E
270°	070°	087°	17°E
285°	069°	087°	18°E
300°	070°	087°	17°E
315°	072°	087°	15°E
330°	075°	087°	12°E
345°	078°	087°	9°E

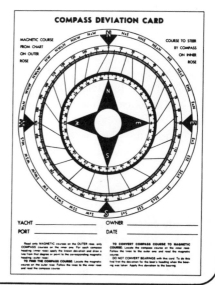

Figure 4.10

tion's announcements are scheduled to coincide with the other's tones, and vice versa.

The first 7.5-second segment following the 45-second period is used by WWVH to announce Greenwich Mean Time, while WWV is silent. The second 7.5-second segment is used by WWV to announce the time, while WWVH is silent. WWVH uses a feminine voice, and WWV a masculine.

Special Publication 236 describes in detail the standard frequency and time service of the National Bureau of Standards. Single copies may be obtained upon request from the National Bureau of Standards, Boulder, CO 80302. Quantities may be obtained from the Superintendent of Documents, U.S. Government Printing Office, Washington, D.C. 20402 at fifteen cents per copy.

Time Zones

Time all over the world is based on the 0° meridian which passes through Greenwich, England. Starting from the 0° meridian, the earth is divided up into twelve time zones eastward and twelve zones westward, each consisting of 15° of the total 360° (36:15 = 24) or—in time—one hour. (The 180° meridian forms the International Date Line being both + 12 hours and − 12 hours from the 0° meridian.) Each time zone is equally divided by its meridian. This means that the time boundary lines are 7.5° east and west of the zone meridian. There are, however, deviations from the time according to this system and official local time. The Benelux countries, France, and Spain are located in the 0-zone with Western European Time but—in practice—these countries use Central European Time. Similar conditions prevail in other areas such as Argentina, Chile, Mexico, and the Pacific coast in Canada. This does not affect astronomical navigation since all calculations are based on standard time in the form of Greenwich Time.

How to Use a Watch as a Compass

In an emergency, you can get an approximate compass reading from a clock or watch, if the sun is visible and the timepiece is reasonably accurate. Hold the clock or watch so the face is up and point the *hour* hand in the direction of the sun. South will be midway between the hour hand the numeral 12.

5.

WEATHER

WEATHER MAP

The weather map provides a bird's-eye view of the weather over a large area. With its many figures, symbols, and lines, the map at first appears to be puzzling. But with a little study of these markings and an understanding of their meaning, the map becomes a picture that gives you a good idea of what's in store.

Some boatmen may receive the weekly compilations of daily weather maps mailed to subscribers by the National Weather Service, Washington, D.C. Most, however, must depend on newspaper maps for their information. These are drawn from Weather Service master weather charts. Four times each day, the Weather Service in Washington prepares and analyzes surface- and upper-air weather charts for the entire Northern Hemisphere.

On surface charts, weather data are plotted as received every six hours from more than 750 reporting stations in North America, more than 200 ships at sea, and 1,500 stations in other countries. Each station reports the amount of sky covered by cloud, direction and speed of wind, visibility distance in miles, present weather, weather during the last three hours, sea level barometric pressure, air temperature, kinds of low, middle and high clouds, dew-point temperature, character and amount of pressure change in the last

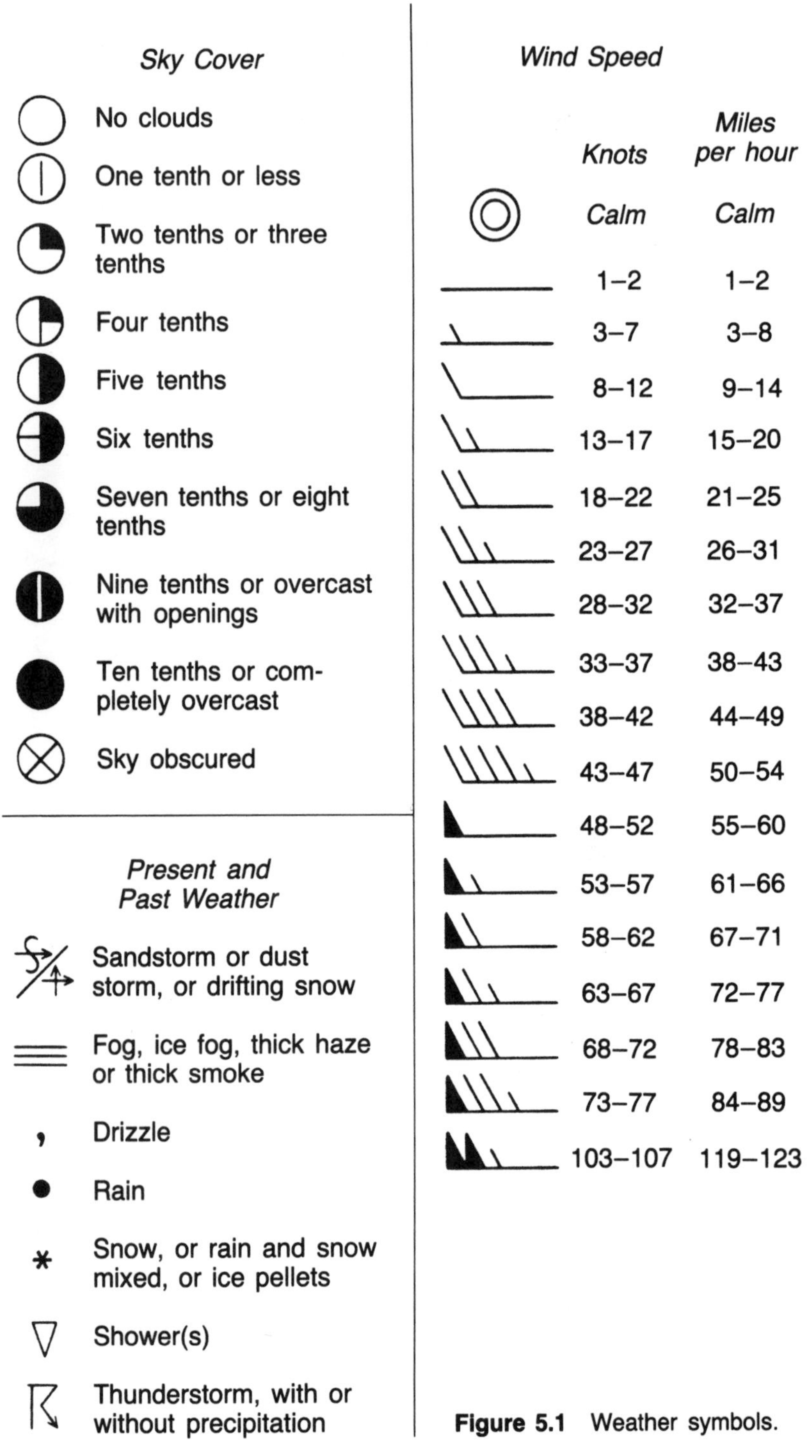

Sky Cover

○	No clouds
◔ (one tenth)	One tenth or less
◔	Two tenths or three tenths
◑	Four tenths
◑	Five tenths
◉	Six tenths
◖	Seven tenths or eight tenths
◕	Nine tenths or overcast with openings
●	Ten tenths or completely overcast
⊗	Sky obscured

Present and Past Weather

⟆⁄⁺	Sandstorm or dust storm, or drifting snow
≡	Fog, ice fog, thick haze or thick smoke
,	Drizzle
●	Rain
✱	Snow, or rain and snow mixed, or ice pellets
▽	Shower(s)
⥼	Thunderstorm, with or without precipitation

Wind Speed

Symbol	Knots	Miles per hour
◎	Calm	Calm
———	1–2	1–2
⟍	3–7	3–8
⟍	8–12	9–14
⟍	13–17	15–20
⟍	18–22	21–25
⟍	23–27	26–31
⟍	28–32	32–37
⟍	33–37	38–43
⟍	38–42	44–49
⟍	43–47	50–54
◣	48–52	55–60
◣	53–57	61–66
◣	58–62	67–71
◣	63–67	72–77
◣	68–72	78–83
◣	73–77	84–89
◣	103–107	119–123

Figure 5.1 Weather symbols.

Low Clouds

Cumulus of fair weather, little vertical development and seemingly flattened

Cumulus of considerable development, generally towering, with or without either cumulus or stratocumulus bases all at the same level

Stratocumulus formed by spreading out of cumulus; cumulus often present also

Cumulonimbus having a clearly fibrous (cirroform) top, often anvil-shaped, with or without cumulus, stratocumulus, stratus, or scud

Middle Clouds

Thin altostratus (most of cloud layer semi-transparent)

Thin altocumulus in patches; cloud elements continually changing and/or occurring at more than one level

Thin altocumulus in bands or in a layer gradually spreading over the sky and usually thickening as a whole

Altocumulus of a chaotic sky, usually at different levels; patches of dense cirrus are usually present also

High Clouds

Filaments of cirrus, or "mares' tails," scattered and not increasing

Dense cirrus in patches or twisted sheaves, usually not increasing, sometimes like remains of cumulonimbus; or towers or tufts

Cirrus, often hook-shaped, gradually spreading over the sky and usually thickening as a whole

Cirrus and cirrostratus, often in converging bands, or cirrostratus alone; generally overspreading and growing denser

Cirrostratus not increasing and not covering entire sky

three hours, and the character, duration and amount of rainfall in the last six hours. Many of these stations also furnish twelve-hour reports of pressure, temperature, moisture, and wind conditions for several levels of upper air. Thus, the central weatherman with his daily surface- and several upper-air charts has a detailed picture of the weather occurring at the same time over the entire Northern Hemisphere. These charts are used in issuing the daily weather forecasts and warnings of approaching storms.

Over 150 *symbols* are used in entering data on weather maps. Although you may never need to know what all the symbols mean, nor have occasion to plot them on a weather map, a knowledge of those used most often will help you to understand and interpret the daily maps appearing in newspapers. See Figure 5.1

The Station Model

Figure 5.2 shows the *"station model,"* a system weathermen the world over developed for entering data on weather maps. It presents a "model" or picture of the weather at a station, using symbols and numbers, which can be understood in any language. Not only the symbols and numbers but their positions around the station circle tell what each item means.

For example, starting with the "station circle" itself (the black dot in the middle)—the fact that this circle is solid black indicates that the sky is completely covered with clouds here.

Let's go counterclockwise around the station circle to examine and understand what's shown. Take the wind first. The symbol indicates a pretty windy day, the wind being from the northwest at 21 to 25 mph. The wind arrows always "fly" with the wind.

Next is temperature in degrees Fahrenheit. As you can see, it was relatively cold, the thermometer registering only 31°F.

Since we know the sky was completely overcast, the next two markings—Visibility and Present Weather—begin to give us a picture of conditions at the station. It was a nasty day with a stiff, cold wind blowing light snow all over the place.

Precipitation Symbols

A word about precipitation symbols is in order here. Figure 5.1 shows the symbols used to indicate different forms of precipitation—drizzle, rain, snow, etc. Increasing precipitation is indicated by more than one symbol being plotted, the range being from one to four identical symbols.

In Figure 5.2 the use of the two stars (or asterisks) tell you that it is snowing continuously but lightly at this station. If there had been three stars, the snow would have been moderate to heavy. Now, if the *shower* symbol (a triangle) had been shown instead of the star it would have carried a star symbol above it to indicate that the showers were *snow* showers. If the showers were *rain,* the shower symbol would have carried a dot (the rain symbol) above it.

Hail is indicated by a small triangle (inverted shower symbol) above the thunderstorm symbol. Fog is represented by three horizontal lines.

Other symbols around the station circle in Figure 5.2 are interest-

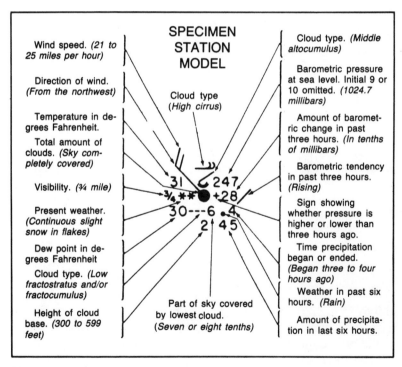

Figure 5.2 Station model.

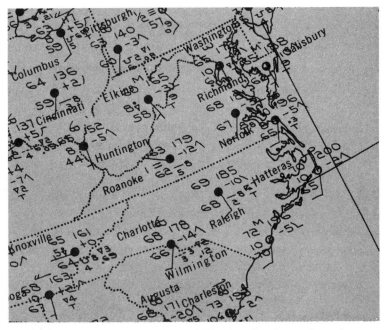

Figure 5.3   Section from a National Weather Service surface chart.

ing and important to weathermen and anyone wishing to use the information. They are worth studying but since most of them do not appear on the abbreviated maps appearing in newspapers, we won't go into a detailed description here. Figure 5.2 does provide a brief explanation of each.

Figure 5.3 shows a small portion of a Weather Service surface chart with data plotted for several stations. By referring to Figures 5.1 and 5.2 you can tell what the weather conditions at any given station are. Let's take Raleigh, NC, as a case in point:

You can see that the sky is completely overcast, the wind is south, at 9 to 14 mph, the temperature is 69°F., the dew point is 68°F., the numeral 2 indicates the clouds are low, the letter *T* says that precipitation in the past six hours was very slight, T standing for "Trace," the barometer has fallen 1.0 millibar during the past three hours, there were thunderstorms at the station during the past six hours, and the pressure is 1018.5 millibars or 30.08 inches of mercury.

Figure 5.4 provides a conversion table for changing millibars to inches and vice versa.

Isobars and Fronts

When data from all stations are entered on the map, the weatherman draws black lines, called *isobars*. These are lines drawn through points having the same ("iso-" means "equal") barometric pressure. For example, a 1020 millibar (30.12 inches) isobar is a line drawn through all points having a barometric pressure of 1020 millibars. Additional isobars are drawn for every four millibar intervals. The purpose of the isobars is to position the centers of low and high pressure—the familiar "LOWS" and "HIGHS" which govern our weather. The centers of high pressures are marked "H" or "High" and the low pressures are marked "L" or "Low." It is the movement of these HIGHS and LOWS that enables the weatherman to

WEATHER

INCHES	MILLIBARS	INCHES	MILLIBARS
28.44	963	29.77	1008
28.53	966	29.86	1011
28.62	969	29.94	1014
28.70	972	30.03	1017
28.79	975	30.12	1020
28.88	978	30.21	1023
28.97	981	30.30	1026
29.06	984	30.39	1029
29.15	987	30.48	1032
29.24	990	30.56	1035
29.32	993	30.65	1038
29.41	996	30.74	1041
29.50	999	30.83	1044
29.59	1002	30.92	1047
29.68	1005	31.01	1050

Figure 5.4 Conversion table for a weather map's millibars.

forecast weather, taking into consideration, of course, the various data supplied by the weather stations.

The heavier lines in Figure 5.5 are drawn to indicate *"fronts"*— the boundaries between different air streams. Triangles and half circles are attached to these heavier lines pointing in the direction in which the fronts are moving. The triangle indicates a *"cold front,"* the half circle a *"warm front."* (See also Figure 5.6)

A front that is not moving, one that is *"stationary,"* is shown by attaching triangles on one side of the line and half circles on the opposite side. An *"occluded front"* is indicated by attaching both triangles and half circles to one side of the line.

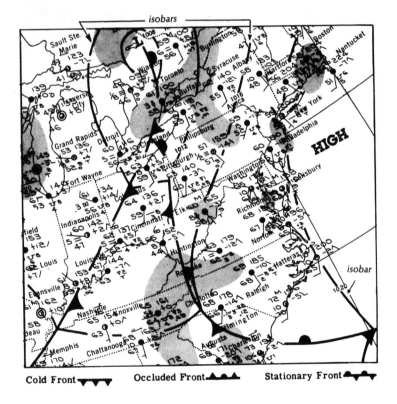

Figure 5.5 Section of weather map with fronts, isobars, Highs, Lows, and direction of fronts plotted on it.

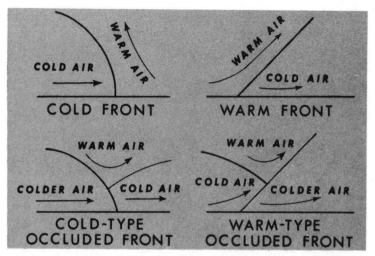

Figure 5.6 Diagrams indicate action of cold and warm fronts and show how their interaction form occluded fronts.

Newspaper Weather Maps

Because of their reduced size, it is impossible to include on newspaper maps all of the data usually entered on a map prepared at a National Weather Service office. To permit easier reading, only sky covered by cloud or other forms of present weather, wind direction and speed, and air temperature are plotted for each station. Barometric pressure at each station is omitted because it can be estimated for any place from the nearest isobar. Incidentally, on some weather maps, isobars may be drawn for 3 millibar intervals; for example, 996, 999, 1002, etc., rather than the 4 millibar intervals. Some maps show isobars marked at one end with the millibar pressure and at the other end in inches. Symbols used for entry of all this information, including those for types of fronts, are usually shown in the margin of newspaper maps. See Figure 5.7

Morning newspapers usually contain the weather map prepared from data collected the evening before, while afternoon editions publish the early morning chart.

Figure 5.7

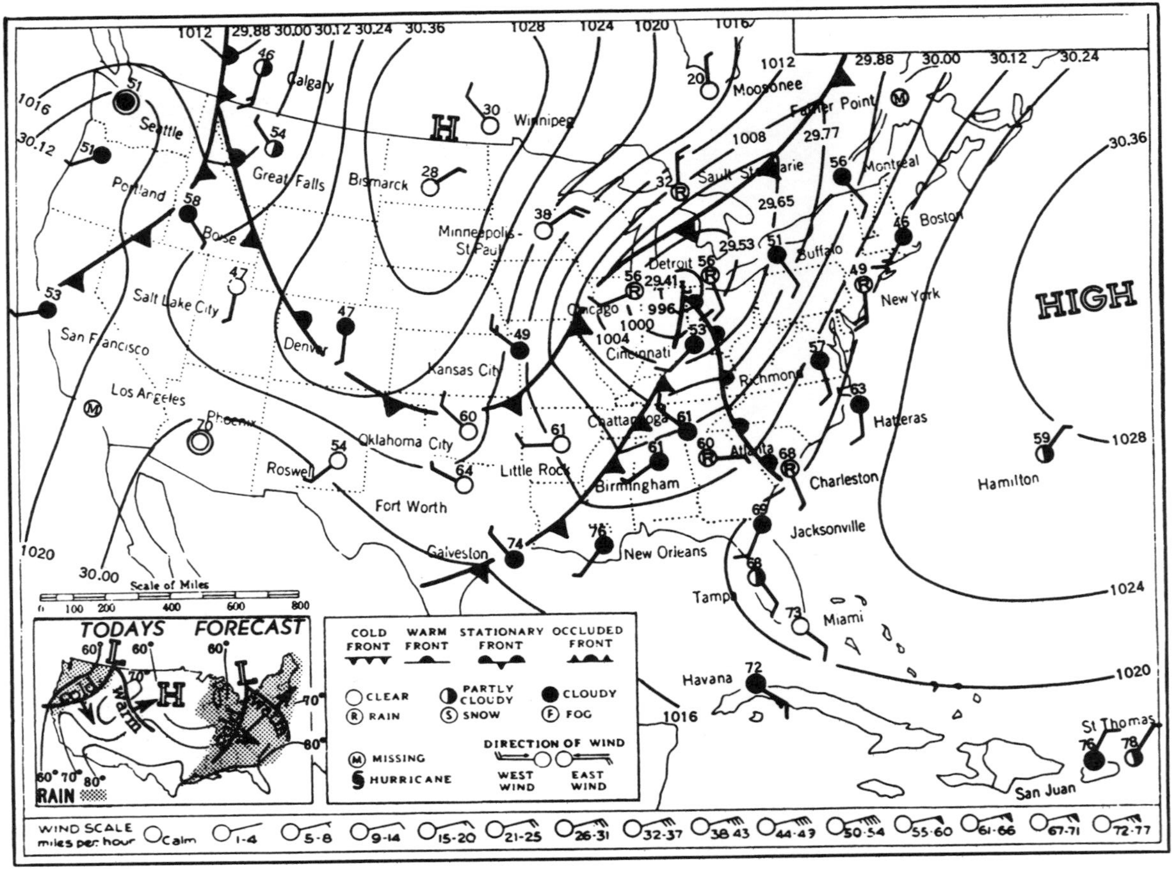

STORM-SIGNAL DISPLAYS

Small Craft Advisory: One red pennant displayed by day and a red light above a white light at night to indicate winds up to 38 MPH (33 knots) and/or sea conditions dangerous to small craft operations are forecast for the area. See Figure 5.8

Gale Warning: Two red pennants displayed by day and a white light above a red light at night to indicate winds ranging from 39 to 54 mph (34 to 47 knots) are forecast.

Storm Warning: A single square red flag with black center displayed by day and two red lights at night indicate winds 55 mph (48 knots) and above (*no matter how high the velocity*) are forecast for the area. NOTE: If winds are associated with a tropical cyclone (hurricane) the *storm-warning* display indicates forecast winds of 55 to 73 mph (48 to 63 knots). The *hurricane warning* is displayed only in connection with a hurricane.

Hurricane Warning: Two square red flags with black centers displayed by day and a white light between two red lights at night to indicate that winds 75 mph (64 knots) and above are forecast for the area.

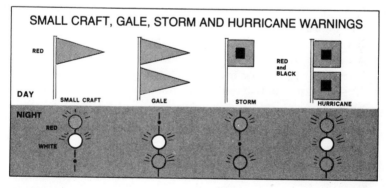

Figure 5.8

WEATHER INFORMATION

Storm warnings and storm advisories issued by the National Weather Service are broadcast by designated U.S. naval and Coast Guard radio stations. A large number of commercial radio stations also broadcast storm warnings, although at somewhat irregular intervals.

The display of storm-warning signals from lightships is now authorized. These signals consist of the standard Weather Service flag hoists, displayed by day in the same manner as from shore stations. No night signals are displayed by lightships, and the day storm flags are displayed only while the lightship is on station, not while preceding to or from station.

National Weather Service Broadcasts

The latest forecasts, weather observations from both the National Weather Service and U.S. Coast Guard stations, and emergency weather warning bulletins are broadcast on stations operated by the National Weather Service. Since frequencies used are above the standard FM band, special receivers are necessary. These are available from manufacturers of marine radioelectronic equipment, in a variety of models.

Each station is in continuous twenty-four-hour operation, with a taped weather message that recycles when completed. Tapes are updated regularly to include the latest forecasts or observations. Routine reports are interrupted when necessary for severe weather warnings.

A typical broadcast contains the following information:

1. The overall weather picture.
2. A radar weather summary.
3. Marine forecasts.
4. Observations of wind, weather, visibility, and sea conditions from U.S. Coast Guard stations.
5. A local area forecast.
6. A regional forecast.

Table 5.1

Beaufort Wind Scale

BEAUFORT NUMBER OR FORCE	WIND SPEED			WORLD METEOROLOGICAL ORGANIZATION Description	EFFECTS OBSERVED AT SEA	ESTIMATING WIND SPEED	EFFECTS OBSERVED ON LAND
	KNOTS	MPH	KM/HR			EFFECTS OBSERVED NEAR LAND	
0	under 1	under 1	under 1	Calm	Sea like a mirror	Calm	Calm; smoke rises vertically
1	1–3	1–3	1–5	Light Air	Ripples with appearance of scales; no foam crests	Small sailboat just has steerage way	Smoke drift indicates wind direction; vanes do not move
2	4–6	4–7	6–11	Light Breeze	Small wavelets; crests of glassy appearance, not breaking	Wind fills the sails of small boats which then travel at about 1 to 2 knots	Wind felt on face; leaves rustle; vanes begin to move
3	7–10	8–12	12–19	Gentle Breeze	Large wavelets; crests begin to break, scattered whitecaps	Sailboats begin to heel and travel at about 3 to 4 knots	Leaves, small twigs in constant motion; light flags extended
4	11–16	13–18	20–28	Moderate Breeze	Small waves 0.5 to 1.25 meters high, becoming longer; numerous whitecaps	Good working breeze, sailboats carry all sail with good heel	Dust, leaves, and loose paper raised up; small branches move

BEAUFORT NUMBER OR FORCE	WIND SPEED			WORLD METEOROLOGICAL ORGANIZATION DESCRIPTION	ESTIMATING WIND SPEED		
	KNOTS	MPH	KM/HR		EFFECTS OBSERVED AT SEA	EFFECTS OBSERVED NEAR LAND	EFFECTS OBSERVED ON LAND
5	17–21	19–24	29–38	Fresh Breeze	Moderate waves of 1.25 to 2.5 meters taking longer form; many whitecaps; some spray	Sailboats shorten sail	Small trees in leaf begin to sway
6	22–27	25–31	39–49	Strong Breeze	Larger waves 2.5 to 4 meters forming; whitecaps everywhere; more spray	Sailboats have double-reefed mainsails	Larger branches of trees in motion; whistling heard in wires
7	28–33	32–38	50–61	Near Gale	Sea heaps up, waves 4 to 6 meters; white foam from breaking waves begins to be blown in streaks	Boats remain in harbor; those at sea heave-to	Whole trees in motion; resistance felt in walking against wind
8	34–40	39–46	62–74	Gale	Moderately high (4 to 6 meter) waves of greater length; edges of crests begin to break into spindrift; foam is blown in well-marked streaks	All boats make for harbor, if near	Twigs and small branches broken off trees; progress generally impaired

				Sea conditions	Land effects
9	41–47	47–54	Strong Gale	High waves (6 meters); sea begins to roll; dense streaks of foam; spray may reduce visibility	Slight structural damage occurs; slate blown from roofs
10	48–55	55–63	Storm	Very high waves (6 to 9 meters) with overhanging crests; sea takes a white appearance as foam is blown in very dense streaks; rolling is heavy and visibility is reduced	Seldom experienced on land; trees broken or uprooted; considerable structural damage occurs
11	56–63	64–72	Violent Storm	Exceptionally high (9 to 14 meters) waves; sea covered with white foam patches; visibility still more reduced	Very rarely experienced on land; usually accompanied by widespread damage
12	64 and over	73 and over	Hurricane	Air filled with foam; waves over 14 meters; sea completely white with driving spray; visibility greatly reduced	

7. Degree-day information during winter months.

8. The extended outlook.

9. Occasional notices to mariners.

10. All pertinent weather warnings.

11. Selected weather reports from National Weather Service stations.

Marine Weather Services Chart

Coast Guard vessels now display storm-warning signals. Headquarters of the Coast Guard are supplied with weather information by the National Weather Service and Coast Guard vessels receive instructions to fly the proper signals when bad weather is approaching.

The shore stations where storm-warning signals are displayed are prominently marked on the *Marine Weather Services Charts,* a series that is published annually by the Weather Service. These charts also contain detailed information concerning the times of weather broadcasts from commercial stations, the radio frequencies of marine broadcast stations, the specific type of storm warnings issued, and the visual display signals that are used in connection with the warnings. This series consists of fourteen charts, twelve of which cover the coastal waters of the United States and the Great Lakes. The remaining two charts are for the Hawaiian Islands, and Puerto Rico and the Virgin Islands. They can be purchased from the Superintendent of Documents, Government Printing Office, Washington, D.C. 20402.

FOG

Fog is merely a cloud whose base rests upon the earth, be the latter land or water. It consists of water droplets suspended in the air, each droplet so small that it cannot be distinguished individually, yet present in such tremendous numbers that objects close at hand are obscured.

If we are to have innumerable water droplets suspended in the air, there must be plenty of water vapor originally in that air. If droplets are to form from this vapor, the air must be cooled by

Table 5.2

Wind and Barometer Indications

WIND DIRECTION	BAROMETER REDUCED TO SEA LEVEL	CHARACTER OF WEATHER INDICATED
SW. to NW.	30.10 to 30.20 and steady	Fair, with slight temperature changes, for one to two days.
SW. to NW.	30.10 to 30.20 and rising rapidly	Fair, followed within two days by rain.
SW. to NW.	30.20 and above and stationary	Continued fair, with no decided temperature change.
SW. to NW.	30.20 and above and falling slowly	Slowly rising temperature and fair for two days.
S. to SE.	30.10 to 30.20 and falling slowly	Rain within twenty-four hours.
S. to SE.	30.10 to 30.20 and falling rapidly	Wind increasing in force, with rain within twelve to twenty-four hours.
SE. to NE.	30.10 to 30.20 and falling slowly	Rain in twelve to eighteen hours.
SE. to NE.	30.10 to 30.20 and falling rapidly	Increasing wind, and rain within twelve hours.
E. to NE.	30.10 and above and falling slowly	In summer, with light winds, rain may not fall for several days. In winter, rain within twenty-four hours.
E. to NE.	30.10 and above and falling rapidly	In summer, rain probable within twelve to twenty-four hours. In winter, rain or snow, with increasing winds, will often set in when the barometer begins to fall and the winds set in from the NE.
SE. to NE.	30.00 or below and falling slowly	Rain will continue one to two days.
SE. to NE.	30.00 or below and falling rapidly	Rain with high wind, followed, within thirty-six hours, by clearing, and in winter by colder weather.
S. to SW.	30.00 or below and rising slowly	Clearing within a few hours, and fair for several days.
S. to E.	29.80 or below and falling rapidly	Severe storm imminent, followed, within twenty-four hours, by clearing, and in winter by colder weather.
E. to N.	29.80 or below and falling rapidly	Severe northeast gale and heavy precipitation; in winter, heavy snow, followed by a cold wave.
Going to W.	29.80 or below and rising rapidly	Clearing and colder.

some means so that the vapor will condense. If the droplets are to condense in the air next to the earth, the cooling must take place at the surface of the earth. If the fog is to have any depth, successively higher layers of air must be cooled sufficiently to cause condensation in them. Fog forms from the ground up. Thus, the land or water must be colder than the air next to it; the lower layers of air must be progressively colder than the layers above them.

If water vapor is to condense out of the air, then the temperature of the air must be lowered to or below the *dew-point temperature;* that is, the temperature at which the air is saturated with water vapor and below which condensation of water vapor will occur.

Air is said to be *saturated* with water vapor when its water-vapor content would remain unchanged if it was placed above a level surface of pure water at its own temperature. The amount of water vapor that is required to saturate a given volume of air depends on the temperature of the air and increases as the temperature increases. The higher the temperatures, the more water vapor the air can hold before it becomes saturated, and the lower the temperature, the less water vapor the air can hold before it becomes saturated.

If a mass of air is originally in an unsaturated state, it can be saturated by cooling it down to a temperature at which its content of water vapor is the maximum containable amount; that is to say, to the dew-point temperature. Or we can saturate it by causing more water to evaporate into it, thereby raising the dew-point temperature to a value equal to the air temperature. In regard to the latter process, unsaturated air, as it passes over rivers and lakes, over the oceans or over wet ground, picks up water vapor and has its dew point raised. Also, rain falling from higher clouds will increase the amount of water vapor in unsaturated air near the earth.

WEATHER INSTRUMENTS

Sling Psychrometer

How do we determine the dew point? By means of a simple-to-operate, inexpensive little gadget known as a *sling psychrometer*. A sling psychrometer is merely two thermometers mounted in a single holder with a handle that permits it to be whirled overhead. One thermometer, known as the *dry bulb,* has its bulb of mercury exposed directly to the air. This thermometer shows the actual temperature of the air. The other thermometer, known as the *wet bulb,* has its bulb covered with a piece of gauze. We soak this gauze in water so that the bulb is moistened. If the air is not saturated with water vapor, evaporation then takes place from the wet-bulb thermometer, and the wet bulb is cooled, since the process of evaporation requires the expenditure of heat. The reduced temperature shown by the wet-bulb thermometer, the so-called wet-bulb temperature, represents the lowest temperature to which the air can be cooled by evaporating water into it.

When we whirl the psychrometer we create a draft around the instrument. The ventilation so produced increases the efficiency of the evaporation process and makes the wet-bulb reading more reliable than it would be if there were little or no air movement past the wet bulb. This is the reason why the psychrometer is designed for whirling.

From the wet-bulb temperature and dry-bulb temperature, the dew point may be determined by referring to a suitable table. As we are far more interested, however, in knowing the *spread, or difference, between the air temperature and dew point,* we will save ourselves some work by using another table (Table 5.4).

If the air is already actually saturated with water vapor, then no water can evaporate from the gauze and both thermometers must show the same value. The dew point then has this same numerical value and so the spread between air temperature and dew point must be zero. But, as explained above, if the air is not already saturated with water vapor, the wet-bulb thermometer will give a lower reading than the dry-bulb thermometer. We subtract the wet-bulb temperature from the dry-bulb temperature. With this difference and the dry-bulb (the air) temperature, we consult Table 5.4 and find directly the corresponding spread between the air temperature and the dew-point temperature. This is the figure we want.

If, in the late afternoon or early evening, the spread between the air temperature and dew point is less than approximately 6°F, and the air temperature is falling, fog or greatly restricted visibility will probably be experienced in a few hours. These critical values are emphasized by the heavy line above which they lie in Table 5.4.

Table 5.3

Cloud Formations

Type and description	Approximate height (feet)	Weather portent
Cirrus—Very high white strands of cloud; commonly known as mares' tails.	25,000– 35,000	Probable approach of a depression with wind and rain
Cirrostratus—Spreading white film or veil through which the sun can still be seen, probably with a halo effect.	Ditto.	More definite forecast of rain
Cirrocumulus — Compressed bunches of cloud forming a more clearly defined pattern; commonly known as a mackerel sky.	Ditto.	Changeable
Altostratus—Watery gray layer or heavy veil of cloud; sun usually just visible.	10,000–20,000	Almost certain rain
Altocumulus—An even layer of fairly dense cloud, often resembling the pattern of sand on the sea bed. Also sometimes called a mackerel sky.	Ditto.	Usually more settled weather; perhaps a chance of thunder
Stratocumulus—A lower version of altocumulus, with perhaps a more distinct definition.	5,000– 10,000	Fairly settled conditions
Cumulus—Clearly defined fleecy clouds with a firm, dark base, often increasing in size and number during the day.	2,000–5,000	Fair conditions
Cumulonimbus—Larger, more menacing development of cumulus, with towering gray-and-white masses, often rising to an anvil-shaped plateau.	Rising from a fairly low base up to perhaps 25,000	Big air disturbances with possibility of thunder, heavy showers or hail
Nimbostratus—Heavy, dark, amorphous cloud, driving hard with the wind.	Mostly below 7,000	Prolonged rain likely; fresh or strong wind certain
Stratus—Blanket of fog or mist-like cloud suspended low in the sky.	500– 20,000	Generally humid with prospect of rain or mist

Incidentally, should we ever want to know the dew-point temperature itself, all we need do is to subtract the spread figure given in the table from the temperature shown by the dry-bulb thermometer. Thus, when the dry-bulb thermometer indicates an air temperature of 70°F and the difference between the dry-bulb and wet-bulb temperatures is 11°F, the spread is 19°F and the dew point is 51°F.

Table 5.4

Air Temperature—Dew-Point Spread

(All figures are in degrees Fahrenheit at 30 inches pressure)

Difference Dry-Bulb Minus Wet-Bulb	Air Temperature Shown By Dry-Bulb Thermometer												
	35	40	45	50	55	60	65	70	75	80	85	90	95
1	2	2	2	2	2	2	2	1	1	1	1	1	1
2	5	5	4	4	4	3	3	3	3	3	3	3	2
3	7	7	7	6	5	5	5	4	4	4	4	4	4
4	10	10	9	8	7	7	6	6	6	6	5	5	5
5	14	12	11	10	10	9	8	8	7	7	7	7	6
6	18	15	14	13	12	11	10	9	9	8	8	8	8
7	22	19	17	16	14	13	12	11	11	10	10	9	9
8	28	22	20	18	17	15	14	13	12	12	11	11	10
9	35	27	23	21	19	17	16	15	14	13	13	12	12
10	—	33	27	24	22	20	18	17	16	15	14	14	13
11	—	40	32	28	25	22	20	19	18	17	16	15	15
12	—	—	38	32	28	25	23	21	20	18	17	17	16
13	—	—	45	37	31	28	25	23	21	20	19	18	17
14	—	—	—	42	35	31	28	26	24	22	21	20	19
15	—	—	—	50	40	35	31	28	26	24	23	21	21

Opposite—Difference Dry-Bulb Minus Wet-Bulb and
Under —Air Temperature Shown by Dry-Bulb Thermometer
Read —Value of Spread: Air Temperature minus Dew-Point Temperature

Based on U.S. Weather Service Psychrometric Tables

Table 5.5

BOAT WEATHER LOG

Yact_____At/Passage_____ to _____
Day_____ Date_____ Time Zone_____ Skipper_____

1. Latest Weather Map: Date_____Time_____Summary of forecast and of
   principal regional weather features: _____
   _____
   _____
   _____
   _____
   _____

2. Radio Weather Reports Received (state source and time): _____
   _____
   _____
   _____
   _____
   _____

3. Local Weather Observations
4. Remarks and Local Forecast for Next_____Hours (state time forecast
   effective):_____
   _____
   _____
   _____
   _____
   _____
   _____
   _____
   _____
   _____

Table 5.6

LOCAL WEATHER OBSERVATIONS

Time

Latitude—degrees, minutes

Longitude—degrees, minutes

Course—degrees mag.

    —degrees true

Speed—Knots

Barometer—in. or mb.

    —tendency

Clouds—form

    —moving from

    —amount

    —changing to

Sea—condition

  —swells

  —moving from

Temperatures—air, dry bulb

    —dew-point

    —water

Visibility

Wind—direction, true

  —shifting to

  —velocity, true

  —force (Beaufort)

Weather—present

The Barometer

Another weather instrument is the *aneroid barometer*. A good instrument will have *pressure scales*. Barometric pressure is often expressed in terms of *inches of mercury,* so the outer scale is graduated in these units. Weather maps are now printed with the pressures shown in *millibars* and many radio weather reports specify this value. Consequently, the inner scale is graduated in millibars. Also, it has the usual reference hand, so you can keep track of changes in pressure.

The words "Fair—Change—Rain," in themselves, when they appear on the face of an aneroid barometer, are meaningless. It is not the actual barometric pressure that is so important in forecasting: it is the *direction* and *rate of change of pressure.*

The Anemometer

For measuring *wind velocity* we need something else. This is an *anemometer.* The anemometer is essentially a speedometer. It consists of a rotor with conical cups attached to the ends of spokes and is designed for mounting at the masthead, where the wind is caught by the cups, causing them to turn at a speed proportional to the speed of the wind. Indications of the rotor's speed are transmitted to an indicator which may be mounted in the cabin.

DESTRUCTIVE WAVES

Unusual sudden changes in water level can be caused by tsunamis or violent storms. These two types of destructive wave have become commonly known as tidal waves, a name that is technically incorrect as they are not the result of tide-producing forces.

Tsunamis (seismic sea waves) are set up by submarine earthquakes. Many such seismic disturbances do not produce sea waves and often those produced are small, but the occasional large waves can be very damaging to shore installations and dangerous to ships in harbors.

These waves travel great distances and can cause tremendous damage on coasts far from their source. The wave of April 1, 1946, which originated in the Aleutian Trench, demolished nearby Scotch

Cap Lighthouse and caused damages of $25 million in the Hawaiian Islands two thousand miles away. The wave of May 22–23, 1960, which originated off southern Chile, caused widespread death and destruction in islands and countries throughout the Pacific.

The speed of tsunamis, reaching 300 to 500 knots in the deep water of the open ocean, varies with the depth of the water. In the open sea they cannot be detected from a ship or from the air because their length is so great, sometimes a hundred miles, as compared to their height, which is usually only a few feet. Only on certain types of shelving coasts do they build up into waves of disastrous proportions.

There is usually a series of waves with crests ten to forty minutes apart, and the highest may occur several hours after the first wave. Sometimes the first noticeable part of the wave is the trough that causes a recession of the water from the shore, and people who have gone out to investigate this unusual exposure of the beach have been engulfed by the oncoming crest. Such an unexplained withdrawal of the sea should be considered as nature's warning of an approaching wave.

Improvements have been made in the quick determination and reporting of earthquake epicenters, but no method has yet been perfected for determining whether a sea wave will result from a given earthquake. The Honolulu Observatory of the National Ocean Survey is headquarters of a warning system that has field-reporting stations (seismic and tidal) in most countries around the Pacific. When a warning is broadcast, waterfront areas should be vacated for higher ground, and ships in the vicinity of land should head for the deep water of the open sea so they will not be driven ashore.

Storm waves—A considerable rise or fall in the level of the sea along a particular coast may result from strong winds and sharp change in barometric pressure. In cases where the water level is raised, higher waves can form with greater depth and the combination can be destructive to low regions, particularly at high stages of tide. Extreme low levels can result in depths that are considerably less than those shown on nautical charts. This type of wave occurs especially in coastal regions bordering on shallow waters that are subject to tropical storms.

Seiche is a stationary vertical-wave oscillation with a period vary-

Table 5.7

WIND CHILL TABLE

Prepared by the National Center for Atmospheric Research
Boulder, Colorado

Little Danger		Increasing Danger		Great Danger That Exposed Flesh will Freeze						
				Wind Velocity (MPH)						

Temp. °F	0	5	10	15	20	25	30	35	40	45	50
—10	—10	—15	—31	—45	—52	—58	—63	—67	—69	—70	—70
—5	—5	—11	—27	—40	—46	—52	—56	—60	—62	—63	—63
0	0	—6	—22	—33	—40	—45	—49	—52	—54	—54	—56
5	5	1	—15	—25	—32	—37	—41	—43	—45	—46	—47
10	10	7	—9	—18	—24	—29	—33	—35	—36	—38	—38
15	15	12	—2	—11	—17	—22	—26	—27	—29	—31	—31
20	20	16	2	—6	—9	—15	—18	—20	—22	—24	—24
25	25	21	9	1	—4	—7	—11	—13	—15	—17	—17
30	30	27	16	11	3	0	—2	—4	—4	—6	—7
35	35	33	21	16	12	7	5	3	1	1	0
40	40	37	28	22	18	16	13	11	10	9	8

ing from a few minutes to an hour or more, but somewhat less than the tidal periods. It is usually attributed to external forces such as strong winds, changes in barometric pressure, swells, or seismic sea waves disturbing the equilibrium of the water surface. Seiche is found both in enclosed bodies of water and superimposed upon the tides of the open ocean. When the external forces cause a short-period horizontal oscillation of the water, it is called *surge*.

The combined effect of seiche and surge sometimes makes it difficult to maintain a ship in its position alongside a pier, even though the water may appear to be completely undisturbed, and heavy mooring lines have been parted repeatedly under such conditions. Pilots advise taut lines to reduce the effect of the surge.

6.

ELECTRONICS

ELECTRICAL UNITS

Volts, ohms, amperes, and watts are the terms used to describe electromotive force, electrical resistance, current strength, and electric power, respectively. One volt is the force that will produce a current of one ampere in a conductor with a resistance of one ohm. One watt is the power developed by one ampere of current at one volt.

RADIO TERMINOLOGY

Amplitude: The height of a radio wave.

Frequency: The number of times per second that a radio wave goes through its cycle. All radio waves travel at the speed of light. The shorter the wavelength, the more times per second it will go through its cycle, or the higher the frequency.

Carrier Wave: A radio wave of constant amplitude and constant frequency that is emitted by the transmitter when you press the button but do not speak into the microphone.

Modulation: The manner in which the carrier wave is changed or varied when you speak into the microphone.

FM stands for Frequency Modulation, a process by which speech waves are impressed on the carrier wave by varying its frequency.

AM stands for Amplitude Modulation. A process by which speech waves are impressed on the carrier wave by varying the amplitude of the carrier wave.

Side Bands are produced when speech frequencies are added to the carrier frequency. In conventional amplitude modulation (AM) two side bands are produced, an upper side band containing the carrier-wave frequency *plus* all the speech frequencies present, and a lower side band containing the carrier-wave frequency *minus* all the speech frequencies present.

SSB stands for Single Side Band, a newer method of radiotelephony. In SSB transmission, the carrier wave and one side band are suppressed, only one side band being transmitted. All the power can then be put into this one side band, increasing the "speech power" six times. Thus, a 30-watt SSB radiotelephone would be equivalent to a 180-watt DSB radiotelephone.

RADIOTELEPHONES

Three types of radio systems are used aboard boats; two of these are designed and licensed specifically for marine use. The third is the Citizens Band radio system.

VHF-FM marine radios are considered to be the prime system for marine communications over distances of up to about thirty miles. There are fifty-five channels in the VHF band for marine use; some of these are special-purpose bands for commercial use only; others are for linkup with shoreside telephone systems. Two channels are mandatory for all boats: channel 6 (156.300 MHz), for inter-ship safety communications, and channel 16 (156.800 MHz), the distress, safety, and calling frequency. There also are channels for linkup with shoreside facilities such as marinas and yacht clubs.

For long-distance communications, a Single Side Band (SSB) marine radio is required, but it can be installed only if the boat is equipped with a VHF-FM set, and the owner can demonstrate a

Table 6.1

Priority List of VHF-FM Channels for Recreational Boats

CHANNEL NUMBER	FREQUENCY (MHz) TRANSMIT	RECEIVE	COMMUNICATIONS PURPOSE
16	156.800	156.800	DISTRESS SAFETY and CALLING (mandatory)
06	156.300	156.300	Inter-ship safety communications (mandatory)
22	157.100	157.100	Primary liaison with USCG vessels and USCG shore stations, and for Coast Guard marine information broadcasts
68	156.425	156.425	Noncommercial inter-ship and ship to coast (marinas, yacht clubs, etc.)
09	156.450	156.450	Commercial and noncommercial inter-ship and ship to coast (commercial docks, marinas, and some clubs)
26	157.300	161.900	Public telephone, first priority
28	157.400	162.000	Public telephone, first priority
25	157.250	161.850	Public telephone (also 24, 84, 85, 86, 87, 88)
27	157.350	161.950	Public telephone
13	156.650	156.650	Navigational—bridge to bridge (1 watt only). Mandatory for ocean vessels, dredges in channels, and large tugs while towing. Army installing for communications with boats in their locks. Will be found, also, on Army operated bridges.

ELECTRONICS

CHANNEL NUMBER	FREQUENCY (MHz) TRANSMIT	RECEIVE	COMMUNICATIONS PURPOSE
14	156.700	156.700	Port Operations channel for communications with bridge and lock tenders. Some Coast Guard shore stations have this channel for working.
70	156.525	156.525	Noncommercial only, inter-ship
12	156.600	156.600	Port Operations—traffic advisory—still being used as channel to work USCG shore stations
72	156.625	156.625	Noncommercial inter-ship, second priority
WX-1		162.550	Weather broadcasts
WX-2		162.400	Weather broadcasts
WX-3		162.475	Weather broadcasts
69	156.475	156.475	Noncommercial inter-ship and ship to coast
71	156.575	156.575	Noncommercial inter-ship and ship to coast
78	156.925	156.925	Noncommercial inter-ship and ship to coast

need for the long-range set. On this equipment, the international-distress and calling frequency is 2182 kHz. Pleasure boats can operate with sets having about 80 to 100 watts output power, giving a range of more than one hundred miles.

Citizens Band radios are often used as an adjunct to the normal marine radios, for informal, short-distance communication. There is no CB channel monitored by the U.S. Coast Guard, and there is no linkup with the telephone system ashore. CB range is about ten to fifteen miles, but the distance may be greater to a base station ashore with a high antenna. Since a CB license permits operation of up to five sets, an owner may set up such a base station at home, or carry walkie-talkie type sets for use in communicating with part of the crew ashore. While true marine radios must be used only for ship's business, there is no such restriction on the CB sets.

In areas where the Coast Guard is not operating, CB radios provide the only means for calling for help in an emergency.

Installation and Maintenance

Radio equipment may be physically installed and electrically connected by the boat owner or any person. Before it is put on the air, however, the set must be checked out by a person holding a first- or second-class license who will make certain tests required by FCC rules. Radio installations on gasoline-powered boats will generally require some form of ignition-noise suppression or shielding; this is a job for a technician. With regard to maintenance, an unlicensed person is limited to matters that will not affect the quality of the signal on the air. For example, he can replace bad fuses, tubes, etc., but cannot change crystals or adjust antenna loading.

RADIO LICENSES

To control the use of radio stations, hold down interference, and make possible emergency and essential communications, a system of licenses is used. Recognizing that harmful interference could result from either malfunctioning equipment or from misuse of a properly operating set, licenses are required for both the station and the person operating it. Although it is termed a station license, the FCC authorization is essentially concerned with the transmitting component only. The set owner need not concern himself with the many technical requirements for equipment provided that he has a set that is "type accepted."

The Station License

A station license may be issued to a U.S. citizen, corporation, or an alien individual, but not to the government of another nation or its representative. Application is made on form 506 which should be mailed to the FCC, P.O. Box 1040, Gettysburg, PA 17325. Issuing the license may take as long as sixty days; if you need immediate use of the radio, complete Form 506-A for temporary operating authority and keep it aboard. This form allows legal use of your set and provides a temporary call sign based on your boat's documentation or state registration number.

Radio station licenses in the United States are issued in the name of the *owner* and the *vessel*. A station license is not automatically transferred to another person upon sale of the boat, nor may a license be moved with the radio set to a new boat owned by the same person. A simple change in the name of the boat or licensee (but not a change in ownership) or his address does *not* require license modification. Just send a letter to the FCC advising them of the change; a copy of this letter must be posted on board with the license.

FCC regulations require that a station license be conspicuously posted aboard the vessel. You must apply for renewal before expiration of its five-year term, using Form 504-B. If you did make timely application for renewal, operation may continue even if you have not received the renewed license before the expiration date. If the use of the radio station is ever permanently discontinued, you must return the license to the FCC in Washington for cancellation.

The Operator's Permit

You need a personal license to operate any marine-band radio station. For operation of a radio on board a private recreational boat, or one carrying six or fewer passengers for hire, the lowest grade of radio operator license—a RESTRICTED RADIOTELEPHONE OPERATOR PERMIT—is adequate. For vessels carrying more than six passengers in commercial service, the operator must have a MARINE (formerly "Third Class") RADIOTELEPHONE OPERATOR PERMIT. A higher class license is available for people with technical training and experience, but they are needed only for making tuning adjustments and repairs. An unlicensed person may talk into the microphone of a radio, but a licensed operator must be present and responsible for the proper use of the station.

An applicant for any grade of U.S. operator's license may be a citizen of any nation. A Restricted Permit is obtained by submitting an application on FCC Form 753, which is mailed to the FCC, P.O. Box 1050, Gettysburg, PA 17325. You do not need to appear in person at any FCC office. The permit is issued, without test or examination, by declaration. The applicant must be at least fourteen years old and certify that he (1) can receive and transmit spoken messages in the English language; (2) can keep a rough log in English, or in a foreign language translatable into English; (3) is familiar with the applicable laws, treaty provisions, rules, and regulations; and (4) understands his responsibility to keep currently informed of the regulations, etc. The Restricted Permit is valid for the lifetime of the person to whom issued, unless it is suspended or revoked. A temporary operator permit is also obtained when Form 506-A is filed for a temporary station license.

For the Marine Radio Operator Permit, there is no age limit, but an examination is required and so you must visit an FCC office. This test is nontechnical, covering only operating rules and procedures; questions are of the multiple-choice type. You will find the examination not at all difficult if you prepare for it properly. A free Study Guide is available from FCC offices. For skippers of recreational boats, the privileges of this higher class license are no greater than those of a Restricted Permit, but for many it is a matter of pride to qualify and post it on their craft.

The Radio Log

Log keeping for a radio station on a voluntarily equipped boat has been made much easier than it used to be, but don't let this simplification stop you from meeting the present minimum requirements of the FCC. Each page of the log must show the name of the vessel and the radio call sign; each entry must be signed by the person making it. Entries are required for all distress calls heard or transmitted, for all urgent and safety communications transmitted, and any information related to maritime safety. The log must also show the time of starting and ending a listening watch on 2182 kHz or 156.8 MHz, *but remember that the keeping of such a watch is not mandatory on recreational boats.*

All installation, service, and maintenance work performed on the radio equipment must be logged. It is *not* necessary to make entries for ordinary communications to other boats, the Coast Guard, or shore stations. Logs must be retained for one year following the last entry, except for unusual circumstances described in the Rules.

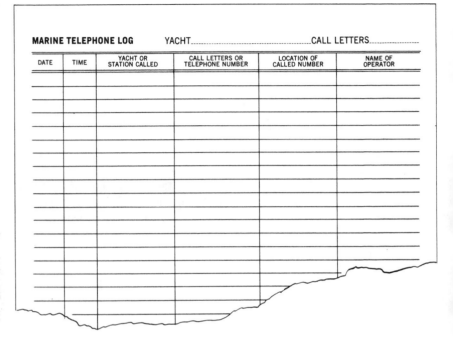

Figure 6.1 Sample radio log.

Logs must be made available for inspection upon request from any authorized FCC representative. Inspection of the station by such an official must be permitted at any reasonable hour, and at such frequent intervals as may be determined necessary in the discretion of the FCC.

How to Make a Call

Listen carefully to make sure that the channel you want to use is not busy. If it is busy, you will hear voices, or from most public shore stations, an intermittent busy tone. Except in a safety emergency, don't interrupt.

When the conversation is to take place on a ship-to-ship frequency—unless you have reached an agreement in advance as to the time and frequency—establish contact on 2182 kHz (or 156.8 MHz) and then shift to the agreed-upon inter-ship channel.

Table 6.2

Standard Phonetic Spelling Alphabet

A	ALFA	**N**	NOVEMBER
B	BRAVO	**O**	OSCAR
C	CHARLIE	**P**	PAPA
D	DELTA	**Q**	QUEBEC
E	ECHO	**R**	ROMEO
F	FOXTROT	**S**	SIERRA
G	GOLF	**T**	TANGO
H	HOTEL	**U**	UNIFORM
I	INDIA	**V**	VICTOR
J	JULIETT	**W**	WHISKEY
K	KILO	**X**	X RAY
L	LIMA	**Y**	YANKEE
M	MIKE	**Z**	ZULU

ELECTRONICS

When the conversation is to take place through a commercial shore station, make your initial contact on a working frequency of that station; this will speed your call.

Both of these practices are designed to relieve the load on 2182 kHz and 156.8 MHz and keep them clear for safety purposes.

Steps to Follow in Making a Call
(Other Than a Distress, Urgency, or Safety Call)

Boat-to-boat calls—Make sure 156.8 MHz (or 2182 kHz) is not busy. If it is free, put your transmitter on the air and say:

"(Name of boat called) This is (name of your boat and call sign), over." To avoid confusion, always observe the proper sequence of call signs—state the name or call sign of the *other station first,* then give your own identification after saying "This is."

(If necessary, the identification of the station called, and your boat's name and call sign may each be given two or three times, but not more; the entire calling transmission must not take longer than thirty seconds.)

Listen for a reply. If no contact is made, repeat the above after an interval of at least two minutes. After establishing contact, switch to the agreed-upon inter-ship working channel. One exchange of communications shall not exceed three minutes after establishing contact on the working frequency. After conversation is completed, say: "This is (name of your boat and call sign), out."

You shall not establish contact thereafter with the same boat until ten minutes has elapsed.

Ship-to-Shore Service

Listen to make sure that the working channel you wish to use is not busy. If it is clear, put your transmitter on the air and say: "(Location) Marine Operator, this is (name of your boat and call sign), over."

Listen for a reply. If no contact is made, repeat after an interval of at least two minutes.

When the Marine Operator answers, say: "This is (name of your boat and call sign) calling (telephone number desired), over."

After the telephone conversation is completed say: "This is (name and call sign of your boat), out."

How to Receive a Call

Your boat can be reached only when your receiver is turned on and tuned to the frequency over which you expect calls.

The receiver you use to maintain watch on 156.8 MHz (or 2182 kHz) will assure that you get calls addressed to you by other boats. For calls from public shore stations, you will generally need to keep a receiver tuned to a working frequency of the station for that area. It is urged that you have one receiver for watch keeping and a second one to ensure that you can be reached by a public shore station over a working channel. This will help to keep 156.8 MHz and 2182 kHz free for their primary purpose.

Steps in Receiving a Call

Boat-to-boat calls—When you hear your boat called, put your transmitter on the air and say: "(Name of boat that called) This is (name of your boat and call sign), over."

Switch to the agreed-upon inter-ship channel. After the conversation is completed, say: "This is (name of your boat and call sign), out."

Shore-to-ship calls—When you hear the name of your boat called, put your transmitter on the air and say: "(Name of station that called) This is (name of your boat and call sign), over."

After the conversation is completed, say: "This is (name of your boat and call sign), out."

DEPTH SOUNDERS

Depth sounders are a modern replacement for the hand-held lead line used for uncounted centuries to determine the depth of water beneath a ship. This electronic device furnishes a vastly greater amount of information and does it with much greater ease, especially in nasty weather. It provides safety as well as convenience in boating, and so is doubly advantageous to have on board.

How Depth Is Measured

Depth is determined by measuring the round-trip time for a pulse of ultrasonic energy to travel from the boat to the bottom of the water and be reflected back to the point of origin. See Figure 6.2. The frequency of the audio pulses generally lies between 50,000 and 200,000 cycles per second, too high to be heard by human ears. Their average velocity through the water is approximately 4,800 feet per second; slight variations in speed will occur between salt and fresh water and with different temperatures. The resulting small errors, however, can be safely ignored for the relatively shallow depths of interest to the operators of recreational boats.

Probably the greatest advantage of the electronic device over the hand-held line is essentially continuous nature of the information furnished. Depth sounders vary widely in the rate at which readings are taken, but in all cases many more soundings are taken than could be accomplished by hand. Current equipment takes readings at rates between one and thirty *each second..*

Components of a Depth Sounder

The major components of a depth sounder are a source of energy (transmitter), a means of sending out the pulses and picking up the echoes (transducer), a receiver to amplify the weak echoes, and a visual presentation of the information. The transducer usually takes the form of a round block of hard ceramic material several inches in diameter and an inch or so thick. In many cases, it is given an oblong, streamline shape to reduce drag.

The visual presentation of information on the depth of the water is accomplished by an "indicator," a "recorder," or a video display. The indicator provides a nonpermanent indication of the depth, in some cases by the use of a flashing light; in many units an ordinary

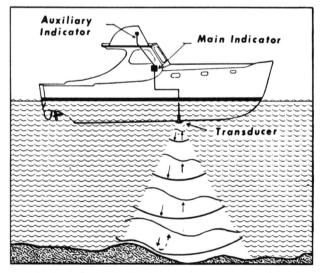

Figure 6.2 An electronic depth sounder measures depth by sending pulses of high-frequency sound waves, reflected back from bottom. Distance is measured by time taken by pulses for the round trip.

electric meter is used with a suitably calibrated dial. Some new units provide a direct readout in digital numbers. The flashing light is mounted on the end of an arm that rotates around a scale much like the second hand of a clock, only much faster. The zero of the scale is usually at the top of the dial and a flash of light occurs there when the outgoing pulse leaves the transducer on the boat's bottom. A second flash occurs when the pulse is received back at the transducer, having been reflected back from the bottom of the water. The deeper the water, the longer it will take for the echo to return to the boat; the longer this takes, the farther the arm will have rotated around the dial. Thus, the scale of depths increases clockwise around the face of the indicator.

The most sophisticated depth sounders are designed more for the serious fishing enthusiast than for actual depth measurement in conjunction with piloting. Features include a white-line display to help separate low-lying fish from the bottom itself, the use of color in a video display to help identify types of fish, and readouts of water temperature, and even position when hooked to Loran-C equipment.

RADIO DIRECTION FINDERS

On the seacoasts of the United States, and on the Great Lakes and other large inland bodies of water, a *radio direction finder* (RDF) is an important piece of electronic equipment. Primarily installed as a safety item, it can also be a great convenience to the boat operator. It is the primary radio aid to navigation for small craft.

A complete radio direction finding system consists of four components:

1. One or more radio transmitters at known locations.
2. An RDF set on the boat.
3. Charts covering both the location of the transmitters and the area of operation of the boat.
4. A person who knows the operation of the system.

To be fully effective, the RDF system must be used with competence and confidence—an incorrect radio bearing can lead to disaster; a correct bearing that is ignored because of mistrust can be equally disastrous.

Special RDF Features

Basically, an RDF is a radio receiver with two additional features. First and vitally important is the directional antenna. Usually, this antenna is rotatable so that the set may be secured firmly in a convenient location. The directional antenna employed with an RDF set is an improved version of the simple loop used on portable receivers, the directional characteristics of which are familiar to most boatmen. This antenna may take the form of a loop, a foot or so in diameter, or it may appear as a plastic bar measuring about an inch square by some six inches in length. Both types will be mounted on top of the set; either will do the job.

As the antenna is rotated through 360 degrees, these directional antennas show two positions of maximum signal strength and two positions of minimum sensitivity called nulls. With properly balanced construction and no local interfering objects, the two maximum signal positions will be separated by 180 degrees, as will be the nulls, which are found 90 degrees in either direction from the maximums. It is characteristic of these antennas that the maximum signal points are broad and poorly defined, while the nulls are marked and precise. For this reason, the nulls are used for direction finding.

The second feature of RDFs is a visual null indicator. While the operator can judge by ear the position of the antenna at minimum signal with fair accuracy, a more precise bearing can be obtained by observing a visual indicator. This is normally a small electric meter, read for either a maximum or minimum deflection of its needle in accordance with the instructions for the particular set being used.

How to Take a Radio Bearing

To take a radio bearing, follow these steps:

1. Set the scale built into the set, usually around the base of the antenna, so that 000 degrees is dead ahead.
2. Rotate the directional antenna until a null point is precisely

located, read the angle from the scale; this is the uncor-
rected relative radio bearing. *Caution:* The boat must be
directly on course at the moment that the bearing is taken
as any error in heading will be reflected in the resultant
radio bearing.

3. If there is any doubt as to whether the reading just taken is
the direct or reciprocal bearing, use the sense antenna to
identify it. If the reading is the reciprocal, do *not* add or
subtract 180 degrees; take a new bearing.

4. Having determined the direct bearing angle, apply the
proper deviation correction; the sum is the corrected relative radio bearing.

5. Add the boat's *true* heading, subtracting 360 degrees if the
sum exceeds that amount; this is now the true radio bearing
from the boat; plot in the same manner as a visual bearing.

The above steps outline in basic terms the correct procedures to
be followed in taking a radio bearing. In the use of any particular
RDF set, however, the manufacturer's manual should be studied
and the instructions followed closely.

Automatic Radio Direction Finders

An automatic radio direction finder (ADF) indicates on a dial the
direction to a transmitter once it has been tuned in—no swinging of
a loop, no 180 degree ambiguity.

ADFs cover the same frequency bands as manual RDFs and use
the same type of transmitting stations. They are, of course, more
complex in circuitry and thus more expensive. The antenna is continuously rotated, either mechanically or electronically, whenever
the set is turned on. Often such equipment is a fixed installation
with a remote antenna, but portable models are available.

The advantages of ADFs lie in their ease and speed of operation.
They are, however, subject to the same radio deviation as manual
RDFs and a correction table must be prepared.

ELECTRONICS

RADAR

Radar is an excellent means of marine navigation and is used on vessels of all sizes, down to boats about thirty feet in length. Although size, power requirements, and cost limit its use on recreational boats, its capabilities and limitations should be known to all boatmen for their own safety when cruising on waters navigated by radar-equipped vessels.

Radar Principles

A radar set sends out brief pulses of super-high frequency radio waves that are reflected by objects at a distance. The time that it takes for the pulse to go out and the echo to return is a measure of the distance to the reflecting object. In broad principles, this is the same technique as previously described for depth sounders, except that transmission is through air rather than water, and radio waves have been substituted for ultrasonic pulses. A refinement has been made in that the radar pulses are sent out in a very narrow beam that can be pointed in any direction around the horizon and used to determine direction as well as distance.

Components of a Radar Set

The major components of a radar set are:

1. The *transmitter*, which generates the radio waves; it includes the *modulator*, which causes the energy to be sent out in brief pulses.

2. The *antenna*, which radiates the pulses and collects the returning echoes. The antenna is highly directional in its horizontal characteristics, but eight to ten times wider vertically. The beam pattern can be thought of as being like a fan turned up on edge. The beam's narrow horizontal directivity gives it a fairly good angle-measuring capability, while its broadness in the vertical plane helps keep the beam on an object despite any rolling or pitching of the vessel.

3. The *receiver,* which detects the returned reflections and amplifies them to a usable strength.

4. The *indicator,* which provides a visual display of objects sending back reflections.

Radars operate at frequencies far above the usual radio communications bands. At such super-high frequencies, radar pulses act much like light waves in that they travel in essentially straight lines. They travel at the speed of light, 186,000 miles per second. For each nautical mile of distance to the target, only a fraction more than twelve microseconds is required for the round trip of the outgoing pulse and the returned echo. Pulses, each of which lasts for only a fraction of a microsecond (one millionth of a second), are sent out at a rate of from six hundred to four thousand each second depending upon the design of the equipment. The directional antenna rotates at a rate of one revolution in about four seconds. The round-trip time for a pulse is so short that the antenna has not appreciably moved before the reflection is returned.

The Plan Position Indicator (PPI)

Marine navigational radars use a Plan Position Indicator (PPI) type of display. A circular cathode ray tube of a special type from five to twenty inches in diameter is used. The center of the face represents the position of the radar-equipped vessel and the presentation is roughly like that of a navigational chart.

A bright radial line on the face of the tube represents the radar beam; it rotates in synchronism with the antenna. Reflections show up as points or patches of light depending upon the size of the echo-producing object. The persistence of the screen is such that the points and patches of light do not completely fade out before the antenna has made another rotation and they are restored to brilliance. Thus the picture on the radarscope is repainted every few seconds.

Radar Range Scales

The relative bearing of an object is indicated directly on the screen; a position corresponding to the 12 on a clock face is directly ahead. The distance to the object is proportional to the distance from the center of the screen to the point of light which is the echo. On most radars, concentric circles of light are used as range markers to make the estimation of distances both easier and more accurate. All radar sets have multiple-range scales that may be selected to suit the purpose for which the radar is being used. Longer range scales provide coverage of greater areas, but at a cost of less detail and poorer definition.

Radar sets have both a maximum and a minimum range, each of which is of importance in the operation of the equipment. The maximum range is determined by the transmitter power and the receiver sensitivity, provided, of course, that the antenna is at a sufficient height above water that the range is not limited by the distance to the horizon. (The radar pulses normally travel with just a slight amount of bending; thus the radar horizon is about 15 percent farther away than the visual horizon.)

Because a radar pulse has a definite duration, and therefore occupies a definite length in space as it moves outward from the antenna, there is a minimum range within which objects cannot be detected. This minimum range, usually between twenty and fifty yards, is important when maneuvering in close quarters, as when passing buoys at the side of a narrow channel.

Units for Small Craft

Radar sets for small craft usually consist of two units. Modern design of the components makes it possible to combine the antenna, transmitter, and a portion of the receiver into a single unit installed on a mast or on the pilothouse. This unit, usually weighing between 60 and 120 pounds, should be located as high as possible in order to avoid limiting the range of the set. The antenna should have an unobstructed "look" in all directions. The remainder of the receiver and the indicator are located near the helmsman's position. Improved design techniques have resulted in indicator units so small that they may be fitted into a pilothouse in any number of positions.

Because radar sets radiate radio frequency energy, they must be licensed by the FCC, but this is not difficult to do for commerically produced equipment. No license is required to operate a radar, but for its installation and maintenance, the technician must have a second- or first-class radio operator's license with a special "ship radar" endorsement. The owner and station licensee of a marine radar installation is responsible that only a properly licensed individual does all of the technical work on the equipment.

Principal Applications

Radars have two principal applications aboard ships and small craft. They are often thought of primarily as anticollision devices, but are even more often used to assist in the piloting of the vessel.

Radar was originally conceived for the detection and tracking of ships and aircraft. It offers an excellent means of extending the coverage of a visual lookout, especially at night and under conditions of reduced visibility. This greater range of detection affords more time for a ship to maneuver to avoid another craft or an obstacle.

Radar serves another valuable function in the piloting of a vessel approaching a coastline or traveling in confined waters. It has real advantages even in the daytime, and, of course, becomes particularly helpful at night or in fog.

Passive Radar Reflectors

The motorboat owner who does not have a radar can still do something to increase his safety in relation to this item of electronic equipment. He can equip his craft with a *passive radar reflector.* This simple and inexpensive item consists of thin lightweight metal sheets, or areas of fine-mesh metal screening, arranged in mutually perpendicular planes. These may fold for storage, but must remain rigid with respect to each other when opened for use. A relatively small reflector with each metal surface only about two feet square will provide a radar reflection as strong as that from a medium-size steel ship. The echo from the wooden hull of a small craft is so weak as to be easily overlooked in the echoes from the waves if a reflector is not used. With a passive reflector hoisted as high as possible, the ôperator of a small craft can be sure that his boat will be detected on the radar screens of passing ships. Often Coast Guard or other rescue craft searching for a boat in distress are radar-equipped; the use of a passive radar reflector greatly increases the chances of being quickly spotted.

ELECTRONIC NAVIGATION
SYSTEMS

There are a number of electronic navigation systems that are available to skippers of offshore cruising and fishing boats as well as to navigators of larger ships. These vary in degree of complexity and cost of receiving equipment. Many boatmen will probably never use any of them personally, but it is desirable to have a general familiarity with their method of operation, and their advantages and disadvantages.

The most widely used electronic navigation system is Loran-C. Another system is *Omega,* which is now operational with only eight transmitting stations needed to provide coverage on all navigable ocean waters of the world.

Decca is a short-range, high-accuracy electronic navigation system that is available only in limited areas; it is more widely used in Europe than North America. Decca is unique in that in the United States it is commercially operated rather than by a governmental agency.

The aeronautical VHF navigations system called *VOR,* or *Omnirange,* is sometimes used by boats, but its short range is a severe limitation. (Aircraft can use this system out to hundreds of miles by reason of their high altitudes; Omni-equipped boats are limited to about ten to twenty miles by the line-of-sight characteristics of the signals.)

There is also an electronic navigation system based on the use of satellites, but the complexity and cost of equipment have limited its use by boatmen.

LORAN

LORAN—the name derived from LOng RAnge Navigation—is an electronic system using shore-based radio transmitters and shipboard receivers to allow mariners to determine their position at sea. Loran works in all kinds of weather, twenty-four hours a day.

Loran-C Principles. The transmitters of Loran-C all operate on 100 kHz in *chain of a master station* (M), plus two to four *secondary stations* designated as W, X, Y, and Z. Stations of a chain are located so as to provide electronic coverage over a wide coastal area. Each station transmits groups of pulses on the same frequency; signals from secondaries follow those from the master station at very precise time intervals. Chains are identified by their individual pulse group repetition intervals (GRI)—the time, in microseconds, between transmissions of the master signal. All Loran-C transmitters are frequency and time stabilized by atomic standards; if the signals of a pair should get out of tolerance, however, the chain will "blink" in a code that indicates the nature of the trouble.

The *difference* in the time of arrival at the receiver of pulse groups from the master and each secondary is measured precisely by electronic circuitry, and this information is used to determine a line of position. The use of two or more master-secondary pairs of signals yields the same number of LOPs and thus a Loran-C fix.

Loran-C has a ground-wave (most reliable) range of up to 1,200 miles (2,200 km), with sky-wave reception out to as far as 3,000 miles (5,600 km). The accuracy of Loran-C positions from ground-wave signals varies from 0.1 to 0.25 miles (0.2 to 0.5 km) depending upon where the receiver is in the coverage area; positional errors on sky-wave signals may be as much as eight times greater. A significant feature of Loran-C is the "repeatability" of positions obtained with this system. Ground-wave signals are very stable and a boat should be able to return to a prior position within 50 to 200 feet (15 to 60 m).

Loran-C readings are highly accurate on or near the baseline between the master and secondary stations, but are subject to significant errors on or near the extensions of the baseline beyond each station. Using sky waves within 250 miles of a station being used is not recommended.

Loran-C Receivers. Loran-C receivers automatically acquire and track the signals from the chain to which the set is tuned. The system is complex, but such complexity is handled internally by advanced solid-state circuits—all the operator has to do is turn the set on and tune to the proper GRI. (The coverage of a single chain is quite great and many boats will never need to change the GRI setting.) The Loran-C receiver will take several minutes to "settle down" and give steady readings; then the operator merely reads out the measured time differences and uses this information to plot his position on a chart that has been overprinted with Loran-C lines of position.

The simplest Loran-C receivers have only a single display of time differences; readings of various station pairs appear sequentially at about two-second intervals. Many sets have two displays, allowing for a simultaneous readout of the two time differences required for a fix; at least one manufacturer has a model with three displays. Often a receiver will automatically make measurements on three or four station pairs with these additional readings being displayed sequentially.

More expensive Loran-C receivers include a microprocessor that gives a direct readout in latitude and longitude, plus direction and distance to a preset destination; also speed along the track, cross-track error, time to go, and even a destination arrival signal when almost there. Some caution must be used with Loran-C sets that give position in latitude and longitude, because their computations are based on theoretical propagation conditions and actual conditions may differ. Computers in some sets now adjust lat/long discrepancies automatically.

Omega

The *Omega* electronic navigation system uses very low frequency (VLF) radio waves; three different frequencies from 10.2 to 13.6 kHz are used. Such VLF signals have considerable range and stability over day and night paths. An advantage of the system is that complete global coverage can be obtained by the use of only six transmitters properly situated. Ideally, stations would be located at the North and South Poles and 90 degrees apart on the Equator; such a requirement must, of course, be modified to meet practical considerations. In actual practice, the Omega network will have eight transmitting sites to allow for possible equipment failures and off-air time for routine maintenance. The transmitters are located approximately six thousand miles apart and at any point signals from at least four stations will be usable. As the global network of stations is established, transmitters will be operated by the United States (by USCG personnel) and by foreign nations.

The Omega System. The Omega system was originally developed by the U.S. Navy for its submarines, surfaced or submerged (VLF signals can be received while under water), as well as for surface vessels and aircraft. Receiving equipment is now available, however, for civilian ships and aircraft, including fishing and recreational boats. Omega equipment is now quite expensive, but advancing technology and increased production can be expected to bring price reductions.

Omega Fixes. Omega stations transmit continuous-wave signals, rather than pulses, for approximately one second out of every ten seconds on each frequency used. Signals from a single pair of stations on a single frequency can furnish a hyperbolic line of position, but rough position knowledge is required to within about eight miles to identify the set of lines, called a lane, within which the receiver is located. Use of a second frequency reduces the need for position knowledge to twenty-four miles, and use of a third frequency extends this to seventy-two miles.

Two or more lines of position are combined in the normal manner to obtain an Omega fix. Station pairs should be selected so as to get lines crossing at large angles, as near 90 degrees as possible for two lines, or 60 degrees for three lines. As with Loran, special charts are used with overprinted Omega lines of position. Receivers have lane counters to keep a record of the number of lanes crossed since the counter was reset after a fix was established, and so lessen the problem of lane identification.

Omega signals are affected by sky-wave propagation conditions and it is necessary to refer to published correction tables in the use of this system. The nominal all-weather accuracy is one mile in the daytime and two miles at night. Special techniques are available within local areas for increased degree of precision in position fixing; this is known as *differential omega,* and is useful for high-accuracy work such as surveys.

Decca

The Decca electronic navigation system depends on radio signals sent out by four transmitters: a master station and three "slaves." The three slaves are located at the corners of an approximately equal-sided triangle, and the master station is in the center. Distance from master to each slave is about sixty miles. For convenience in identification, the slaves are known as red, green, and purple, and the Decca charts show lines in these colors.

In operation, the Decca receiver compares the wave arriving from each slave with that arriving from the master. This comparison is made possible by a natural phenomenon known as standing waves. When two waves of slightly different frequencies are imposed together, the confluence is marked by many points at which one either amplifies or neutralizes the other. At these points there will be a peak or valley that does not move with the waves. The Decca receiver takes the intervals developed by these standing waves and translates them into a pulse, which rotates a scale pointer to give a line of position reading.

The pulses arrive in a definite order: master, red, green, and purple, with a two-and-a-half second gap between each.

A "Minidec" unit is available for recreational craft installation that can operate off the boat's battery. A whip antenna and a good ground are required. The crystal for the desired chain is inserted, and the selection knob is set to the "sync" position. The first pulse should set the pointer at zero; if not, the "hold" button is pushed while a manual reset knob is turned to make the correction.

Turn the selector knob to "coarse" and the readings will appear at their two-and-a-half second intervals. Find the corresponding Decca lines on the special chart, and you have a fix. If necessary, the selector knob can be turned to the "fine" position to provide the last two significant digits in the coordinates.

7.

RACING

Speed always has been a challenge for many boatmen, whether to see how fast a given boat could go, or in competition with other boats. Here are some of the outstanding records for speed on the water—power and sail, commercial and recreational vessels, in solo runs or passages, and in races.

Here, too, is information on the major power and sail races and the organizations that conduct them.

AMERICAN POWER BOAT ASSOCIATION

Powerboat Racing

All major power racing in the United States is sanctioned and governed by the American Power Boat Association. The APBA is also the United States national authority representing this country in races sanctioned here and abroad by the Union Internationale Motonautique (UIM).

APBA racing classifications include Unlimited Hydroplanes, Cruiser (predicted log racing), Drag, Inboard, Outboard, Stock Outboard, Outboard Performance Craft, and Offshore. Profiles of typical boats are shown in Figure 7.1. Most races are conducted by

PROFILES OF SOME APBA CLASSES

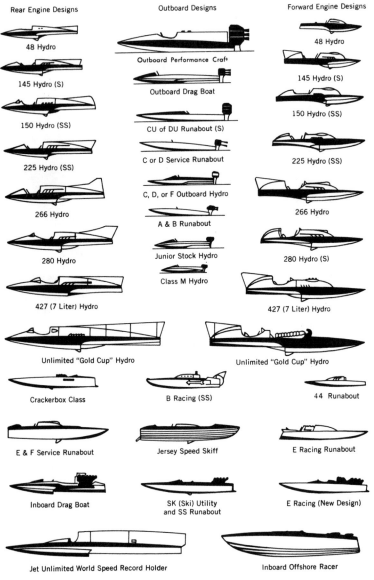

Figure 7.1 Profiles of some APBA classes.

clubs and officials within the various APBA regions, which are shown in Figure 7.2.

The prestigious Gold Cup is one of about ten races held each year on the Unlimited Hydroplane circuit. Officially called the Gold Cup Challenge Trophy, it is meant to be the award for the world's fastest water competition.

Most of the big Unlimited boats are powered by World War II Rolls-Royce or Allison aircraft engines that can provide straight-away speeds close to 200 mph, and lap speeds of well over 100 mph. However, in one 1983 race, an outboard-powered craft managed a second-place finish.

Offshore powerboat racing is done over courses of approximately two hundred miles for Class I boats, and one hundred miles for Class II through Class V boats. The big Class I boats, with two or more engines of more than 600 horsepower each, can reach speeds of close to 100 mph, and an average speed of more than 80 mph over a two hundred-mile course is not unusual.

The circuit for Class I boats is eight to ten races each year; many more races for the smaller classes are held on a regional basis.

Cruiser events do not involve speed, but rather precision piloting. Skippers and navigators file "predicted logs" prior to an event, list-ing the exact times they expect to pass each checkpoint and to cross the finish line. The "race" is run without any timepieces on board, except for that in the possession of an official observer, who is not part of the crew and who does not permit the crew to see or other-wise use it. Over courses of several miles involving a number of checkpoints, errors for the proficient skippers are usually within a few seconds of the predicted times.

Racing for other APBA categories is of the closed-course type, where the boats do laps around oval courses of specific lengths. In each class there are regional and national championship events, as well as high-point honors for overall excellence in the course of a season.

SAILBOAT RACING

The North American Yacht Racing Union is an association of yacht clubs and individual members that, in an advisory capacity,

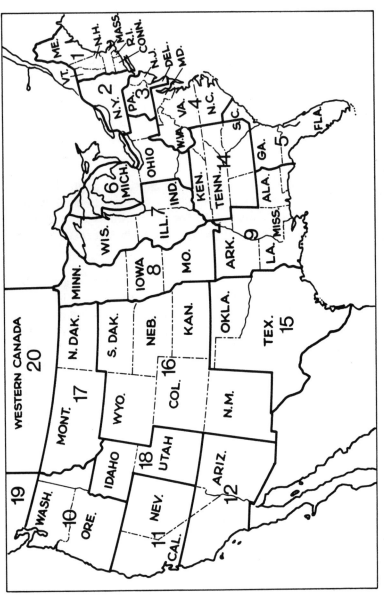

Figure 7.2 American Power Boat Association Regions.

encourages and promotes the racing of sailing yachts, as well as the unification of rules in the United States. The International Yacht Racing Union, based in London, is the world governing body for sail racing. Its membership includes eighty-five national yachting authorities, and it meets annually to resolve rules problems governing racing as well as construction of certain yachts raced internationally. Many individual yacht clubs, or organizations such as the Cruising Club of America, also sponsor major sailing races.

THE AMERICA'S CUP

The *America's Cup* is international yachting's most coveted award. The trophy itself, put up by the Royal Yacht Squadron of England for a race around the Isle of Wight, was first won in 1853 by the U.S. schooner *America*. Deeded to the New York Yacht Club, its possession was successfully defended against English, Irish, Scottish, Canadian, and Australian challengers for 130 years. In 1983 the American defender, *Liberty,* lost the cup to *Australia II,* and the defending yacht club is now in Perth, Australia.

Although original value of the "Ould Mug" was only five hundred dollars, millions of dollars have been spent by defenders, would-be defenders, challengers, and would-be challengers. Until 1970, all challenges were from English-speaking people, but since then France, Italy, and Sweden have made unsuccessful bids to challenge for the cup.

When the yacht *America* won the cup, it defeated a large fleet of boats in the race around the Isle of Wight. In the first challenge, the British boat *Cambria* raced a fleet from the New York Yacht Club in 1870. It finished tenth; the winner was the U.S. yacht *Magic;* the aging *America,* which had seen service in the Civil War, finished fourth.

In subsequent races, the challenger faced only one boat, although in 1871, the New York Yacht Club reserved the right to name the boat on the day of each race of what was then the best two out of three events. *Columbia* and *Sappho* were the successful defenders against the English *Livonia.*

Prior to World War II, contenders for the America's Cup were large yachts, averaging about 120 feet in overall length; the 1903

Table 7.1

Unrestricted Class World Water Speed Records Since 1928

```
1928  Gar Wood, Miss America VII, at Detroit ....................... 92.862
1930  Sir Henry Segrave, Miss England II at Windermere (died
      immediately after). ......................................... 98.7
1931  Kaye Don, Miss England II, in Argentina ..................... 103.48
1931  Kaye Don, Miss England II, Lake Garda ...................... 110.24
1932  Gar Wood, Miss America IX, Miami, Florida .................. 111.65
1932  Kay Don, Miss England III, Loch Lomond (first man to reach 100
      knots) ..................................................... 119.75
1932  Gar Wood, Miss America X, at Detroit ....................... 124.86
1937  Sir Malcolm Campbell, Blue Bird, Lake Maggiore ............. 129.5
1938  Sir Malcolm Campbell, Blue Bird, Lake Hallwil, Switzerland; ... 130.94
1939  Sir Malcolm Campbell, Blue Bird, Lake Coniston ............. 141.74
1950  Stanley Sayres, Slo-mo-shun IV, Lake Washington ........... 160.323
1952  Stanley Sayres, Slo-mo-shun IV, Lake Washington ........... 178.497
1955  (July 23) Donald Campbell, Bluebird, Ullswater ............ 202.32
1955  (Nov. 16) Donald Campbell, Bluebird, Lake Mead, Nevada ..... 216.25
1956  (Sept. 19) Donald Campbell, Bluebird, Coniston Water ........ 225.63
1957  (Nov. 7) Donald Campbell, Bluebird, Coniston Water .......... 239.07
1958  (Nov. 10) Donald Campbell, Bluebird, Coniston Water ........ 248.62
1959  (May 14) Donald Campbell, Bluebird, Coniston Water ......... 260.35
1964  (Dec. 31) Donald Campbell, Bluebird, Lake Dumbleyung,
      Australia .................................................. 276.33
1968  (June 30) Lee Taylor, Jr., Hustler, Guntersville, Alabama ....... 285.21
```

Table 7.2

Record Ocean Passages

DATE	SHIP	FROM	TO	NAUT. MILE DISTANCE	TIME
SAILING VESSELS					
1854	*James Blaine*	Boston Light	Light Rock	—	12d 6h
1854	*Flying Cloud*	New York	San Francisco	15,091	89d
1860	*And. Jackson*	New York	San Francisco	13,700	89d 20h
1868– 69	*Thermopylae*	Liverpool	Melbourne	—	63d 18h
1853	*Northern Light*	San Francisco	Boston	—	76d 6h
—	*Red Jacket*	New York	Liverpool	3,150	13d 1h
1846	*Yorkshire*	Liverpool	New York	3,150	16d
1905	*Atlantic*	Sandy Hook	England	3,054	12d 4h
1981	*Elf Aquitane*	Sandy Hook	England	3,054	9d 6h
POWER VESSELS					
1819	*Savannah*	Savannah	Liverpool	—	16d
1838	*Great Western*	Bristol	New York	—	15d
1910	*Mauretania*	Queenstown	New York	2,780	4d 10h 42m
1933	*Rex*	Gibraltar	Ambrose Light	3,181	4d 13h 58m
1934	*Bremen*	Cherbourg	Ambrose Light	3,092	4d 14h 27m
1937	*Normandie*	New York	Southampton	2,936	3d 22h 07m
1938	*Queen Mary*	Ambrose Light	Bishop's Rock	3,120	3d 20h 42m
1952	*United States*	Ambrose Light	Bishop's Rock	2,942	3d 10h 40m

defender, *Reliance,* carried about 16,000 square feet of sail. A modern 12-Meter yacht, of the type now used in cup racing, carries about 1,850 square feet of sail.

Competition for the America's Cup is now a best four of seven race series, and the next series will be sailed in the waters off Perth, Australia, in 1986 or 1987. Potential Australian defenders will compete to select the actual defender, and yachts of all challenging nations will compete to select the actual challenger for the cup itself.

AMERICA'S CUP SUMMARIES

Year	Winner (U.S.)	Challenger
1851	*America*	U.S. schooner *America* defeated Royal Yacht Squadron fleet in race around the Isle of Wight, England.
1870	*Magic*	*Cambria,* England
1871	*Columbia, Sappho*	*Livonia,* England
1876	*Madeline*	*Countess of Dufferin,* Canada
1881	*Mischief*	*Atalanta,* Canada
1885	*Puritan*	*Genesta,* England
1886	*Mayflower*	*Galatea,* Scotland
1887	*Volunteer*	*Thistle,* Scotland
1893	*Vigilant*	*Valkyrie II,* England
1895	*Defender*	*Valkyrie III,* England
1899	*Columbia*	*Shamrock,* Ireland
1901	*Columbia*	*Shamrock II,* Ireland
1903	*Reliance*	*Shamrock III,* Ireland
1920	*Resolute*	*Shamrock IV,* Ireland
1929	*Enterprise*	*Shamrock V,* Ireland
1934	*Rainbow*	*Endeavor,* England
1937	*Ranger*	*Endeavor II,* England
1958	*Columbia*	*Sceptre,* England
1962	*Weatherly*	*Gretel,* Australia
1964	*Constellation*	*Sovereign,* England
1967	*Intrepid*	*Dame Pattie,* Australia
1970	*Intrepid*	*Gretel II,* Australia
1974	*Courageous*	*Southern Cross,* Australia
1977	*Courageous*	*Australia,* Australia
1980	*Freedom*	*Australia,* Australia
	Winner (Australia)	Defender
1983	*Australia II*	*Liberty* (U.S.)

OTHER MAJOR SAIL RACES

Newport–Bermuda Race

Sailed biennially in June (alternating with the Annapolis to Newport Race), the 635-mile race starts at Brenton Reef Tower off
Newport, R.I., and finishes at Mount Hill Light on St. David's
Head, Bermuda. The event, open to sailing yachts and under rules
of the Cruising Club of America, is sponsored by the CCA and the
Royal Bermuda Yacht Club. Yachts are handicapped according to
rating of the International Offshore Yacht Racing Rules.

Annapolis to Newport Yacht Race

Sailed in June every other year, alternating with the Newport–Bermuda Race, the Annapolis, Md., to Newport, R.I., ocean
race is 473 miles long and is sponsored by the New York Yacht
Club, the Annapolis Yacht Club, and the U.S. Naval Academy Sailing Squadron.

Transpacific Race

This sailing race is held every odd-numbered year in July, going
from Los Angeles to Honolulu. It is sponsored by the Transpacific
Yacht Racing Association.

Transpacific Catamaran Race

Alternating with the Transpacific Race, this event is for multihulls
every July in even-numbered years. It is sponsored by the Seal
Beach, Cal., Yacht Club and the Ocean Racing Catamaran Association.

Chicago to Mackinac

This 333-mile freshwater sailboat race is sponsored annually by
the Chicago Yacht Club in July.

Southern Ocean Racing Conference

This series of races generally consists of six events, five of which count toward a high-point championship. The races are: St. Petersburg to Venice, Fla.; St. Petersburg to Ft. Lauderdale; Miami to Lucaya; Sir Thomas Lipton Cup (day race off Miami); Miami to Nassau; and the Nassau Cup Race, off Nassau, Bahamas. Racing is conducted under International Offshore Rules during the first two or three months of the year.

Acapulco Race

Sponsor of this 1,430-mile sail is the San Diego Yacht Club, which runs it every even-numbered year in February.

Ensenada Race

A highly popular (over five hundred yachts) sailing event going from Newport Beach, Cal., to Ensenada, Mexico, a distance of about 130 miles, the Ensenada Race is sponsored by the Newport Ocean Sailing Association on the weekend closest to May 5 each year.

Congressional Cup

Round-robin match racing among the nation's top sailors is sponsored each year by the Long Beach, Cal., Yacht Club. The trophy for this invitational series was created by the United States Congress.

World Ocean Racing Championship

In 1969, the St. Petersburg, Fla., Yacht Club established a three-year competition for a world's championship for ocean-racing yachts. A low-point system is used, with seven out of eighteen possible races counted. Of the eighteen, two are mandatory, the St. Petersburg–Ft. Lauderdale Race and the Miami to Montego Bay Race; the other five are optional. The eighteen sanctioned races are held in nine different countries. The boat and owner, or charterer, must be the same for three years in order to be eligible.

Fastnet Race

Sponsored by the Royal Ocean Racing Club, this race is run in

the years alternating with the Newport–Bermuda Race. First run in
1925, the event is over a 600-mile course with the start at Cowes on
the Isle of Wight, and the finish at Plymouth, after rounding Fastnet
Rock off the southwest corner of Ireland.

Sidney–Hobart Race

This event is over a 600-mile course from Sidney, Australia, to
Hobart, Tasmania, south to the Australian continent. It is sponsored by the Cruising Yacht Club of Australia.

La Petite Fastnet de la Méditerranée

This race is run from San Remo to Toulon, France, in even years,
and the reverse in odd years, in each case rounding Giraglia Rock
off Corsica. The race usually takes place in mid-July.

Little America's Cup

This is match racing for catamarans in a competition similar to
that for the America's Cup. The series was started in 1961 and has
been dominated by British catamarans.

8.

AMENITIES AND DIVERSIONS

A lot of little things can add to the pleasure of boating. Making life aboard more comfortable is one of them; another is knowledge of common boating customs and etiquette. Here are a number of useful tips in the galley and housekeeping departments, suggestions for the boatman's library ashore and afloat, information on pets and boats, and even a short course on photography for the boatman. In short, here are boating's amenities and diversions.

HOUSEKEEPING HINTS*

Those Wire Clothes Hangers Can Be Rust-Proofed

A good coat of colorless nail polish prevents the hanger from rusting. This type of rust-free hanger takes up much less room than plastic or wooden ones. And bear in mind that where the hanging hook is attached to the plastic and wooden hangers is where the neck of the terry cloth robe or cotton sweatshirt always touches, making a most identifiable rust mark.

*From Ruth Lundgren Williamson's column, "The Companionway," which appeared for several years in *Motor Boating & Sailing* magazine.

Table 8.1

Table of Equivalents

Beans, dried	1 cup	½ lb.
Butter	2 cups	1 lb.
	1 stick	½ cup
	1 stick	8 tablespoons
Chocolate	1 square	1 oz.
Cheese	5 cups, grated	1 lb.
Dates	2 cups, pitted	1 lb.
Eggs	5 whole	About 1 cup
Egg whites	8	About 1 cup
Egg yolks	16	About 1 cup
Meat	2 cups, diced	1 lb.
Nut meats	4 cups, chopped	1 lb.
Raisins	3 cups, seedless	1 lb.
Rice	1 cup, raw	3 to 4 cups cooked

SUBSTITUTIONS

Baking powder	1 teaspoon	=	¼ teaspoon baking soda plus ½ teaspoon cream of tartar
Butter	1 cup	=	⅞ cup cottonseed, corn, nut oil, or lard
Chocolate	1 square	=	3 tablespoons cocoa plus 1½ teaspoons fat
Cornstarch	1 tablespoon	=	2 tablespoons flour when used for thickening purposes
Cracker crumbs	¾ cup	=	1 cup bread crumbs
Cream, sour, heavy	1 cup	=	⅓ cup butter and ⅔ cup milk in any sour-milk recipe
Flour, cake, sifted	1 cup	=	⅞ cup sifted all-purpose flour (1 cup less two tablespoons)
Milk	1 cup	=	½ cup evaporated milk and ½ cup water

When It Comes to Pots and Pans

It is generally felt that rust-resistant stainless steel or enamel cookware is best for the boat. We have always been for high, fairly narrow cookware. It saves space in a galley and prevents liquids from sloshing over when the going gets rough. Shop for the widest two pots that will fit on a two-burner. Water boils faster in a wide pot (the same amount, of course) and, with the pot covered, one-dish meals simmer in absolutely no time. Both time and alcohol are conserved.

About Ice Chests

They leak and sweat. They also rot—which isn't so much their fault as the ice that's in them. Ice melts and chests have to be drained. On some boats they drain through the hull, but on many boats the drain goes into the bilge. Of course, what makes the ice chests rot is that this is fresh water. Some people carry this rotten idea further. Like down the bilge. A famous boating woman from Puerto Rico mentions cow licks. She suggests you get a cow lick and put it directly under the drain. Every drop from the ice chest is converted into salt water before it settles into those dark recesses in the bilge beyond the reach of the probing penknife. They can be ordered from a farm supply house. If you don't know a farm supply house, call up your local Department of Agriculture Extension Service office. If you don't have room for a cow lick, simple rock salt of the sort you sprinkle on winter sidewalks, generously distributed, will work pretty well.

How to Prevent and Remove Mildew

A useful little pamphlet, *Mold and Mildew,* is available from the Office of Information, U.S. Department of Agriculture in Washington, D.C. Mildew is caused by molds that grow on anything from which they can get enough food. Boat wives do not need to be told that as the molds grow they cause damage and have a musty odor. Obviously, it's pretty hard to get rid of the dampness that encourages the mildew but there are some things you can do to protect your interests. Providing ventilation is the first rule. Give some articles special care. Plastic bags are a joy here. Boat sheets, pil-

Table 8.2

Roasting Time

ROAST	WEIGHT	OVEN TEMP. CONSTANT	TEMP. INSIDE MEAT	MINUTES PER POUND
BEEF				
standing ribs	6–8	300°F.	140°F.	18-20
			160°F.	25-27
			170°F.	27-30
standing ribs (1 rib)	1–8	350°F.	140°F.	33
			160°F.	45
			170°F.	50
rolled ribs	6–8	300°F.	140°F.	30-32
			160°F.	45-48
chuck ribs	5–8	300°F.	150–170°F.	25-30
rump	5–7	300°F.	150–170°F.	25-30
PORK—FRESH				
loin—center	3–4	350°F.	185°F.	35-45
whole	12–15	350°F.	185°F.	15-20
ends	3–4	350°F.	185°F.	45-50
shoulder—whole	12–14	350°F.	185°F.	30-35
boned and rolled	4–6	350°F.	185°F.	40-45
cushion	4–6	350°F.	185°F.	35-40
pork butt	4–6	350°F.	185°F.	45-50
fresh ham	10–12	350°F.	185°F.	30-35
LAMB				
leg	6½–7½	300°F.	165–180°F.	30-35
shoulder-rolled	3–4	300°F.	165–180°F.	40-45
shoulder	4½–5½	300°F.	165–180°F.	30-35
VEAL				
leg roast	7–8	300°F.	165–170°F.	25
loin	4½–5	300°F.	165-170°F	30-35
rack—4 to 6 ribs	2½–3	300°F	165-170°F	30-35
shoulder	7	300°F.	165–170°F.	25
shoulder—rolled	5	300°F.	165–170°F.	40-45

This chart can be used for both the searing and constant temperature methods.

lowcases, towels, and extra blankets should always be stored in plastic bags when they're on the boat and if anybody lives on the waterfront, it's a good idea to keep all home and boat linens in plastic. It reduces the dampness—never known or had a piece of cloth mildew in a plastic bag. In season, these bags also keep leather and canvas shoes dry and mildew-free. And plastic covers are a must for cotton mattresses. Nice on foam, too, but essential on cotton. There are now mildew-resistant finishes that can be put on some surfaces to protect them. The little pamphlet suggests the following to remove mildew already present on fabrics: Use lemon juice and salt solution, perborate bleach, or chlorine bleach. And use talcum powder in books.

Reusable-Disposable Bed Sheets

These bed sheets and pillowcases can be slept on for seven nights before throwing them away. Soft and cozy the whole week long, with nary a rip or tear, and they're attractive to boating wives for another reason: They store in about a quarter of the space of ordinary bed linen.

A Boat Bucket with a Lid

Rubbermaid puts out such a bucket. It's rectangular, has a 14-quart capacity, and is handy for a dozen things aboard. It can be used to hold bait one day, for icing beverages the next, and for mopping the deck after that—it's that easy to keep clean. The lid is what gives it added value.

Pressure Cookers

Some boat wives seem to feel that for cooking in a hurry, they're great. They reduce cooking time for just about everything by two thirds or more. Sometimes this is important. Sometimes it's not, especially if you're looking forward to a long, beautiful cruising day and have plenty of time to spare. At any rate, you can use a pressure cooker as long as there's a steady source of heat and cold water. Some recipes for quick-cooking foods like fresh vegetables require the cold water for reducing pressure immediately after the recommended cooking time to prevent overcooking. Otherwise, you let the pressure drop of its own accord. It doesn't take much cold water, though. Running the cooker under the water faucet or pouring cold water over it is enough. Or even just placing it in a pan of cold water. National Presto Industries, Eau Claire, Wisconsin, makes one of the most popular cookers; you can get them electric or nonelectric, with or without Teflon.

Table 8.3
PURCHASING GUIDE FOR FRESH VEGETABLES

Item	Market Unit	Approx. Measure as Purchased	Approx. No. of Servings per Unit
Asparagus	1 lb.	16-20 stalks	6
Beans, lima shelled	1 lb.	2 cups	6
Beans, snap	1 lb.	3 cups	5
Beets	1 lb.	2 cups diced	4
Broccoli	1 lb.	—	3
Brussels sprouts	1 lb.	1 quart or less	5
Cabbage—Served raw	1 lb.	1/2 small head	7
Served cooked	1 lb.	—	4
Carrots	1 lb.	4 cups diced or shredded	5
Cauliflower	1 lb.	1½ cups	2
Celery	1 lb.	2 med. bunches 4 cups diced	4 (cooked)
Corn, ears	12 medium	3 cups cut	6
Greens	1 lb.	—	4
Mushrooms	1 lb.	35-45	6
Onions	1 lb.	3 large	4
Peas, in pod	1 lb.	1 cup shelled	2
Potato, sweet	1 lb.	3 medium	3
Potato, white	1 lb.	3 medium	3
		2½ cups diced	
Rutabaga	1 lb.	2⅔ cups sliced	4
Squash, summer	1 lb.	—	3
Tomato	1 lb.	4 small	3 (cooked)
Turnip	1 lb.	3 medium	4

Table 8.4

COOKING MEASURES	COOKING TEMPERATURES
3 teaspoons............1 tablespoon	Simmering (water)............180° F.
4 tablespoons............1/4 cup	Boiling (water)............212° F.
5⅓ tablespoons............1/3 cup	Soft Ball stage
16 tablespoons............1 cup	(candies and sauces)....234°-240° F.
7/8 cup.....3/4 cup plus 2 tablespoons	Jellying stage............220°-222° F.
	Very slow oven............250°F.
2 cups............1 pint	Slow oven............300° F.
2 pints............1 quart	Moderately slow oven............325° F.
4 quarts............1 gallon	Moderate oven............350° F.
8 quarts............1 peck	Moderately hot oven............375° F.
16 ounces............1 pound	Very hot oven............450°-500° F.
4 pecks............1 bushel	Hot oven............400° F.

Galley Stoves

Galley stoves should never be taken lightly. Something you're going to be fooling with every day deserves some thought, even if it does not contribute greatly to your comfort and pleasure. Most boat women will agree, and many ask for the final answer as to type, fuel, size, etc. Many stoves have many good qualities, depending somewhat on the space available, your own temperament, your budget for stoves, etc. However, the more burners the better. Some cooks can do all right with one burner, but darn few. And of those few, all could do better with more burners. It may be pointed out (because boating people are such literal people) that when camping one fire can be made to make do. But a camp fire is many fires and, properly made, can serve many purposes. With one burner you have one source, one heat—and that's it. Sometimes we have little choice because of space, but most of the time things can be rearranged oh so little to accommodate two burners rather than one. You can give up on almost anything else and if by doing so you could get the kind of galley stove to suit you, it would be worth the effort.

Use Your Laundry Marker

To label the tops of all cans aboard. It is to be pointed out that moisture can cause labels to fall off and "pot luck" ceases to be fun after a day or two. Any kind of paper packaging is not for boats. Transfer things like flour and sugar to airtight plastic containers (Tupperware is a fine choice). Or else put the paper package into a tightly tied plastic bag. If you've got some good heavy plastic bags, incidentally, you can stuff them with canned foods, seal them, and drop them into the bilge for storage. In that way, you'll never be without variety for your menus. And it's in the best tradition of the sea.

Coffee and Tea Canisters

You have discovered Tupperware somewhere along the line but you'll be happy to learn about new canisters they have added to their line. They're brown and big and labeled. One for coffee holds a whole pound and the matching tea canister stores from seventy-five to one hundred tea bags. The unique Tupperware seal can be counted on, as most boating women know, not only to keep things fresh but to keep things in, in case of a heavy sea.

SKIPPER'S HOME AND ON-BOARD LIBRARIES

The only thing more impossible than picking someone else's neckwear is choosing his reading matter. People who love books are very touchy (and rightly so, I think) about others telling them what they ought to be reading. So this list is offered very tentatively as one man's opinion, in the hope that it will inspire readers to seek out their own favorites.

One other point: The titles listed here are for the most part older books that are either still in print or generally available at good public libraries. If you're interested in buying any of the volumes listed, one of the major mail-order nautical book specialists will probably be able to help you.

On Board

The number of books you can (and want) to carry aboard your boat will depend a lot on how much room you have to stow them (for suggestions, see below). Assuming you've got a bare minimum of dry lockerage, you'll want to keep your library down to basic, operational books.

Engine Book: It may be that your particular engine's service manual covers this heading—some of them, like the excellent book on the Universal Atomic-4, are all the engine literature you need. But if your owner's manual is inadequate or missing, you may want to carry a substitute. Outboard skippers cannot do better, I think, than the appropriate volume of *Glenn's Outboard Motor Repair and Tune-Up Guide.* These complete, hardcover books now cover all the major U.S. outboards—Chrysler, Evinrude, Johnson, McCulloch, Mercury, and Sears, one book to a manufacturer.

The owner of an inboard has nothing so specific. Very small engines are covered by Boyd Daugherty's *Servicing Small Gasoline Engines,* a good, clear introduction. More elaborate installations are a problem. At this writing, the best book in the field is the text of the U.S. Power Squadrons' *Engine Maintenance Course*—so if you're already a Squadron member, it would certainly help you to take the course and have the book aboard for reference.

Log Book: Basically, the boating world seems to be divided between log keepers and non-log keepers—with the latter in the great majority. Even if you're not the systematic type, it can pay you to keep some records of your boat's operation, and some of her vital statistics—major equipment serial numbers, sail plans, stowage plan, etc.

For both the cruising sail- or powerboat skipper, *Chapman's Log & Owner's Manual* provides standard trip-notation pages, radiotelephone log pages, and a guest register as well as a great deal of specific information on boat care, and forms for logging technical information about your boat, its engine(s), electronic gear, and other accessories. Compiled and edited by John R. Whiting and Tom Bottomley, it is published by Hearst Marine Books, 105 Madison Avenue, New York, NY 10016.

For the cruising sailor, I can think of no better log than the loose-leaf version, in large and small sizes, published by West Products (161 Prescott Street, E. Boston, MA 02128). Its removable pages include many sections peculiar to sailing skippers, for recording sail inventory or racing records.

If your vessel has a radiotelephone, you'll need a radio log, and it must be permanently bound to be legal. There are probably enough pages in the Chapman's log referred to above to handle most skippers' loggable messages, but you may also want to invest in a small, informative booklet called *Marine Radio Telephony,* available from Radio Technical Commission for Marine Services, % FCC, Washington, D.C. 20554. While having this book aboard will not relieve you of the obligation to carry the relevant FCC Rules, those rules are incomprehensible to just about everyone except the people who wrote them. *Marine Radio Telephony* tells you how to operate your R/T legally and effectively.

Medical Emergencies: Most good marine first-aid kits come with a pamphlet-size manual enclosed. If you feel yours isn't good enough—and it probably isn't—there are several books you can get to supplement it. Two titles are put out by the American Red Cross—*First Aid* and *Life Saving and Water Safety.* Another very fine book, of special pertinence to the yachtsman, is *First Aid Afloat,* by Paul Sheldon, M.D. Whichever first-aid book you decide on, check the ingredients of your first-aid kit against those noted in the book to make sure you'll have what you need to follow the doctor's orders.

Forecasting: The complete pleasure boatman's weather book is yet to be published. In the meantime, however, there are three worthy volumes to consider. For on-board use, one of the most helpful publications I've ever encountered is *Sager Weathercaster*. It has a set of cardboard dials on the front cover, which can be set to correspond to the present weather conditions and trend, and the resultant coded readout will provide the skipper with a local forecast for the next twelve to twenty-four hours. All you need besides the book is a reliable barometer.

One-Volume Reference: If your shoreside nautical library was restricted to a single book, you could do far worse than make it a copy of the revised *Piloting, Seamanship and Small Boat Handling,* by Charles F. Chapman. Virtually everything you need to know is in *Chapman's,* and a recent overhaul, now complete, makes the book both thoroughly up to date and far easier to use than ever before.

Beyond the basics, there are literally hundreds of worthy volumes the skipper can consider for home or boat. There's only room to list the most outstanding ones here—ones known personally to the compiler or by reliable recommendation.

For information on the many good new books that are being published, it is a good idea to get the current catalog from a specialist publisher, such as Hearst Marine Books, 105 Madison Avenue, New York, NY 10016, or a distributor that handles books of all publishers, such as International Marine Books, 21 Elm Street, Camden, ME 04843.

Learning to Sail

Basic Sailing, by M. B. George. A self-teaching text for beginners.

Sailing, by Peter Heaton. Also for the beginner, but with a pronounced British flavor.

Glenans Sailing Manual, by the staff of the Glenans Sea Centre. The textbook of France's Glenans sailing school in translation. Practical and thorough.

Practical Sailing, by Tony Gibbs. How to sail and why, plus some information on boats and equipment currently available.

Hand, Reef and Steer, by Richard Henderson. Perhaps the best young person's introduction to sailing.

You Can Sail, by John R. Whiting. Well-illustrated instructions for the beginner.

More Advanced Sailing and Racing

Yachtsman's Omnibus, by H. A. Calahan. The famous writer's *Learning to Sail, Race and Cruise* in one volume. Old-fashioned but charming.

Yacht Racing, by Manfred Curry. First of the great yachting theorists and still controversial and thought-provoking.

Sailing to Win, by Robert N. Bavier, Jr. An excellent introduction to competitive sailing.

Race Your Boat Right, by Arthur Knapp. A classic for those learning to race.

Sailing Theory and Practice, by C. A. Marchaj. Intellectual in the extreme, but fascinating if you have the advanced math to follow the author's arguments.

Cornelius Shields on Sailing. Another racing classic; like golf books, there never seem to be enough.

Wind and Sailing Boats, by Alan Watts. A theoretical approach, but not too technical for the intelligent reader.

Offshore Boats and Sailing

Cruising, by Peter Heaton. A charming paperback introduction to the sport. Very old-fashioned and British.

Heavy Weather Sailing, by Adlard Coles. There are few hard-and-fast rules when the going gets tough. Most of them are here.

Cruising Under Sail and *Voyaging Under Sail,* by Eric Hiscock. How it's done, by a man who has made most of the significant voyages there are.

Practical Boating, by W. S. Kals. Not specifically for sailors alone, this is a compendium of useful information for far voyagers.

The Racing-Cruiser, by Richard Henderson. A new and very good introduction to the sport of distance racing, by an American author.

Further Offshore, by John Illingworth. Successor to the classic *Offshore,* this is a revision of the earlier volume. American readers will find it still useful but incomplete.

Storm Sailing, by Gary Jobson. An important book for all sailors, big boat or small, off-shore or weekend, racer or cruiser. It details the information needed to make fast and accurate decisions during storm conditions.

The Compleat Cruiser, by L. Francis Herreshoff. The author is a man of many strong opinions—but who is more entitled to hold them? Lots of useful hints and tips.

The Proper Yacht, by Arthur Beiser. An experienced cruising man's informed ideas on what goes into a liveaboard sailing boat.

Boatbuilding and Design

Boatbuilding, by Howard I. Chapelle. A classic, if somewhat dated.

Boatbuilding Manual, by Robert Steward. An excellent and up-to-date volume that goes from A to Z. Mostly about wooden craft.

Ferro-Cement Boat Construction, by Jack R. Whitener. Covers every detail of concrete boatbuilding from the trowel up.

Boatkeeper, edited by Bernie Gladstone and by Tom Bottomley. Ideas and specifications for modifications, improvements, and installations on all types of boats.

Your Boat's Electrical System, by Conrad Miller. The layman's book that deals at a practical level with everything electrical aboard a boat, power or sail.

Skene's Elements of Yacht Design, by Francis Kinney. The great classic in the field.

Understanding Boat Design, by Brewer and Betts. A very good introduction to elementary factors of design.

Sailor's Skills

Ashley Book of Knots. Perhaps the most complete knot book ever compiled, though most of it is of use only to antiquarians.

Knight's Modern Seamanship. Another of the nonfiction classics of the sea, this one is not of great pertinence to the pleasure boatman.

Arts of the Sailor, by Hervey Garrett Smith. Fancy rope work—a small gem of a book.

Celestial Navigation for Yachtsmen, by Mary Blewitt. A method of approaching deep-water navigation that may appeal to amateurs because of its simplicity.

The Coastal Navigator's Handbook, by Tony Gibbs. Tables, shortcuts, and memory hints for piloting in coastal waters. Book is spiral-bound to lie flat on a chart table or cockpit seat.

Practical Piloting, by Tom Bottomley. Basic piloting procedures and theory, with examples and problems for the reader.

Practical Celestial Navigation, by Tom Bottomley. Theory and practice of navigation by sextant, using any of the available almanacs and sight-reduction tables, or a pocket calculator.

Primer of Navigation, by G. W. Mixter. A navigation text designed for class use.

Art of Knotting and Splicing, by Cyrus Dey. A good, complete book—if not so complete as Ashley.

Dutton's Navigation and Piloting, by E. S. Maloney. The latest revision of an old classic.

Knots & Lines Illustrated, by Paul and Arthur Snyder. How to handle most rope-and-line situations on a modern sailboat. Highly practical.

Reference

Safety Standards for Small Craft, issued periodically by the American Boat & Yacht Council. Recommended construction, design, and installation practices for pleasure boats. Technical but sound.

International Maritime Directory, by René de Kerchove. Heavily weighted toward commercial shipping terms, it is still the only game in town.

Modern Powerboats, by Jack West. The boats themselves, the equipment for them, and how to install and care for it.

Sailboat & Sailboat Equipment Directory, by Institute for Advancement of Sailing. Annual paperback directory.

Sails, by Jeremy Howard-Williams. With a British bias, this is still the best general book on the design and construction of sails.

Mariner's Notebook, by William Crawford. A self-teaching course in piloting and boat handling.

American Practical Navigator, better known as *Bowditch.* Not really very useful to the pleasure boatman, but fun to have just the same.

Power Boat Annual. Not as good as the *Sailboat Directory,* but adequate.

Boat Owner's Buyer's Guide, by the editors of *Yachting.* Annual compendium of where-to-get-it information. A lot easier than trying to keep track of individual catalogs.

AMENITIES

Yachtsman's Eight Language Dictionary. Most pleasure boating terms rendered into French, German, Dutch, Danish, Italian, Spanish, Portuguese, and—you guessed it—English.

PETS AND BOATS

Some dog breeds such as retrievers and spaniels take to boating readily. Poodles, beagles, and dachshunds seem to be natural sailors. Short-haired breeds seem to do better than those with long hair, and most puppies can usually acclimate themselves to the water. Old dogs who have a violent dislike of the water should not be forced to go along on boats.

If your dog swims in salt water as part of his boating experience, wash him off with fresh water at least once a day, dry him well, and keep him away from drafts. Salt water, if left on the dog, can cause skin problems.

Some pets will drink excessive amounts of salt water, causing them to become nauseous. Give a small amount of Pepto-Bismol and do not feed the animal for a while. Fresh water should be available at all times; renew it four or five times a day, if necessary, to make sure it is fresh and pure. Avoid excessive ice water, however, as this can lead to diarrhea.

Canned dog foods are ideal for the boat; dry foods tend to pick up the dampness and become soggy. Most table scraps are all right, but avoid all bones, and double-check the condition of leftovers from the ice box or refrigerator. Don't overfeed your pet.

Dogs need plenty of exercise, and should have it, ashore, three or four times a day. Make sure there's a total of at least an hour a day for exercise. Dogs find it necessary to relieve themselves with some degree of regularity, and scheduled times should be provided. Most of them prefer to have this opportunity after they have eaten, so a good walk following the evening meal is recommended.

Don't allow your pet on deck when coming in alongside a pier or another boat. Most dogs regard the boat as family property to be guarded and may try to bite anyone who reaches aboard to take a line or steps aboard for any reason. A dog or cat moving about on deck also could be a tripping hazard.

Don't go off from the boat at night and leave a noisy dog in the cabin, and don't allow your dog to run loose in a marina.

It should be noted that cats make excellent cruising companions.

They do not need trips ashore for exercise, and an on-board Kitty Litter pan serves them very well. They can swim, too, in case one falls overboard.

PHOTOGRAPHY AFLOAT

It's easy to take good pictures of boats and boating—*good* pictures, not the blurred, improperly exposed and composed snapshots or slides that are seen so often. Here are a few tips that will put you on the right track. Photography magazines and your camera dealer can help fill in the details.

Camera

An inexpensive Instamatic-type camera cannot produce pictures that are as sharp as those shot with expensive equipment. But the expensive camera *can* produce results that are worse than those from the Instamatic.

Basic to the inexpensive cameras are fixed-focus lenses and slow, single-speed shutters. If the scene is too bright for the film being used, the picture will be overexposed; if there's not enough light, it will be underexposed. Background detail will be just as sharp as foreground detail.

An increase in camera price generally indicates an increase in the quality of the lens, in addition to other details. The better the lens, the sharper the detail in the finished print or slide. Also, the better lenses can be focused to provide maximum sharpness at a distance from the camera ranging from a few feet to infinity. With the proper lens aperture and shutter adjustments, a picture will have a foreground subject clear and sharp, with a softly blurred background, or sharp detail in the distance framed by a blurred foreground. This is actually the way your eyes operate. It's also possible to have *everything* sharp under normal conditions.

Other advantages of more expensive cameras are the ability to adjust lens apertures to compensate for the amount of existing light, and a range of shutter speeds that permits "stopping" fast action or taking pictures in fairly dim light without a flash attachment.

Another bonus of the more expensive cameras is the availability of interchangeable or add-on lenses for wide-angle and telephoto pictures. The latter is particularly useful in getting close-up detail in subject matter that would be lost with an ordinary lens.

With inexpensive cameras, you don't have to worry about any adjustments; with expensive equipment, you'll get better pictures—if your adjustments are correct.

Film

There are three basic film choices: black and white, color for slides, and color for prints. Most Instamatic-type cameras use a medium-speed black-and-white or color film for prints. Outdoors, these provide good results in the hours of maximum daylight. Faster films are available for the more expensive roll-film cameras to permit taking pictures at speeds up to 1/1000th of a second in normal light, or at slow shutter speeds in dim light.

Choice of color film depends on whether color prints or slides are wanted. For color prints, a film such as Kodacolor should be used; for slides, use Kodachrome or Ektachrome, or their equivalent. Some provide richer colors, others a better grain structure. It's worth experimenting to see which meets your needs. It's also possible to make black-and-white prints from Kodacolor negatives, or black-and-white conversions from color slides. These do not have the quality of prints made from regular black-and-white film negatives.

Filters

A medium yellow filter is recommended for best results when using black-and-white film outdoors. It brings out detail in clouds, darkens the water, and adds sparkle to highlights. Orange or red filters also can be used for more dramatic effects; a deep red filter can transform a bright afternoon into a moonlight scene in the final print.

For color film, an almost clear "skylight" filter can be used, or a polaroid filter, to cut haze and to emphasize cloud detail.

When using a filter, it will be necessary to increase exposure by the applicable "filter factor." As the filter reduces the amount of light hitting the film, you must use a slower shutter speed or a larger aperture to compensate. A skylight filter has no filter factor and normal exposures are used.

Composition

A basic premise of the professional photographer is that film is relatively cheap. Take a lot of pictures, and the law of averages will turn up some that are good, some that are fair, and some that are poor. Still, try to plan your pictures. Decide what is to be the point of interest. See what elements of foreground or background best emphasize it. Try to avoid conflicts of subject and background such as a mast that appears to grow out of the first mate's head.

Scenic shots are plentiful, but make sure you can identify them later. Including an element of crew activity will personalize these. When taking pictures of people or activities on the water, try to move around your subject as much as possible, shooting from various angles and distances. Don't worry about the direction from which the light is coming; except for early morning or late evening, there's no problem. Do try to keep faces in an even light.

Shooting

If you are on a boat, you are in motion unless the boat is hard aground in a flat calm. If you are ashore and taking a picture of a boat in action, it is in motion. With an inexpensive fixed-focus single-speed shutter camera, motion means blurs. Always brace the camera against your face or body with both hands and hold it as steady as possible while you apply even pressure to the shutter release. Don't trip the shutter with a hard snap; you'll jar the camera.

When taking a picture of a boat that's moving at a good clip, "pan" with the action: Move the camera to keep the boat centered. It will come out sharp and clear in the picture, and the background will be slightly blurred. Or get in a position so the boat is coming directly toward you or heading directly away. This minimizes apparent motion.

With cameras that have adjustable shutter speeds and lens apertures, you may use a speed that freezes action—whether your motion or that of your subject. Or you can use a slow speed and pan as above to give the feeling of motion to the finished picture. use of a light meter is recommended. Be sure it is set for the speed of the film you are using, and that you read the light on your subject, not its background.

If you are taking movies or using a video camera, be sure to make fairly frequent changes of angle or scene to provide variety. In observing professionally made movies or television shows, note that the camera remains on a scene no more than three or four seconds before there is a change. It may be from a distant shot to a close-up of the same action, or the action shot from another location—anything that helps to keep the attention of the viewer. Of course, you can hold on a scene longer and edit to the desired length if you have film-editing facilities.

Processing

You can take your exposed black-and-white film to your drugstore and have it sent to a central mass-production laboratory that will grind it out quickly and cheaply. That's the best that can be said about this method. No attempt is made to compensate for differences in type of film or exposure. Even the best exposures, the best compositions, lose a lot.

If possible, send your film to one of the custom processors listed in the Yellow Pages of your phone book. Each roll of film gets individual attention, and you can order contact sheets. A whole roll of film can be printed on one 8″ × 10″ contact sheet. Check the contact sheets to indicate which negatives you want printed, and order the prints in any of the standard sizes available—up to 11″ × 14″ or larger. The larger the print, the higher its cost, but you'll find that you won't want prints of everything you shoot. With the drugstore, you don't have a choice. Every negative that has an image is printed.

Color film can be processed at a local "60-minute"-type facility, or sent by way of drugstore, supermarket, or mail service to a large processing house. For Kodacolor film, many professionals prefer Kodak laboratories to be sure of the best possible results. However, the 60-minute and "Fotolab"-type operations usually provide prints of acceptable quality.

CUSTOMS AND ETIQUETTE

Yachting Etiquette

Etiquette in yachting takes many forms, but all are essentially the act of showing consideration and courtesy to others. The range of correct etiquette extends from simple everyday actions to formal daily routines and official ceremonies.

Daily Color Ceremonies.   If a boatman is at a yacht club or a military or naval base, where formal morning and evening color ceremonies are held, he should follow the actions of local personnel who are not in formation. If he is outdoors when the flag is raised or lowered, and he is wearing a uniform or visored cap, he should face the flag and give a hand salute, holding it until the ceremony is completed. If he is wearing a civilian hat, this should be removed and held over the left breast. If no headgear is worn, the right hand should be placed over the left breast. This is the "breast salute." Women not in uniform stand at attention and give the breast salute. Automobiles are stopped and personnel remain inside.

The above rules do not, of course, apply if the boatman is engaged in hoisting or lowering his own colors. He should complete his actions and then, if the official ceremonies have not ended, he should stand at attention, and salute, if appropriate.

On official occasions, the same salutes as above are given for the playing of the *Star-Spangled Banner* or a national anthem of another country.

Boarding Another Boat.   The etiquette to be observed when coming on board another person's boat is derived from that for boarding a naval vessel. Salutes are seldom exchanged, but a simple request for permission to come aboard is always in good taste. An occasion for saluting might be if the individual boarding was wearing a uniform cap and the craft was that of the commodore of the yacht club or the commander of a Power Squadron.

When leaving another's boat, the naval form of requesting permission is not used. A simple statement of thanks for the hospitality or best wishes for a pleasant cruise is sufficient.

Salutes Between Vessels

In formal ceremonies such as a rendezvous of a yacht club or Power Squadron, the fleet of boats present may pass in review before the flagship of the commodore or USPS commander. In such cases, each craft will salute as it passes. In other isolated instances, joining a club cruise or passing a ship with a high public official embarked, salutes may be exchanged between vessels.

Dipping the Ensign in Salute.   Federal law prohibits dipping the flag of the United States (the fifty-star flag) to any person or thing, and only government vessels are permitted to dip the national ensign in reply to a dip.

The law does, however, permit organizational or institutional flags to be dipped. Thus the U.S. Power Squadrons' ensign, when flown from stern or gaff, may be dipped to salute another craft, or dipped in reply to a dip.

The status of the yacht ensign (thirteen stars in a circle around an anchor on a blue field) is not spelled out clearly, but since the law specifically covers only the flag of the United States, the assumption has been made that the yacht ensign may be dipped.

In a fleet review of a unit of the Power Squadrons, the USPS ensign should be flown from the stern staff or gaff if a suitable-size flag is available. In this way, the flag dipped would be that of the organization holding the review.

All vessels in any review, flying either the USPS or yacht ensign at the stern or gaff, should dip that flag when their bow comes abreast of the stern of the flagship and return it to full height when their stern clears the bow of the flagship.

On this occasion, the flag of the United States should *not* be flown, but if it is, *do not dip it* and use only the hand salute described below. Do not dip any flag other than the flag being flown at the stern staff or the gaff (including the equivalent position on a Marconi sail).

Hand Saluting.   When a vessel is officially reviewing a parade of other vessels, the senior officer present stands on the deck of the reviewing ship with his staff in formation behind him. Only he gives the hand salute in return to salutes rendered him.

On a boat passing in review, if the skipper has his crew and guests in formation behind him, only he gives the hand salute. If the crew and guests are in uniform and standing at attention at the rail facing the reviewing boat as they pass, they all give the hand salute. The criterion is whether or not the other persons aboard are in formation. If in formation, only the skipper salutes; but if not in formation, all salute.

For both situations, the hand salute is given as the flag is dipped and is held until it is raised again.

Gun Salutes.   Guns should not be used in salutes between yachts unless ordered by a national authority or by the senior officer present.

Yacht Routines

The following regulations, particularly applicable to a consideration of yachting etiquette, are taken from that portion of the New York Yacht Club code entitled *Yacht Routine*. These deal with salutes, boats (meaning tenders and dinghies), and general courtesies. Other sections, not given here, relate primarily to the display of flags, signaling, and lights.

The routines of other yacht clubs may be considerably less formal and detailed than that which follow, but whatever routines are used they are likely to have been derived from the procedures of the New York Yacht Club.

Salutes.   All salutes shall be made by dipping the ensign once, lowering the ensign to the dip, and hoisting it when the salute is returned. All salutes shall be returned.

Whistles shall never be used in saluting.

Guns may be used to call attention to signals, but their use otherwise shall be avoided as much as possible.

Vessels of the United States and foreign navies shall be saluted.

When a flag officer of the club comes to anchor, he shall be saluted by all yachts present, except where there is a senior flag officer present.

When a yacht comes to anchor where a flag officer is present, such officer shall be saluted. A junior flag officer anchoring in the presence of a senior shall salute.

Yachts passing shall salute, the junior saluting first.

All salutes shall be answered in kind.

A yacht acting as race committee boat should neither salute nor be saluted while displaying the committee flag.

Boats.   Upon entering and leaving boats, deference is shown seniors by juniors entering first and leaving last.

When in boats, flag officers display their flags, captains (owners) their private signals, and members (nonowners) the club burgee. When on duty, the fleet captain and race committee display their distinctive flags. The flag of the senior officer embarked takes precedence. A flag officer embarked in a boat not displaying his distinctive flag should be considered as present in an unofficial capacity.

When two boats are approaching the same gangway or landing stage, flag officers shall have the right-of-way in order of seniority.

Whenever possible, boat booms shall be rigged in at night. Otherwise, a white light shall be shown at the end. All boats made fast to the stern of a yacht at anchor shall show a white light at night.

Courtesies.   When a flag officer makes an official visit, his flag, if senior to that of the yacht visited, shall be displayed in place of the burgee while he is on board.

A yacht may display the personal flag of a national, state, or local official when such individual is on board, or the national ensign of a distinguished foreign visitor. This flag should be displayed in place of the private signal or officer's flag for the President of the United States, and in place of the burgee, for all other officials and visitors.

On Independence Day, and when ordered on other occasions, a yacht shall, when at anchor and the weather permits, *dress ship* from morning to evening colors.

After joining the squadron during the annual cruise, a yacht shall request permission before leaving.

Cruising

When cruising away from home waters, the wise skipper keeps a sharp eye out for local customs. It is a mark of courtesy to conform to local procedures and practices.

While visiting at a yacht club of which you are not a member, observe the actions and routines of the local owner-members, and particularly the club officers. This is especially important with respect to evening colors. Not all clubs strictly calculate the daily time of sunset, and some may be earlier than you would normally expect.

If you will be off your boat at the time of evening colors—in the clubhouse for dinner, for example—be sure to take down your flags before you leave your craft.

Be a Good Neighbor. Consideration of the other skipper is an important element of yachting etiquette. Don't anchor too close to another boat so as to give cause for concern for the safety of both craft; consider the state of the tide and the effect of its range on the radius about which you will swing. Use a guest mooring only with permission; tie up to a fuel pier only briefly.

In the evening hours at an anchorage, don't disturb your neighbors on other boats. Sound travels exceptionally well across water and many cruising boatmen turn in early for dawn departures. Keep voices down and play radios only at low levels. If you should be one of the early departees, leave with an absolute minimum of noise.

Be a good neighbor in other ways, too. Don't throw trash and garbage overboard. Secure flapping halyards; they can be a most annoying source of noise for some distance. When coming into or leaving an anchorage area, do so at a dead slow speed to keep your wake and wash at an absolute minimum.

Passing Other Boats. A faster boat overtaking and passing a slower one in a narrow channel should slow down *sufficiently* to cause no damage or discomfort. Often overlooked is the fact that it may be necessary for the *slower* boat itself to reduce speed. If that boat is making, say, 8 knots, the faster boat can only slow down to about 10 knots in order to have enough speed differential left to get past. At this speed, the passing boat may unavoidably make a wake that is uncomfortable to the other craft. In such cases, the overtaken boat should slow to 4 or 5 knots to allow herself to be passed at 6 or 7 knots with little wake.

If adequate depths of water extend outward on one or both sides of the course, it is the courteous thing for the passing boat to swing well out to a safe side to minimize the discomfort of the overtaken boat.

Proper etiquette calls for powerboats to pass sailing craft astern or well to leeward.

Guests Aboard

If you are invited to go cruising for a day, a weekend, or a more

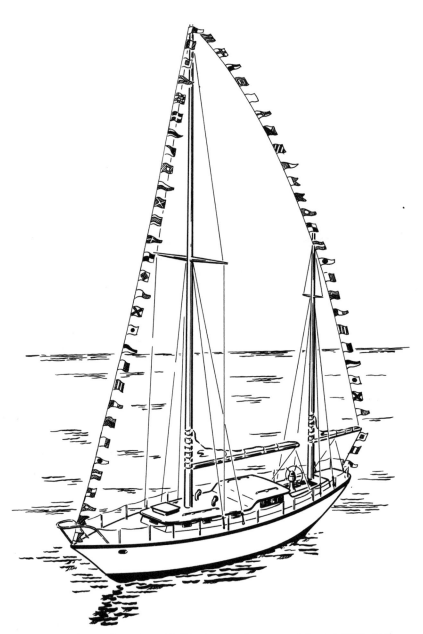

Figure 8.1 "Dressing ship" is done only on special occasions, and the proper procedures must be followed to be correct. Although the pattern is in effect random, flags should be in sequence shown.

extended period, there are many things to be considered—clothes, promptness, gifts, aids, noise, smoking, privacy, and time.

Take a minimum of *clothes,* packed in collapsible containers, or at least in suitcases that will nest inside each other when empty—storage space is severely limited aboard boats. Bring one outfit of "city clothes" for use at those places ashore requiring such dress. Bring two bathing suits if you plan to do much swimming—at times, things dry slowly around a boat.

For the *stowage of clothing* you bring aboard, the skipper may assign a special locker, which he has cleared for your convenience. Don't scatter gear and clothing all over the boat. Use the locker provided, keep it orderly, and thus help the skipper keep things shipshape.

When a *sailing time* is given, be there ahead of time. The skipper generally chooses a time with a purpose in mind—the tides and currents, normal weather patterns, the length of the planned run, etc.

Meal times are set for the convenience of the galley hand. It is inconsiderate for a tardy guest to delay meals. In any event, it is bad manners to be late for a meal.

Rising and *bedtimes* are a matter of convenience to everyone aboard because of the generally limited washing and toilet facilities. Get up promptly when the skipper or paid hands are heard moving about. Use the head as expeditiously as possible, make up your bunk, stow any loose gear about the cabin, and appear on deck. When the skipper suggests that it is time to retire for the evening, take the hint and bed down.

Noise on a boat seems to amplify, so walk and speak softly and your shipmates will be glad you're aboard.

Smoking is stopped, of course, when gasoline is to be taken aboard, but care is the order of the day even when smoking is permissible. A carelessly flicked cigarette ash or butt has started many a fire in a chair, awning, or compartment. Cigars leave a particularly unpleasant after-odor and should be enjoyed only in the open air.

Many small particles—pipe tobacco and ashes, peanut shells, bits of potato chip, crumbs, etc.—have a way of getting into cracks, crevices, and corners, thereby defying the ordinary cleaning facilities found on a boat. Use care with all of these things.

Privacy becomes valuable on a protracted cruise. Part of every day should be set aside for getting away from everyone else aboard.

AMENITIES

Your cruise mates will be more glad of your company if it is not constant.

Should occasions arise where you board the boat from a *dinghy,* or have an opportunity to use the skipper's dinghy (with his permission, of course), use care in coming alongside. Unship oarlocks which could scar the boat's topside, and stow oars in the boat; never leave them in the oarlocks.

Gifts are certainly not expected, but are always acceptable. Be sure, however, that they are appropriate for boating—if in doubt, make it liquid and consumable. When invited on board for a day or a week, ask what you can bring. If the owner wants to provide all of the food and drink, the guest might take the cruising party ashore for a good dinner at the first port of call. Buying part of the fuel is looked upon as a partial charter by some government agencies, but bringing food or liquid refreshment is not so regarded.

Assistance on board a boat can be useful, or it can do more harm than good. If you don't know what to do, sit down out of the way and be quiet. Always keep out of the line of vision of the helmsman and be particularly quiet and unobtrusive when the craft is being docked or undocked.

If being on board is not a new experience, or you wish to learn to be more useful, you may ask what you can do to help. Ask, however, when things are calm and uneventful; don't ask in the midst of getting under way or coming alongside a pier.

Above all, if you are assigned to do something, do exactly that. If you think that the instructions were wrong, say so, but don't go off on your own when the skipper thinks that you are doing what he asked.

9.

INFORMATION SOURCES

ORGANIZATIONS

One way to get more pleasure from your boating is to join with others with similar boating interests. And if you need special information, or want your voice as a boatman heard in legislative councils, there are organizations that can provide the help you need.

Listed here are major national organizations and a brief statement of purpose of each. For complete details, write to the group's headquarters.

General Organizations

United States Coast Guard Auxiliary,% Commandant (G-BAU), Washington, DC 20593. This civilian volunteer arm of the Coast Guard provides boating classes and courtesy safety-related examinations of pleasure boats. It also assists in search and rescue operations under Coast Guard orders.

United States Power Squadrons, P.O. Box 30423, Raleigh, NC 27622. This is a fraternal organization of boatmen that provides free basic boating classes to the public, as well as advanced courses in seamanship and navigation practices to its members, along with courses covering such topics as weather, engine maintenance, and marine electronics.

American National Red Cross, 17th and D Streets, N.W., Washington DC 20006. Safe-boating classes offered at local Red Cross chapters are: Basic Rowing, Basic Canoeing, Basic Sailing, and Basic Outboard Boating. Swimming and water-safety courses are also offered, ranging from Beginner to Advanced, as well as a variety of first-aid courses.

Boat Owners Association of the United States (BOAT/U.S.), 880 S. Pickett St., Alexandria, VA 22304. Richard Schwartz, executive director. A full-service representational membership organization of recreational boatmen, offering group-rate marine insurance, a boating-equipment savings program, charts, books, cruise planning, consumer-complaint bureau, theft protection, correspondence courses, and other services for members. It is active in legislative and conservation programs related to boating and waterways.

National Boating Federation, 2550 M Street N.W., Washington, DC 20037. A federation of national, state, and regional boating organizations, yacht clubs, and individuals that keeps members informed of news on boating legislation, etc., and provides an elected, responsible voice of the boating public nationally.

Racing Organizations, Power

American Power Boat Association, 17640 E. Nine Mile Rd., East Detroit, MI 48021. This organization sanctions all major powerboat races in the United States.

Union Internationale Motonautique, Centre International Rogier, Passage International, 29, Residence "HERA" 8me étage, B-1000, Brussels, Belgium. The Union of International Motorboating sanctions all major international powerboat races. It is represented in the United States by the American Power Boat Association.

Racing Organizations, Sail

Cruising Club of America, % Pratt, Read & Co., Ivoryton, CT 06442. Peter H. Comstock, chairman, membership committee. This club sponsors selected races.

U.S. Yacht Racing Union, 1133 Avenue of the Americas, New York, NY 10036. Henry H. Anderson, Jr., executive director. An association of individual members and yacht clubs that encourages and promotes the racing of sailing yachts, and the unification of rules, in an advisory capacity. Thirteen major championship races are sailed under its auspices each year.

International Yacht Racing Union, 60 Knightsbridge, Westminster, London SW 1X 7JX, England. The world governing body for sailing. Its membership includes eighty-five national yachting authorities. Meets annually in London to resolve the rules for sail racing, and the construction of International yachts.

Slocum Society, P.O. Box 76, Port Townsend, WA 98369. Don Holm, secretary. An organization established in 1955 to record, encourage, and support long-distance passages in small boats. Publishes a periodic journal, *The Spray,* and bimonthly newsletters. Dues: regular $15/year; cruising and senior citizen, $10/year.

United States International Sailing Association, 1133 Avenue of the Americas, New York, NY 10036. Henry H. Anderson, Jr., executive secretary. Membership fees help to provide boats, training for participants, for Olympic and other international sailing events.

United States Olympic Yachting Committee, 527 Lexington Ave., New York, N.Y. 10017. Paul H. Smart, chairman. This organization helps to raise funds to facilitate U.S. participation in Olympic yachting competition.

Government Agencies

National Oceanic and Atmospheric Administration (NOAA), Rockville, MD 20852. This branch of the Department of Commerce includes the National Weather Service and the National Ocean Service, among other services. It publishes nautical charts and a wealth of other material useful in piloting and seamanship. See the listings of available publications and chart sources in this section.

Corps of Engineers, Department of the Army, Washington, DC 20314. This branch of the U.S. Army is charged with the maintenance of all federal navigation projects within the United States.

National Association of State Boating Law Administrators, Embassy Square, 2000 N Street N.W., Washington, DC 20036. Morris Rosenbloom, executive secretary. Organization is instrumental in development of uniform boating legislation at the state level.

United States Coast Guard, Coast Guard Headquarters, 400 7th Street, N.W., Washington DC 20591. This is the government organization charged with responsibility for pleasure-boating safety and regulation on a national level.

SOURCES

Industry Associations

American Boat and Yacht Council, Inc., P.O. Box 806, 190 Ketcham Ave., Amityville, NY 11701. G. James Lippmann, executive director. Technical society develops safety standards and recommended practices for design, construction, equipment, and maintenance of all types of recreational boats to 65 feet in length.

American Boat Builders and Repairers Association, 715 Boyleston St., Boston, MA 02116.

International Council of Marine Industry Associations, Boating Industry House, Vale Road, Oatlands, Weybridge, Surrey, England. Antony Skinner, secretary general. Purpose of this group is to promote recreational boating on an international basis.

National Marine Bankers Association (NMBA), 401 N. Michigan Ave., Chicago, IL 60611. Don W. Mattocks, president; Gregory Proteau, executive secretary. NMBA represents the North American marine lending community. Membership includes commercial banks, savings and loan associations, and financial service companies. Associate members include those providing service to the marine lending trade. Provides statistics on marine lending activities of its members, publishes guides, and conducts marine lending seminars.

National Marine Manufacturers Association (NMMA), 401 N. Michigan Ave., Chicago, IL 60611; 353 Lexington Ave., New York, NY 10016. Jeff W. Napier, president; Frank Scalpone, executive vice-president. NMMA represents the North American recreational boating industry, with membership that includes manufacturers of boats, marine engines and outboard motors, boating accessories, publishers, original equipment manufacture (OEM) suppliers, and local and regional trade associations. Provides services and benefits to improve the profitability of members through government relations activities, standards and engineering programs, group insurance plans, marketing statistics, market promotions, public relations, and management education. It owns and produces two trade and six consumer boat shows across the United States.

Secretary, National Safe Boating Council, U.S. Coast Guard HQ G-BBS-4, 2100 2nd St. S.W., Washington, DC 20593. Council is made up of representatives of organizations which coordinate the presidentially proclaimed National Safe Boating Week. Information can be obtained by writing to the above address.

Society of Small Craft Designers, % NMMA, Suite 2950, 401 N. Michigan Ave., Chicago, IL 60611. David Beech, secretary.

Underwriters Laboratories, Marine Department, 2602 Tampa East Boulevard, Tampa, FLA 33619. This UL department was formerly the Yacht Safety Bureau. The facility evaluates products or systems intended for marine use with respect to safety. For products found to comply with the Laboratories' requirements, manufacturers are authorized to use an appropriate listing mark on or in conjunction with such products, contingent upon the establishment of UL's Follow-Up Service, which is designed to check on manufacturer compliance on a continuing basis.

Yacht Architects and Brokers Association, 49 Tiffany Rd., Norwell, MA 02061.

PUBLICATIONS

Notices to Mariners

Notice to Mariners. Weekly publication: Defense Mapping Agency Hydrographic/Topographic Center, Washington, DC 20390.

Local Notices to Mariners. Issued as necessary by the commanders of Coast Guard districts, and available at district offices. ˙

Coast Pilots

U.S. Waters. Atlantic, Gulf, and Pacific coasts; Atlantic and Gulf Intracoastal Waterways; the Great Lakes; National Ocean Service, Rockville, MD 20852, its distribution offices, or sales agents as listed semiannually in *Notice to Mariners.*

Canadian Waters. Chart Distribution Office, Department of the Environment, P.O. Box 8080, 1675 Russel Road, Ottawa, Ontario K1G 3H6. Coastal and Inland Waters Catalog gives details. Descriptive list of *Pilots and Sailing Directions* is also available.

Light Lists

Light Lists. Published by the U.S. Coast Guard; Superintendent of Documents, Washington, DC 20402, or many of the sales agents listed in NOS Chart Catalogs.

Tide and Current Tables

Tide Tables, Current Tables, Tidal Current Charts, Tidal Current Diagrams. National Ocean Service, Rockville, MD 20852, its dis-

SOURCES

tribution offices, or many of the sales agents listed in the NOS chart catalogs.

Rules of the Road

Rules of the Road. COMDTINST 16672.2. Booklet contains full text of the 1972 International Rules of the Road and the 1980 U.S. Inland Navigational Rules, and all Annexes; illustrated. Also contains information on Demarcation Lines separating the two sets of Rules, and the text of the Bridge-to-Bridge Radiotelephone Act. Sold by local chart sales agents and regional bookstores of the Government Printing Office.

U.S. Coast Guard Publications

This is the Seal of Safety . . . Get a Free Motorboat Examination. Aux-204. Flyer explains the Auxiliary Courtesy Marine Examination and the standards which must be met to be awarded a CME decal. Commandant (G-BAU) U.S. Coast Guard, Washington, DC 20593.

Marine Aids to Navigation. CG193. Brief explanation of the significance of colors of beacons and buoys, of the variety of light and fog signal characteristics, and of the system of electronic aids to navigation. Commandant (G-NSR), U.S. Coast Guard, Washington, DC 20593.

Federal Requirements for Recreational Boats. Digest of boating laws and regulations covering numbering, accidents, sales to aliens, law enforcement, documentation, and equipment requirements, plus safety suggestions. Available at all Coast Guard offices.

Visual Distress Signals. CG-152. Illustrated booklet provides description and guidance for use of distress signals suitable for boats. Free from Coast Guard district offices, or Headquarters, U.S. Coast Guard, Washington, DC 20593.

The Skipper's Course. Booklet is a do-it-yourself program in basic boating safety, with informal text and an exam at the end of the course. A certificate is awarded to all who pass. Bookstore #15, P.O. Box 713, Pueblo, CO 81002.

Modifications (for a new look in U.S. Aids to Navigation). ANSC SN 3022. Illustrated information on the changes to U.S. aids to navigation that are being made to bring them into conformity with the IALA-B system. Copies free from Coast Guard offices or Commandant (G-NSR-1), U.S. Coast Guard Headquarters, Washington, DC 20593.

Publications of the Defense Mapping Agency Hydrographic/Topographic Center

DMAHTC publications are available from its Office of Distribution Services (DDCP), 6500 Brooks Lane, Washington, DC 20315, or its authorized sales agents.

DMA Catalog of Maps, Charts and Related Products, Part 2, Vol. X. Catalog lists some of the more popular index charts, world charts, general nautical charts, magnetic charts, oceanographic and bottom sediment charts, aeronautical charts, Loran charts published by the agency.

Sailing Directions. Books supplementing DMAHTC charts contain descriptions of coastlines, harbors, dangers, aids, port facilities, and other data that cannot be shown conveniently on charts.

Daily Memorandum. A synopsis of the latest information relating to dangers and aids to navigation, together with advance items that will appear in *Notices to Mariners.* Issued locally by Branch Hydrographic Offices. Most urgent items are also broadcast by radio.

Pilot Charts

No. 16. Pilot Chart of the North Atlantic Ocean (monthly).
No. 55. Pilot Chart of the North Pacific Ocean (monthly).
No. 106. Atlas of Pilot Charts, South Atlantic Ocean and Central America waters.
No. 107. Atlas of Pilot Charts, South Pacific and Indian Oceans.

Lists of Lights and Fog Signals

Pub. 110 and 111. Coast of North and South America (only the seacoast lights of the United States), the West Indies, and Hawaiian Islands.
Pub. 112. Islands of the Pacific and Indian oceans, Australia, Asia, and the east coast of Africa.
Pub. 113. West coasts of Europe and Africa, the Mediterranean Sea, Black Sea, and the Sea of Azov.
Pub. 114. Britain and Ireland, English Channel, and North Sea.
Pub. 115. Norway, Iceland, and Arctic Ocean.
Pub. 116. Baltic Sea with Kattegat, Belts and Sound, and Gulf of Bosnia.

SOURCES

National Oceanographic Office

Pub. 234. Breakers and Surf; Principles in forecasting.

Pub. 601. Wind, Sea, and Swells; Theory of Relations in Forecasting.

Pub. 602. Wind, Waves at Sea, Breakers, and Surf.

Miscellaneous DMAHTC Publications

Chart No. 1. Nautical Chart Symbols and Abbreviations.

Pub. 9. American Practical Navigator, originally by Nathaniel Bowditch.

Pub. 102. International Code of Signals.

Pub. 117A and 117B. Radio Navigation Aids, Marine Direction-Finding Stations, Radio Beacons, Time Signals, Navigational Warnings, Distress Signals, Medical Advice and Quarantine Stations, Loran, and Regulations Covering the Use of Radio in Territorial Waters.

Pub. 150. World Port Index.

Pub. 217. Maneuvering Board Manual.

Pub. 226. Handbook of Magnetic Compass Adjustment and Compensation.

Pub. 1310. Radar Navigation Manual.

Weather Publications

Marine Weather Service Charts. A series of fifteen charts contains broadcast schedules of radio stations, National Weather Service telephone numbers, and locations of warning-display stations. Charts cover the Atlantic, Gulf, and Pacific coasts, and waters adjacent to Hawaii, Puerto Rico, the Virgin Islands, and Alaska. Distribution Division (C44), National Ocean Service, 6501 Lafayette Ave., Riverdale, MD 20854.

Marine Weather Services and High Seas Storm Information Service. Brochures contain marine weather information in capsule form. Distribution Division (C44), National Ocean Service, 6501 Lafayette Ave., Riverdale, MD 20854.

Worldwide Marine Weather Broadcasts. Broadcast schedules of marine weather information from all areas of the world where such service is available. Superintendent of Documents, U.S. Government Printing Office, Washington, DC 20402.

Hurricane, the Greatest Storm on Earth. Updated hurricane information, thirty-four pages; Stock Number 003-018-00018-1. Superintendent of Documents, Government Printing Office, Washington, DC 20402.

The Daily Weather Map, Weekly Series. Available by annual subscription. A complete explanation of the maps, including all symbols and tables, appears on the reverse side of the Sunday map only. Published by National Weather Service. Superintendent of Documents, Washington, DC 20402.

Miscellaneous Publications

The American Nautical Almanac. Compact publication from the United States Naval Observatory contains all ephemeris material essential to the solution of problems of navigational position; star chart is included. Superintendent of Documents, Washington, DC 20402, or sales agents.

A Mariner's Guide to Rules of the Road. By William H. Tate. A concise and comprehensive presentation of the 1972 International Rules of the Road and current U.S. Inland Rules; extensively illustrated. U.S. Naval Institute, Annapolis, MD 21402.

First Aid. Illustrated 160-page manual provides only first-aid instruction. Superintendent of Documents, Government Printing Office, Washington, DC 20402.

Miscellaneous Publication No. 9. The Ship's Medicine Chest and First Aid at Sea. Book from the United States Health Service includes special instructions for emergency treatment, and first aid by radio; 496 pages, illustrated. Superintendent of Documents, Washington, DC 20402.

Charts of Various Waterways

U.S. Coastal Waters and Great Lakes. Atlantic, Pacific, and Gulf coasts; the Atlantic and Gulf Intracoastal waterways; the Hudson River north to Troy, New York; the Great Lakes and connecting rivers; Lake Champlain; New York State canals; and the Minnesota–Ontario Border Lakes. National Ocean Service, Distribution Division (C44), Riverdale, MD 20840, or local sales agents listed in chart catalogs.

New York State Canals. Bound booklet of charts of the Champlain, Erie, Oswego, and Cayuga–Seneca canals. National Ocean Service Distribution Division, (C44), Riverdale, MD 20840, or local sales agents.

Mississippi River and Tributaries. Middle and Upper Mississippi, Cairo, Illinois, to Minneapolis, Minnesota; Middle Mississippi River from Cairo, Illinois, to Grafton, Illinois; Mississippi River from Cairo, Illinois, to Gulf of Mexico; Small Boat Chart, Alton, Illinois, to Clarksville on the Mississippi River and Grafton, Illinois, to LaGrange, Illinois, on the Illinois River. Illinois Waterways from Grafton, Illinois, to Lake Michigan at Chicago and Calumet Harbor. U.S. Army Engineer District, 210 Tucker Boulevard North, St. Louis, MO 63101.

Mississippi River and Tributaries, below Ohio River. Mississippi River Commission, P.O. Box 80, Vicksburg, MS 39180. This office also has a free booklet, *Mississippi River Navigation,* which discusses its history, development, and navigation.

Mississippi River and Connecting Waterways, North of the Ohio River. U.S. Army Engineer Division, North Central, 219 S. Dearborn St., Chicago, IL 60605.

Ohio River and Tributaries; Pittsburgh, Pennsylvania, to the Mississippi River. U.S. Army Engineer Division, P.O. Box 1159, Cincinnati, OH 45201.

Tennessee and Cumberland Rivers. U.S. Army Engineer District, P.O. Box 1070, Nashville, TN 37202; also Tennessee Valley Authority, Maps and Engineering Records Section, 102A Union Building, Knoxville, TN 37902.

Missouri River and Tributaries. U.S. Army Engineers, Missouri River Division, P.O. Box 103 DTS, Omaha, NB 68101.

Canadian Waters. Charts include coastal waters; Canadian sections of the Great Lakes including Georgian Bay; the St. Lawrence River; Richelieu River; Ottawa River; the Rideau Waterway; and other Canadian lakes and waterways. Indexes of charts for any area are free, and chart prices and details are given in a Coastal and Inland Waters catalog. Chart Distribution Office, Department of the Environment, P.O. Box 8080, 1675 Russell Road, Ottawa, Ontario K1G 3H6.

Waters of Other Nations. Defense Mapping Agency Hydrographic/Topographic Center, Office of Distribution Services (DDCP), 6500 Brooks Lane, Washington, DC 20315, or authorized sales agents. A general catalog (free) and nine regional catalogs are available.

Cruising Guides

Cruising the Canals. Free booklet with map of the New York State canal system. Waterways Maintenance Division, State Department of Transportation, 1220 Washington St., Albany, NY 12232.

Waterway Guide. Publication provides detailed information on inland waterways in four editions: Northern, Maine to New York; Middle Atlantic, New York to Sea Island, Georgia; Southern, Sea Island, Georgia, to Florida and Gulf Coast to New Orleans; Great Lakes, New York to Great Lakes, with connecting Canadian canals and rivers. Waterway Guide, Inc., 93 Main St., Annapolis, MD 21401.

Intracoastal Waterway Booklets. Comprehensive descriptions of the Intracoastal Waterway, with data on navigation, charts, distances. Prepared by U.S. Army Corps of Engineers in two sections: (1) Atlantic, Boston to Key West; (2) Gulf, Key West to Brownsville, Texas. Superintendent of Documents, Washington, DC 20402.

Intracoastal Waterway Bulletins: Frequent bulletins giving latest information on the condition of the Intracoastal Waterway are published by the U.S. Army Corps of Engineers; available from District Offices at: 803 Front St., Norfolk, VA 23510; P.O. Box 1890, Wilmington, NC 28401; P.O. Box 919, Charleston, SC 29402; P.O. Box 889, Savannah, GA 31402; P.O. Box 4970, Jacksonville, FL 32201; P.O. Box 2288, Mobile, AL 36601; and P.O. Box 1229, Galveston, TX 77551.

Cruising the Pacific Coast, Acapulco to Skagway. Carolyn and John West, W. W. Norton & Co., 500 Fifth Ave., New York, NY 10110.

Cruising the San Juan Islands. Bruce Calhoun, W. W. Norton & Co., 500 Fifth Ave., New York, NY 10110.

Yachtsman's Guide to the Greater Antilles. By Harry Kline. Virgin Islands, Puerto Rico, Dominican Republic, and Haiti. Tropic Isle Publishers, Inc., P.O. Box 611141, North Miami, FL 33161.

Cruising Charts, Guides, Booklets. Texas Travel Service, P.O. Box 1459, Houston, TX 77001.

California Coastal Passages. By Brian M. Fagan. Facilities and sailing directions, San Francisco, California, to Ensenada, Mexico.

Capra Press and ChartGuide, Ltd., P.O. Box 2068, Santa Barbara, CA 93120.

Guide for Cruising Maryland Waters. Prepared by Maryland Department of Natural Resources, Tidewater Administration. Twenty full-color charts, with more than 200 courses and distances plotted; marina and facility information reference listing. Department of Natural Resources, Tawes State Office Bldg., Annapolis, MD 21401. A Maryland Basic Boating Course is available from the same address.

Quimby's Harbor Guide. The navigable Mississippi from Minneapolis to New Orleans, plus harbors on the Illinois and Arkansas waterways, and St. Croix and Black rivers. Covers harbors, services, cities, towns, transportation, tourist interests, some history, locks and dams, sources of navigation charts and books, hazards. Mildred Quimby, P.O. Box 85, Prairie du Chien, WS 53821.

Cruising Guide to Lake Ontario. Harbor information, facilities, Lake Ontario and the Thousand Islands area of the St. Lawrence River; Welland Canal lock information. Cruising Guide to Lake Ontario, Box 338, Youngstown, NY 14174.

SCHOOLS

Piloting and Seamanship

American National Red Cross, 17th and D Streets, N.W., Washington, DC 20006.

American Institute of Navigation, Seafarer Group, Sugarloaf Rd., Boulder, CO 80307.

Boat Owners Association of the United States, 880 S. Pickett St., Alexandria, VA 22304.

Captain Van's mail-order pre-Coast Guard exam training for all Motorboat, Ocean & Inland, Deck and Steam/Diesel Engineer License examinations, all grades. Books, instruments, and courses. Write for free catalog. Captain Van, Inc., P.O. Drawer 1510, Mid-City Post Office, Groves, TX 77619–1510. Established 1917.

Charles F. Chapman School of Seamanship, Palm City, FL 33490. Piloting, seamanship, celestial navigation, powerboat handling, diesel- and gasoline-engine maintenance, preparation for Coast Guard license.

Coast Navigation School, 1934 Lincoln Dr., Annapolis, MD 21401.

Crawford Nautical Center, Pier 2, Agricultural Bldg., Box 3656, Rincon Annex, San Francisco, CA 94119. Preparation for Coast Guard examinations.

Florida Maritime Institute, Box 11834-A, St. Petersburg, FL 33733. Captain's license study guide, lessons, practice exercises.

Marine Associates, Box 217, Teaneck, NJ 07666; Box 370396, Miami, FL 33137; Box 710, LaJolla, CA 92038; Box 2221, Ann Arbor, MI 48106. Study guide for Coast Guard examinations.

Maritime Education, Box 9581, Treasure Island, FL 33740. Question/answer study guide for Coast Guard license.

National Small Craft Schools. For information write: American National Red Cross, Washington, DC 20006. See General Organizations listing, this section.

United States Coast Guard Auxiliary, Washington, DC 20593. See General Organizations listing for more details.

Celestial Navigation

Boat Owners Association of the United States, 880 S. Pickett St., Alexandria, VA 22304.

Coast Navigation School, 1934 Lincoln Dr., Annapolis, MD 21401.

Florida Maritime Institute, Box 11834-A, St. Petersburg, FL 33733. Self-study course for offshore navigation. C. Plath North American Division, 222 Severn Ave., Annapolis, MD 21403.

Yacht Design

Westlawn School of Yacht Design, 733 Summer St., Stamford, CT 06904. Jules G. Fleder, president.

YDI Schools, Main St., Blue Hill, ME 04614. Home study course in small craft naval architecture technology; associate degree program in small craft naval architecture technology; and forty-week residential program in naval architecture. Bob Wallstrom, director.

Sailing

Afterguard Marine, 254 Kimberly Ave., New Haven, CT 06519. Windsurfing instruction.

Annapolis Sailing School, Box 3334, Annapolis, MD 21403.
Offshore Sailing School, Ltd., E. Schofield St., City Island, NY
10464.

MUSEUMS AND RESTORATIONS
Maritime Museums

California.   *San Francisco Maritime Museum,* Foot of Polk St., San
Francisco, CA 94102.
   Cabrillo Marine Museum, 3720 Stephen M. White Dr., San Pedro
CA 90731.
   Los Angeles Maritime Museum, Berth 84, San Pedro, CA 90731.
   National Maritime Museum, San Francisco. National Park Ser-
vice, Golden Gate National Recreation Area, Fort Mason, San
Francisco, CA 94123.

Connecticut.   *Mystic Seaport,* Mystic, CT 06355. Village area with
crafts, scrimshaw, models, paintings, prints, navigational instruments, Henry B. duPont Preservation Shipyard. See also Ship Exhibits listing.

District of Columbia.   *Smithsonian Institution,* Constitution Ave.,
N.W., between 12th & 14th Sts., Washington, DC 20560.
   Truxton-Decatur Naval Museum, 1610 H St., N.W., Washington,
DC 20006.
   U.S. Navy Memorial Museum, Building #76, Washington Navy
Yard, Washington, DC 20374.

Maine.   *Maine Maritime Museum,* 963 Washington St., Bath, ME
04530. Sewall Mansion; Winter Street Center; Percy and Small
Shipyard; the Apprenticeship (boatbuilding program); the *Sasanoa*
boat ride on the Kennebec River; and the *Seguin,* oldest surviving
wood tug.
   Penobscot Marine Museum, Searsport, ME 04974. Six buildings
with paintings, prints, American and Oriental furnishings, models of
Maine-built vessels, tools, builders' half-models, navigational instruments, small boats, and nautical memorabilia. Open Memorial Day
through October 15.

Maryland.   *U.S. Naval Academy Museum,* Annapolis, MD 21402.

Open 9 A.M. to 4:50 P.M., Monday through Saturday; 11 A.M. to 4:50 P.M. Sunday. Closed Thanksgiving, Christmas, and New Year's Day.

Chesapeake Bay Maritime Museum, Navy. Point, St. Michaels, MD 21663. Sixteen-acre waterfront complex includes Hooper Strait Lighthouse, working boatshop with antique tool collection, floating historic craft, library, and gift shop. Open daily; weekends only in January through March. Closed Christmas and New Year's Day.

Massachusetts. *Museum of Science,* Science Park, Charles River, Boston, MA 02114.

Francis Russell Hart Nautical Museum, Massachusetts Institute of Technology, 55 Massachusetts Ave., Cambridge, Mass. 02139.

Peabody Museum of Salem, East India Square, Salem, MA 01970.

Whaling Museum, Broad St., Nantucket, MA 02554. Full size brick try-works, completely rigged whale boat, scrimshaw, copper and blacksmith shops, whale skeletons, prints, portraits.

Whaling Museum, 18 Johnny Cake Hill, New Bedford, MA 02740.

Michigan. *Dossin Great Lakes Museum,* Belle Island Park, Detroit, MI 48207.

Rose Hawley Museum, Ludington, MI 49431.

New York. *Adirondack Museum,* Blue Mountain Lake, NY 12812. Guide boats, canoes, small craft, and some launches.

East Hampton Town Marine Museum, Box 858, Bluff Rd., Amagansett, NY 11930.

South Street Seaport Museum, 207 Front St., New York, NY 10038. Building and vessel restorations, restaurants, bookstores, and fish market.

Sag Harbor Whaling and Historical Museum, Main St., Sag Harbor, NY 11963.

Thousand Islands Shipyard Museum, Clayton, NY 13624. Historic small craft including Gold Cup racers and St. Lawrence skiffs. Many motors, including first Johnson outboard ever built. Antique tour boat rides.

The Whaling Museum, Main St., Cold Spring Harbor, NY 11724. Fully rigged whaleboat, dioramas of whaling and harbor scenes, whaling gear, scrimshaw, ship and navigation gear, and paintings. Open daily 11 A.M. to 5 P.M. Memorial Day through Labor Day; closed on Mondays remainder of the year.

Skenesborough Museum, Whitehall, NY 12887.

Ohio. *Ohio River Museum,* Washington and Front Sts., Marietta, OH 45750. Indoor and outdoor exhibits of history of river life, commerce, and travel; steam towboat *W. P. Snyder, Jr.* Admission hours vary; closed December through February.

Oregon. *Columbia River Maritime Museum,* Foot of 17th St., Astoria, OR 97103.

Pennsylvania. *Civic Center Museum,* 34th St. & Convention Ave., Philadelphia, PA 19104.

Philadelphia Maritime Museum, 321 Chestnut St., Philadelphia, PA 19106. Museum's *Workshop on the Water,* Penn's Landing at foot of Lombard St.

Vermont. *Shelburne Museum,* Shelburne, VT 05482. Exhibits include Colchester Reef Lighthouse, with collection of marine prints, paintings, scrimshaw; and Webb Gallery of American Art, with paintings. Admission charged. Free folder sent upon request. See also Ship Exhibit listing.

Virginia. *The Mariners Museum,* Newport News, VA 23606.

Portsmouth Lightship Museum, Water St. at London Slip, P.O. Box 248, Portsmouth, VA 23705. Admission free. Open Tuesday through Saturday, 10 A.M. to 4:45 P.M.; Sundays 2 P.M. to 4:45 P.M. Closed Mondays, Christmas, and New Year's Day.

Portsmouth Naval Shipyard Museum, 2 High St., P.O. Box 248, Portsmouth, VA 23705. Admission free. Open Tuesday through Saturday, 10 A.M. to 5 P.M. Sundays 2 P.M. to 5 P.M. Closed Mondays, Christmas, and New Year's Day.

Washington. *The Museum of History and Industry,* 2161 E. Hamlin St., Seattle, WA 98112. Admission: adults, $1.00; senior citizens, children, handicapped, 50¢; children five and under, free. Open Monday through Saturday, 10 A.M. to 5 P.M.; Sundays noon to 5 P.M. Closed Thanksgiving, Christmas, and New Year's Day.

Ship Exhibits

California.   San Diego Maritime Museum, 1306 N. Harbor Dr., San Diego, CA 92101. 1863 sailing ship *Star of India*, 1898 ferryboat *Berkeley*, 1904 steam yacht *Medea*, plus many exhibits aboard these vessels.

Golden Gate National Recreation Area, National Maritime Museum, 2905 Hyde St., San Francisco, CA 94109. Scow schooner *Alma*, lumber schooner *C. A. Thayer*, paddle-wheel ferry *Eureka*, tug *Hercules*, tug *Eppleton Hall*, square-rigged ship *Balclutha*, Liberty ship *Jeremiah O'Brien*.

Connecticut.   Mystic Seaport, Mystic, CT 06355. Whaler *Charles W. Morgan*, full-rigged ship *Joseph Conrad*, *L. A. Dunton*, *Emma C. Berry*, steamboat *Sabine*, and others.

Coast Guard Cutter *Eagle*, U.S. Coast Guard Academy, New London, CT 06320.

District of Columbia.   *Philadelphia*, U.S. Museum of History and Technology, Smithsonian Institution, Washington, DC 20560.

Florida.   H.M.S. *Bounty* Replica, 345 2nd Ave. N.E., St. Petersburg, FL 33701. Open daily, 9 A.M. to 10 P.M.

Hawaii.   U.S.S. *Arizona* Memorial, National Park Service, #1 Arizona Memorial Dr., Honolulu, HI 96818. Open daily 8 A.M. to 4 P.M. Arrive early to obtain free tickets; children must be six or older. All visitors must have at least shirts, shorts, and footwear as minimum attire.

U.S.S. *Utah* Memorial, Pearl Harbor, HI 96610. U.S. Navy-owned memorial is not open to the public.

Maryland.   Baltimore Seaport, Pratt St., Baltimore, MD. U.S.S. *Constellation*, Constellation Dock, Pier 1; U.S.S. *Torsk*, Submariners Dock, Pier 3; USCG lightship *Five Fathom*, and schooner *Freedom*, Pier 3.

Massachusetts.   U.S.S. *Constitution*, oldest commissioned warship afloat, Charleston, MA 02129. Open daily except Thanksgiving, Christmas, and New Year's Day. Isaac Hull exhibit, continuing demonstrations by the U.S.S. Constitution Model Shipwright Guild in the Preservation Gallery.

Mayflower II, Replica, Box 1620, Plymouth, MA 02360.

U.S.S. *Massachusetts,* State Pier, Fall River, MA 02721. Open all year, 9 A.M. to 5 P.M. daily.

New York. South Street Seaport Museum, 207 Front St., New York, NY 10003. Lightship *Ambrose,* full-rigged ship *Wavertree,* fishing schooner *Lettie G. Howard,* ferryboat *Maj. Gen. Wm. H. Hart,* Delaware Bay freight schooner *Pioneer.*

Clearwater, Hudson River sloop restoration, 112 Market St., Poughkeepsie, NY 12601.

Intrepid Sea-Air Space Museum, 1 Intrepid Square, New York, NY 10036. U.S.S. *Intrepid,* aircraft carrier.

North Carolina. U.S.S. *North Carolina* Battleship Memorial, Cape Fear River, Wilmington, NC 28401.

Oregon. Columbia *Lightship,* Foot of 17th St., Astoria, OR 97103.

Pennsylvania. Philadelphia Ship Preservation Guild, Penn's Landing, Delaware Ave. & Spruce St., Philadelphia, PA 19106. 1883 barkentine *Gazela Primeiro.*

U.S.S. *Olympia,* Pier 11, N. Delaware Ave. & Race St., Philadelphia, PA 19106.

Texas. U.S.S. *Texas,* San Jacinto Battleground, P.O. Box 868, La Porte, TX 77571.

Vermont. S.S. *Ticonderoga,* Rt. 7, Shelburne, VT 05482.

Virginia. Jamestown Festival Park, Route 31 South (Jamestown Road), six miles from Williamsburg; P.O. Drawer JF, Williamsburg, VA 23187. *Susan Constant, Goodspeed,* and *Discovery.*

England. Cutty Sark, Greenwich, London.

H.M.S. *Victory,* Portsmouth, Hampshire.

Sweden. Wasa, Stockholm.

10.

GOVERNMENT REQUIREMENTS

Although you don't need a license (in most cases) to operate your boat, there are certain federal and state laws that govern its registration, equipment, and use.

The major federal legislation is the Boating Act of 1971, which was signed into law on August 10, 1971. It incorporates many provisions of the Motorboat Act of 1940 and the registration provisions of the Federal Boating Act of 1958.

The Motorboat Act of 1940 established a set of minimum equipment requirements (Table 10.1) for boats in each size category. The new act permits the Commandant of the Coast Guard to modify these or make additions that he deems necessary to promote safe boating. In any case, the requirements shown in Table 10.1 should be regarded as an absolute minimum. You should carry at least all the items required for award of the Coast Guard Auxiliary Courtesy Examination sticker, as listed in this section. Note that Table 10.2 shows the classification of fire extinguishers by size and type.

Boat registration, as required by the 1958 act, is retained in the new legislation. State offices that handle the registration, and the fees required, are shown in Table 10.3.

RULES OF THE ROAD

Currently there are two sets of Rules of the Road that cover re-

Table 10.1

EQUIPMENT	CLASS A LESS THAN 16 FEET (4.9M)	CLASS 1 16 FEET TO LESS THAN 26 FEET (4.9–7.9M)
Personal flotation devices	One Type I, II, III, or IV for each person.	One Type I, II, or III for each person on board or being towed on water skis, etc., plus one Type IV available to be thrown.
Fire extinguishers		
When no fixed fire-extinguishing system is installed in machinery space(s)	At least one B-I type approved hand portable fire extinguisher. Not required on outboard motorboats less than 26 feet (7.9 m) in length and not carrying passengers for hire if the construction of such motorboats will not permit the entrapment of flammable gases or vapors. *	
When fixed fire-extinguishing system is installed in machinery space(s)	None.	

Ventilation	At least two ventilator ducts fitted with cowls or their equivalent for the purpose of properly and efficiently ventilating the bilges of every engine and fuel-tank compartment of boats constructed or decked over after April 25, 1940, using gasoline or other fuel having a flashpoint less than 110°F. (43°C). Boats built after July 31, 1981 must have operable power blowers.
Whistle	Boats up to 39.4 feet (12 m)—any device capable of making an "efficient sound signal," audible 1/2 mile.
Bell	Boats up to 39.4 feet (12 m)—any device capable of making an "efficient sound signal."
Backfire flame arrester	One approved device on each carburetor of all gasoline engines installed after April 25, 1940; except outboard motors.
Visual distress signals	Required only when operating at night or carrying six or fewer passengers for hire. Same equipment as for larger boats.	Orange flag with black square-and-disc (D); and an S-O-S electric light (N); or three orange smoke signals, hand-held or floating (D); or three red flares of hand-held, meteor, or parachute type (D/N).

*Dry chemical and carbon dioxide (CO_2) or the most widely used types, in that order. Other approved types are acceptable. Toxic vaporizing-liquid type fire extinguishers, such as those containing tetrachloride or chlorobromomethane, are not acceptable. Fire extinguishers manufactured after January 1, 1965 will be marked "Marine Type____ Size____ Approval No. 162.028/EX____."

EQUIPMENT	CLASS 2 26 FEET TO LESS THAN 40 FEET (7.9–12.2M)	CLASS 3 40 FEET TO NOT MORE THAN 65 FEET (12.2–19.8M)
Personal flotation devices	One Type I, II, or III for each person on board or being towed on water skis, etc., plus one Type IV available to be thrown.	
Fire extinguishers		
When no fixed fire-extinguishing system is installed in machinery space(s)	At least two B-I type approved hand portable fire extinguishers, or at least one B-II type approved hand portable fire extinguisher.	At least three B-I type approved hand portable fire extinguishers, or at least one B-I type plus one B-II type approved hand portable fire extinguisher.
When fixed fire-extinguishing system is installed in machinery space(s)	At least one B-I type approved hand portable fire extinguisher.	At least two B-I type approved hand portable fire extinguishers, or at least one B-II approved unit.
Ventilation	At least two ventilator ducts fitted with cowls or their equivalent for the purpose of properly and efficiently ventilating the bilges of every engine and fuel-tank compartment of boats constructed or decked over after April 25, 1940, using	

gasoline or other fuel having a flashpoint less than 110°F. (43°C). Boats built after July 31, 1981 must have operable power blowers.

EQUIPMENT	CLASS 2 26 FEET TO LESS THAN 40 FEET (7.9–12.2M)	CLASS 3 40 FEET TO NOT MORE THAN 65 FEET (12.2–19.8M)
Whistle	Boats up to 39.4 feet (12 m)—any device capable of making an "efficient sound signal" audible 1/2 mile.	Boats 39.4 to 65.7 feet (12–20 m)—device meeting technical specifications of Inland Rules Annex III, audible 1/2 mile.
Bell	Boats up to 39.4 feet (12 m)—any device capable of making an "efficient sound signal."	Boats 39.4 to 65.7 feet (12–20 m)—bell meeting technical specifications of Inland Rules Annex II; mouth diameter of at least 7.9 inches (200 m).
Backfire flame arrester	One approved device on each carburetor of all gasoline engines installed after April 25, 1940, except outboard motors.	
Visual distress signals	Orange flag with black square-and-disc (D); and an S-O-S electric light (N); or three orange smoke signals, hand-held or floating (D); or three red flares of hand-held, meteor, or parachute type (D/N).	

*Dry chemical and carbon dioxide (CO₂) or the most widely used types, in that order. Other approved types are acceptable. Toxic vaporizing-liquid type fire extinguishers, such as those containing tetrachloride or chlorobromomethane, are not acceptable. Fire extinguishers manufactured after January 1, 1965 will be marked "Marine Type____Size____Approval No. 162.028/EX____."

Table 10.2

Fire Extinguishers

CLASSIFICATION (TYPE-SIZE)	FOAM (MINIMUM GALLONS)	CARBON DIOXIDE (MINIMUM POUNDS)	DRY CHEMICAL (MINIMUM POUNDS)	FREON (MINIMUM POUNDS)
B-I	1¼	4	2	2½
B-II	2½	15	10	

quirements for running lights on all types of vessels and right-of-way under all possible situations. Rules of the *Inland Navigation Act of 1980* cover all U.S. bodies of water open to the sea or connected to it by navigable rivers and channels, as well as bodies of water that overlap or separate two or more states, even though they are not connected with the ocean.

1972 International Rules cover the high seas outside of Demarcation Lines established along the coast, as listed in the "Piloting and Navigation" section of the *Boatman's Handbook.*

Both sets of rules are published in the Coast Guard booklet *Navigation Rules, International—Inland,* which is available at low cost from most chart sales agents.

Individual states often have equipment and operation requirements that supplement those given in the federal legislation, and state laws apply to waters that are not covered by federal acts. Table 10.3 lists the offices from which this type of information is available.

ITEMS REQUIRED FOR USCG AUXILIARY DECAL

In most boating areas, a skipper can obtain a Coast Guard Auxiliary "Courtesy Marine Examination" (CME) of his boat and receive a decal for the current year. The examination is free, and the decal indicates the boat meets equipment and safety standards beyond

Table 10.3

State Registration Requirements

STATE	BOATS AFFECTED	NUMBERING PERIOD	FEE	WHERE TO APPLY
ALABAMA	All motorboats, sailboats, boats for hire	1 year	Under 16 feet: $6 16 feet to 26 feet: $10 26 feet to 40 feet: $20 Over 40 feet: $40	Marine Police Division, Department of Conservation, State Administration Bldg., Montgomery, AL 36104.
ALASKA	All motorboats	3 years	$6	Department of Public Safety, P.O. Box 6188 Annex, Anchorage, AK 99502.
ARIZONA	All watercraft	1 year	Residents: $4 Nonresidents: $10	Game & Fish Department, 2222 W. Greenway Rd., Phoenix, AZ 85023.
ARKANSAS	Boats over 10 hp	1 year	Original: $2 Renewals: $1	Licensing Division, Department of Finance & Administration, P.O. Box 1272, Little Rock, AR 72201.
CALIFORNIA	All vessels except those powered manually, sailboards, and sailboats under 8 feet in length	1 year	Original: $9 Renewals: $5	Department of Motor Vehicles, P.O. Box 11780, Sacramento, CA 95853.

STATE	BOATS AFFECTED	NUMBERING PERIOD	FEE	WHERE TO APPLY
COLORADO	All motorboats and sailboats	1 year	$5	Colorado Division of Parks & Outdoor Recreation, 13787 S. Highway 85, Littleton, CO 80125.
CONNECTICUT	All motorboats	1 year	From $10 for boats less than 12 feet to $700 for boats 65 feet and over.	Motor Vehicle Department, Boating Registration Unit, 60 State St., Wethersfield, CT 06109, or any branch office of the M.V.D.
DELAWARE	All motorboats	1 year	Less than 16 feet: $5 16 feet to 26 feet: $10 26 feet to 40 feet: $15 40 feet to 65 feet: $25 Over 65 feet: not required to be documented, $30	Boating Administrator's Office, Division of Fish & Wildlife, P.O. Box 1401, R&R Bldg., Dover, DE 19903.
DISTRICT of COLUMBIA	All motorboats	1 year	Powered by propulsion machinery: $10 Nonpowered by propulsion machinery: $2	Harbor Patrol Boat Registration Office, 550 Water St. S.W., Washington, DC 20024.

State	Vessels Covered	Period	Fees	Where to Register
FLORIDA	All motorboats	1 year	Less than 12 feet and all canoes with motors: $2 12 feet to 16 feet: $6 16 feet to 26 feet: $11 26 feet to 40 feet: $31 40 feet to 65 feet: $51 65 feet to 110 feet: $61 Over 110 feet: $76 All fees plus $1 service fee	County Tax Collectors.
GEORGIA	All motorized vessels, sailboats over 12 feet	3 years	Under 16 feet: $10 16 feet to 26 feet: $24 26 feet to 40 feet: $60 40 feet and over: $100	Georgia Department of Natural Resources, Game & Fish Division, Law Enforcement Section, Room 711, 270 Washington St., S.W., Atlanta, GA 30334.
HAWAII	All motorboats, sailboats over 8 feet	1 year	Under 16 feet: $1 Over 16 feet: $6 Renewals $3 for first 12 feet; 25 cents for each additional foot.	Harbors Division, Department of Transportation, Box 397, Honolulu, HI 96809.

STATE	BOATS AFFECTED	NUMBERING PERIOD	FEE	WHERE TO APPLY
IDAHO	All motorboats.	3 years	$2	Motor Vehicle Division, Department of Transportation, P.O. Box 34, Boise, ID 83707.
	Annual boat license: sum equal to 1 percent of boat length times horsepower of motor(s), but in no case less than $2.50. Sailboats, including auxiliaries: 50 cents per foot. Depreciation is a factor in license fees, and there are reduced rates for boats not within the state for full year.			
ILLINOIS	All motorboats, sailboats over 12 feet	2 years	$4	Illinois Department of Conservation, Registration Section, 524 S. 2nd St., Room 210, Springfield, IL 62706.
INDIANA	All motorboats	3 years	$3	Department of Natural Resources, 606 State Office Bldg., Indianapolis, IN 46209
IOWA	All boats	2 years	Motor or sail powered: $8 Nonmotor, nonsail: $4	County Recorder.
KANSAS	All boats powered by machinery or sail if used on public waters of Kansas	3 years	$9	Forestry, Fish & Game Commission, RR #2, Box 54A, Pratt, KS 67124.

State	Boats Requiring Registration	Registration Period	Fees	Where to Apply
KENTUCKY	All motorboats	1 year	Under 16 feet: $10 16 feet to 26 feet: $14 26 feet to 40 feet: $20 40 feet and over: $24	Circuit Court Clerk in county of residence of owner, or county where boat is principally used.
LOUISIANA	Boats over 10 horsepower	3 years	Original: $5 Renewals: $3	Department of Wildlife & Fisheries, 7389 Florida Blvd., Baton Rouge, LA 70806.
MAINE	All motorboats	2 years	$6	Bureau of Licensing, State House Station 41, Augusta, ME 04333.
MARYLAND	All motorboats	3 years	16 feet or less with motor 7½ horsepower or less: free	Department of Natural Resources, Licensing & Consumer Services, 580 Taylor Ave., P.O. Box 1869, Annapolis, MD 21401.
		1 year	Boats 16 feet or more with motor more than 7½ horsepower: $12 Documented vessels: $5	

STATE	BOATS AFFECTED	NUMBERING PERIOD	FEE	WHERE TO APPLY
MASSACHUSETTS	All propelled vessels	2 years	Original: $20 Renewal: $20	Department of Fisheries & Wildlife & Recreational Vehicles, Division of Marine & Recreational Vehicles, 100 Cambridge St., Room 2108, Boston, MA 02202.
MICHIGAN	All motorboats; all other boats over 12 feet except those 16 feet or less powered by oars or paddles, and canoes	3 years	From $4.50 to $240 depending on type and length	Bureau of Driver & Vehicle Services, Department of State, 7064 Crowner Dr., Lansing, MI 48919.
MINNESOTA	All watercraft	3 years	Under 19 feet: $12 19 feet to 26 feet: $20 26 feet to 40 feet: $30 Over 40 feet: $40 Canoes, kayaks, sailboats, etc., to 19 feet: $7	Department of Natural Resources License Center, 625 N. Robert, St. Paul, MN 55101.
MISSISSIPPI	Boats over 10 horsepower	2 years	$2.25	Department of Wildlife Conservation, P.O. Box 451, Jackson, MS 39205.

MISSOURI	All motorboats; sailboats over 12 feet	3 years	$5 Outboard motors registered separately (one time only): $2	Missouri State Water Patrol, P.O. Box 603, Jefferson City, MO 65101.
MONTANA	Boats over 8 horsepower	1 year	$1	Registrar's Bureau, Motor Vehicle Division, Department of Justice, Deer Lodge, MT 59722.
NEBRASKA	All boats powered by any mechanical device	3 years	Under 16 feet: $15 16 feet to 26 feet: $30 26 feet to 40 feet: $45 40 feet and over: $75 Canoes: $15 All fees plus $2 issuing fee	Nebraska Game & Parks Commission, P.O. Box 30370, Lincoln, NB 68503.
NEVADA	All motorboats	1 year	$7.50	Nevada Department of Wildlife, P.O. Box 10678, Reno, NV 89520-0022.

STATE	BOATS AFFECTED	NUMBERING PERIOD	FEE	WHERE TO APPLY
NEW HAMPSHIRE	All motorboats, sailboats 12 feet and over on nontidal waters	3 years	Up to 16 feet: $8.50 16.1 feet to 21 feet: $13.50 21.1 feet to 30 feet: $18.50 30.1 feet to 45 feet: $25.50 45.1 feet and over: $33.50	Department of Safety, James H. Hayes Bldg., Hazen Dr., Concord, NH 03305.
	All motorboats 10 horsepower and over on navigable waters of the United States within New Hampshire	3 years	$3	USCG First District, 150 Causeway St., Boston, MA 02114.
NEW JERSEY	All power and sail vessels	1 year	Under 16 feet: $6 16 feet to 26 feet: $14 26 feet to 40 feet: $26 40 feet to 65 feet: $40 65 feet and over: $125	Division of Motor Vehicles, CN-403, 25 S. Montgomery St., Trenton, NJ 08625.

State	Boats Covered	Registration Period	Fees	Where to Apply
NEW MEXICO	All motorboats and sailboats	3 years	Under 16 feet: $28.50 16 feet to 26 feet: $36 26 feet to 40 feet: $43.50 40 feet to 65 feet: $51 65 feet and over: $66	State Park & Recreation Division, P.O. Box 1147, Santa Fe, NM 87504-1147.
NEW YORK	All motorboats	3 years	Under 16 feet: $3 16 feet to 26 feet: $6 Over 26 feet: $10	Any district office of the Department of Motor Vehicles.
NORTH CAROLINA	All powerboats, sailboats over 14 feet LWL	1 year 3 years	$5.50 $13	Wildlife Resources Commission, Archdale Bldg., 512 N. Salisbury St., Raleigh, NC 27611.
NORTH DAKOTA	All motorboats	3 years	Under 16 feet: $6 16 feet and over: $15 Canoes: $6	North Dakota Game and Fish Department, 2121 Lovett Ave., Bismark, ND 58505.

STATE	BOATS AFFECTED	NUMBERING PERIOD	FEE	WHERE TO APPLY
OHIO	All watercraft	3 years	Handpowered: $3/year Boats to 16 feet: $7.50/year 16 feet to 26 feet: $10/year 26 feet to 40 feet: $15/year 40 feet to 65 feet: $15/year Agent fee for each: $1	Ohio Department of Natural Resources, Division of Watercraft, Fountain Square, Building C-2, Columbus, OH 43224.
OKLAHOMA	All watercraft and outboard motors over 10 horsepower	1 year	Based on factory-delivered price, $150 or less: $1 Over $150 add $1 for each $100 or fraction thereof. Then prorated each year thereafter.	Oklahoma Tax Commission, Motor Vehicle Division, Boat & Motor Section, 2501 Lincoln Blvd., Oklahoma City, OK 73194.
OREGON	All motorboats	1 year	Under 12 feet: $3 12 feet to 16 feet: $6 16 feet to 20 feet: $8 Over 20 feet: $8 plus $1 for each foot or fraction thereof	State Marine Board, No. 505, 3000 Market St. N.E., Salem, OR 97310.

State	Vessels	Period	Fees	Address
PENNSYLVANIA	All motorboats	1 year	Under 16 feet: $4 16 feet and over: $6	Pennsylvania Fish Commission, Boat Registration Section, P.O. Box 1852, Harrisburg, PA 17105-1852.
RHODE ISLAND	All motorboats	2 years	Under 16 feet: $4; all others $10	Division of Boating Safety, Department of Environmental Management, Quonset Administration Bldg. 7, Davisville, RI 02854.
SOUTH CAROLINA	All motorboats	3 years	$10	Wildlife Resources Department, P.O. Box 167, Columbia, SC 29202.
SOUTH DAKOTA	All power vessels	3 years	$10	Department of Game, Fish & Parks, 1429 E. Sioux, Pierre, SD 57501.
TENNESSEE	All sailboats, all mechanically propelled vessels	1 year	16 feet and under: $4 16 feet to 26 feet: $8 26 feet to 40 feet: $12 40 feet and over: $16	Tennessee Wildlife Resources Agency, P.O. Box 40474, Nashville, TN 37204.

STATE	BOATS AFFECTED	NUMBERING PERIOD	FEE	WHERE TO APPLY
TEXAS	All motorboats	2 years	Under 16 feet: $12 16 to 26 feet: $18 26 feet to 40 feet: $24 Over 40 feet: $30	Texas Parks & Wildlife Department, 4200 Smith School Rd., Austin, TX 78744.
UTAH	All motorboats and sailboats	1 year	$5	Motor Vehicles Division, 1095 Motor Ave., Salt Lake City, UT 84116.
VERMONT	All motorboats	1 year	Under 16 feet: $2.50 16 feet to 26 feet: $5 26 feet to 40 feet: $10 Over 40 feet: $25	Registration Section, Department of Public Safety, Montpelier, VT 05602.
VIRGINIA	All motorboats	3 years	$11	Boat Section, State Game & Fisheries Commission, P.O. Box 11104, Richmond, VA 23230.
WASHINGTON	All motorboats	3 years	$6	USCG Thirteenth District, 618 Second Ave., Seattle, WA 98104.

WEST VIRGINIA	All motorboats	1 year	Original $5 Renewal $5	Department of Motor Vehicles, State Office Building, Charleston, WV 25305
WISCONSIN	All motorboats and sailboats over 12 feet	2 years	Under 16 feet: $6.50 16 feet to 26 feet: $8.50 26 feet to 40 feet: $10.50 40 feet and over: $22.50	Wisconsin Department of Natural Resources, Box 7236, Madison, WS 53707, Att: Boat Registration.
WYOMING	All motorboats	1 year	$5	Wyoming Game and Fish Department, Cheyenne, WY 82002.
PUERTO RICO	—	—	—	Maritime Department, Puerto Rico Ports Authority, GPO Box 2829, San Juan, PR 00936.
VIRGIN ISLANDS	—	—	—	Department of Conservation & Cultural Affairs, Lagoon Fishing Center, Estate Frydenhoj, St. Thomas, VI 00801.

those legally required. The requirements for the decal, given below, make a good checklist for any well-equipped boat.

Personal Flotation Devices

An approved personal flotation device of the appropriate type is required for *each berth* on the boat; this may be more than the legal requirement of one PFD for each person on board at the time of a check. In addition, a boat with no bunks, or with only one, must still have a minimum of two lifesaving devices aboard.

Fire Extinguishers

The Auxiliary standards for fire extinguishers on smaller boats are likewise more demanding than the legal requirements. Although a boat under 26 feet of open construction, or one which has a built-in fire extinguisher system, need not carry an additional hand-portable extinguisher to meet the legal minimum, it must have one for a CME decal.

Sailboats of 16 feet or more in length, even without any auxiliary power or fuel tanks, must have at least one B-I extinguisher. The letter *B* designates the type of fires on which the extinguisher can be used (see page 22); the roman numeral designates extinguisher capacity. Size I is the smallest; V is the largest.

Additional Fire Extinguishers.   Even the USCG Auxiliary requirements may not be enough to provide an extinguisher at all desirable locations:

1. The helm, where there is always someone when under way.

2. The engine compartment.

3. The galley.

4. Adjacent to the skipper's bunk, for quick reach at night.

Add extinguishers as necessary to meet the needs of your own boat.

Navigation Lights

The law does not require that a boat operated only in the daylight have navigation lights, but these must be fitted and in good working order to meet the Auxiliary's standards for all craft 16 feet or more in length. Proper lights for use both under way and at anchor must be shown. The decal will not be awarded if lights are grossly misplaced, even if they are operable.

A sailboat with an auxiliary engine must be capable of showing the lights of both a sailboat and a motorboat; the lights must be wired so that the display can be changed from one to the other.

Visual Distress Signals

To receive CME approval, *every* boat must have acceptable visual distress signals even if not legally required due to size or waters used. The Auxiliary requirements of types and numbers are the same as the legal requirements.

Anchor and Line

An anchor of suitable type and weight together with line of appropriate size and length is required for the CME decal. This is a valuable safety item should the engine fail and the boat be in danger of drifting or being blown into hazardous waters.

Bilge Pump or Bailer

For the CME decal, all boats must have a bilge pump or bailer of a suitable size for the craft, and it must be in proper operating condition. This will normally be an installed electric pump for boats more than roughly 18 feet in length, and a hand scoop-type bailer on smaller craft.

Smaller Craft Requirements

All Class A boats must carry a second means of propulsion. Normally a paddle or oars is used to meet this requirement, but an alternate mechanical means is acceptable *if* it has both a different starting source (battery) and a separate fuel source.

Requirements for Inflatables

An inflatable boat is eligible for a CME decal if it meets all requirements for a craft of its size, plus certain additional specifications such as a minimum of three separate air chambers that

GOVERNMENT

Table 10.4

Lights for Various Types of Vessels—1980 Inland Rules

DIAGRAM	VESSEL	MASTHEAD (FORWARD)	SIDE	STERN	ADDITIONAL LIGHTS OR REMARKS
1	Power-driven vessel 12 m but less than 20 m in length	White, 225°, vis. 3 mi. At least 2.5 m above gunwale[3]	Separate red and green 112½°, or combination, vis. 2 mi. Above hull at least 1 m below masthead light[2]	White 135°, vis. 2 mi.	[1]After masthead light may be shown but not required. (Exception allowed on Great Lakes.) [2]Fitted with inboard screens if necessary to prevent being seen across bow.
2	Power-driven vessel less than 12 m in length	Can be less than 2.5 m above gunwale, but at least 1 m above side lights[1],[3]	Separate red and green, 112½°, or combination, vis. 1 mi. Above hull at least 1 m below masthead light[2],[3]	White 135°, vis. 2 mi.	[3]Less than 12 m in length, need only have all-round white light, vis. 2 mi, but should have side lights
3	Sailing vessel under 20 m in length	None	Separate red and green, 112½°, or combination, vis. 2 mi.[2], [4]	White 135°, vis. 2 mi.	Optional—two all-round lights at or near top of mast, red over green, separated at least 1 m, vis. 2 mi.
4	Sailing vessel under 12 m in length	None	Separate red and green, 112½°, or combination, vis. 1 mi.[2],[4], [5]	White, 135°, vis. 2 mi.[4], [5]	[4]May be combined into triple combination light at masthead [5]Less than 7 m, need only have flashlight or lantern to show
5	Vessel propelled by oars	None	May show separate red and green, 112½°, or combination, vis. 1 mi.[6]	May show white, 135°, vis. 2 mi.[6]	[6]Need only have flashlight or lantern to show white light

#	Vessel	Masthead lights	Sidelights	Sternlight	Other
6	Power-driven vessel 20 m but less than 50 m in length	White, 225°, vis. 5 mi. Not more than ½ of length aft from stern; 6 m, or beam (up to 10 m) above hull	Red and green, 112½°, vis. 2 mi. At or near sides of vessel; above hull at least 1 m below masthead light	White, 135°, vis. 2 mi.	After masthead light may be shown; at least 4.5 m higher than forward masthead light
7	Power-driven vessel 50 m or more in length	Not more than ½ of length aft from stern; 6 m or beam (up to 10 m) above hull	Red and green, 112½°, vis. 3 mi. At or near sides of vessel; above hull at least 1 m below masthead light	White, 135°, vis. 3 mi.	After masthead light required; at least 4.5 m higher and ¼ of vessel length (up to 50 m) aft of forward masthead light
8	Vessel towing; tow less than 200 m overall from stern of towing vessel. (Also towing alongside or pushing ahead)	Two white, arranged vertically, 225°, vis. determined by length of vessel (not required pushing ahead or towing alongside on Western rivers)	Normal for size of vessel		Towing astern: towing light[7] over stern light. Pushing ahead or towing alongside. Two towing lights[7] vertically. [7]Vis. 3 mi. for vessels 50 m or more in length. 2 mi. for shorter vessels
9	Vessel towing; tow 200 m or more overall length	Three white, arranged vertically, 225°, vis. determined by length of vessel	Normal for size of vessel		Towing light: yellow, 135°, above sternlight[7]
10	Vessel being towed astern, if manned	None	Normal for size of vessel	Normal for size of vessel	
11	Vessel being towed alongside or pushed ahead	None	Normal for size of vessel; at forward end	Normal for size of vessel (not used for pushed ahead)	Also "special flashing light" at center or forward end. A group of vessels is lighted as a single vessel.

DIAGRAM	VESSEL	MASTHEAD (FORWARD)	SIDE	STERN	ADDITIONAL LIGHTS OR REMARKS
12	Vessel engaged in trawling or drift fishing		[8] Show only normal lights of power-driven or sailing vessel		
13	Vessel engaged in trawling	None[12]	When making way through the water, normal for size of vessel		Under way or at anchor, two all-round lights, green over white[7, 9, 10, 11] [9]Vertical spacing 1 m [10]Lower light not less than 4 m (2 m if under 20 m in length) above hull [11]Lower light above sidelights at least twice vertical spacing
14	Vessel engaged in fishing, other than trawling (or trolling)	None[12]	When making way through the water, normal for size of vessel		Under way or at anchor, two all-round lights, red over white[7, 9, 10, 11] [12]When not actually fishing, show normal masthead lights for vessel its size
15	Vessel at anchor, less than 50 m in length	None	None	None	White, all-round light where can best be seen. Vis. 2 mi. (not required if less than 7 m in length and not anchored in a narrow channel or where vessels normally navigate)
16	Vessel at anchor; 50 m or more in length	None	None	None	White, all-round light in fore part of vessel not less than 6 m above hull. A second white, all-round light in after part, not less than 4.5 m lower than forward anchor light. Vis. 3 mi.

17	Vessel aground	None	None	None	Anchor light(s) as line 15 or 16, plus two red all-round lights of same visibility range[7,9,10] (not required if less than 12 m in length)
18	Pilot vessel	None if on pilot duty; normal if under way and not on pilot duty	When under way, normal for size of vessel	When under way, normal for size of vessel	Two all-round lights, white over red, at masthead[7,9,10] If at anchor, normal anchor light(s); line 15 or 16
19	Vessel not under command	None	If making way through the water, normal for size of vessel	If making way through the water, normal for size of vessel	Two red all-round lights, vertically where best can be seen[7,9,10]
20	Vessel restricted in ability to maneuver	None	When making way through the water, normal for size of vessel	When making way through the water, normal for size of vessel	Three all-round lights vertically, red-white-red[7,9] If at anchor, normal anchor light(s). (Not required if less than 12 m in length)

Equivalent measures in customary units

50 m = 164 ft   7 m = 23.0 ft   2 m = 6.6 ft   200 m = 656 ft   20 m = 65.6 ft   4.5 m = 14.8 ft
6 m = 19.7 ft   1 m = 3.3 ft   100 m = 328 ft   12 m = 39.4 ft   2.5 m = 8.2 ft

Table 10.5

Lights for Various Types of Vessels—1972 International Rules

DIAGRAM	VESSEL	MASTHEAD (FORWARD)	SIDE	STERN	ADDITIONAL LIGHTS OR REMARKS
A	Power-driven vessel 12 m but less than 20 m in length	White, 225°, vis. 3 mi. At least 2.5 m above gunwale[3]	Separate red and green, 112½°, or combination, vis. 2 mi. Above hull at least 1 m below masthead light[2]	White, 135°, vis. 2 mi.	[1]After masthead light may be shown but not required. [2]Fitted with inboard screens if necessary to prevent being seen across bow
B	Power-driven vessel less than 12 m in length	White, 225°, vis. 2 mi. Can be less than 2.5 m above gunwale, but at least 1 m above side lights[3]	Separate red and green, 112½°, or combination, vis. 1 mi. Above hull at least 1 m below masthead light[2]	White, 135°, vis. 2 mi.	[3]Less than 7 m and less than 7 kt max speed need only have all-round white light, vis. 2 mi. but should have sidelights
C	Sailing vessel under 20 m in length	None	Separate red and green, 112½°, or combination, vis. 2 mi.	White, 135°, vis. 2 mi.	Optional—two all-round lights at or near top of mast, red over green, separated at least 1 m, vis. 2 mi.
D	Sailing vessel under 12 m in length	None	Separate red and green, 112½°, or combination, vis. 1 mi.[2, 4]	White, 135°, vis. 2 mi.[4, 5]	[4]May be combined into triple combination light at masthead [5]Less than 7 m, need only have flashlight or lantern to show
E	Vessel propelled by oars	None	May show separate red and green, 112½°, or combination, vis. 1 mi.[6]	May show white, 135°, vis. 2 mi.[6]	[6]Need only have flashlight or lantern to show white light

	Vessel	Masthead light	Sidelights	Sternlight	Other lights
F	Power-driven vessel 20 but less than 50 m in length	White, 225°, vis. 5 mi. Not more than ¼ of length aft from stem; 6 m or beam (up to 12 m) above hull	Red and green, 112½°, vis. 2 mi. At or near sides of vessel; not more than ¾ height of masthead light	White, 135°, vis. 2 mi.	After masthead light may be shown; at least 4.5 m higher than forward masthead light
G	Power-driven vessel 50 m or more in length	White, 225°, vis. 6 mi. Not more than ¼ of length aft from stem; 6 m or beam (up to 12 m) above hull	Red and green, 112½°, vis. 3 mi. At or near sides of vessel; not more than ¾ height of forward masthead light	White, 135°, vis. 3 mi.	After masthead light required; at least 4.5 m higher and half of vessel length (up to 100 m) aft of forward masthead light
H	Vessel towing; tow less than 200 m overall vessel. (Also towing alongside or pushing ahead)	Two white, arranged vertically, 225°, vis. determined by length of vessel	Normal for size of vessel	Normal for size of vessel	Towing light[7] over sternlight (not shown when towing alongside or pushing ahead) [7]Vis. 3 mi. for vessels 50 m or more in length; 2 mi. for shorter vessels
I	Vessel towing; tow 200 m or more overall length	Three white, arranged vertically, 225°, vis. determined by length of vessel	Normal for size of vessel	Normal for size of vessel	Towing light[7] over sternlight
J	Vessel being towed astern, if manned	None	Normal for size of vessel		
K	Vessel being towed alongside or pushed ahead	None	Normal for size of vessel; at forward end	Normal for size of vessel (not used for pushed ahead)	A group of vessels is lighted as a single vessel

DIAGRAM	VESSEL	MASTHEAD (FORWARD)	SIDE	STERN	ADDITIONAL LIGHTS OR REMARKS
L	Vessel engaged in trawling or drift fishing		[8]Show only normal lights of power-driven or sailing vessel		
M	Vessel engaged in trawling	None[12]	When making way through the water, normal for size of vessel		Under way or at anchor, two all-round lights, green over white[7, 9, 10, 11] [9]Vertical spacing 2 m for vessels 20 m or more in length, 1 m for shorter vessels [10]Lower light not less than 4 m (2 m if under 20 m in length) above hull [11]Lower light above sidelights at least twice vertical spacing
N	Vessel engaged in fishing, other than trawling (or trolling)	None[12]	When making way through the water, normal for size of vessel		Under way or at anchor, two all-round lights, red over white[7, 9, 10, 11] [12]When not actually fishing, show normal masthead lights for vessel its size
O	Vessel at anchor, less than 50 m in length	None	None	None	White, all-round light where can best be seen. Vis. 2 mi. (not required if less than 7 m in length and not anchored in a narrow channel or where vessels normally navigate)
P	Vessel at anchor; 50 m or more in length	None	None	None	White, all-round light in fore part of vessel not less than 6 m above hull. A second white, all-round light in after part, not less than 4.5 m lower than forward anchor light. Vis. 3 mi.

Q	Vessel aground	None	None	None	Normal anchor light(s) plus two red all-round lights of same visibility range
R	Pilot vessel	None if on pilot duty; normal if under way and not on pilot duty	When under way, normal for size of vessel	None	Two all-round lights, white over red, at masthead[7,9,10] If at anchor, normal anchor light(s); line 15 or 16
S	Vessel not under command	None	If making way through the water, normal for size of vessel	None	Two red all-round lights, vertically where best can be seen[7,9,10]
T	Vessel constrained by her draft	Normal for size of vessel	Normal for size of vessel		Three red all-round lights, arranged vertically and equally spaced[7,9,10]

Equivalent measures in customary units

50 m = 164 ft	7 m = 23.0 ft	2 m = 6.6 ft	200 m = 656 ft	20 m = 65.6 ft	4.5 m = 14.8 ft
6 m = 19.7 ft	1 m = 3.3 ft	100 m = 328 ft	12 m = 39.4 ft	2.5 m = 8.2 ft	

are *not* interconnected and an installed rigid transom (a strap-on outboard motor mount is not acceptable).

Sailboats

Sailboats without mechanical power, either installed or detachable, are required to have personal flotation devices for each person on board; the type of PFD varies with the size of the boat. Sailboats longer than 16 feet are eligible to become Coast Guard Auxiliary Facilities if they meet certain prescribed standards. These requirements can serve as a guide to all owners of sailing craft as to desirable safety equipment.

Sailing Facilities under 26 feet in length are required to have one B-I hand fire extinguisher, and larger ones muct have two such units on board. These sailboats must meet the CME standard of one approved lifesaving device on board for each berth, with a minimum of two such devices. Further, such craft must meet all standards for motorboats other than those relating to propulsion machinery, fuel systems, and ventilation of related compartments. This leaves in the requirements such items as an anchor with line, distress flares, and standards for galley stove installation and general electrical systems, as mentioned below—all matters appropriate to the safe operation of any sailboat.

Installation Standards

In addition to requiring the above items of equipment, the Coast Guard Auxiliary program has established standards for the installation of fuel systems, electrical systems, and galley stoves.

The Auxiliary requires that a galley stove be of a marine type and be installed so as to present no hazard to the craft and its occupants. Any common fuel is acceptable except gasoline and derivatives or distillates of naphtha and benzene. Liquid petroleum (LP) gas stoves or heaters that use an integral fuel container or one that fastens directly to the appliance are not acceptable for award of the decal.

Marine Sanitation Devices

The Courtesy Examination focuses on safety aspects of the boat. No check will be made for the presence or operating condition of an

MSD, although the examiner will be glad to provide information on legal requirements.

EQUIPMENT RECOMMENDED BY THE USCG AUXILIARY

The CME checklist also contains a number of items recommended for the proper operation of a boat or for its safety—items beyond those required for award of the decal. The actual selections of items from this list will vary with the size and use of the boat involved.

This list of generally recommended items includes many that are required for "Facilities" and "Operational Facilities"—the Auxiliary members' own boats that have been brought to higher standards for use in their programs.

Anchors

The CME checklist recommends carrying a second anchor, in addition to the one required to pass the CME check. The additional anchor may be a lighter one for nonemergency daytime use. The checklist also recommends that a length of chain be used between the anchor and the nylon line. Shackles used on either end of this chain should have their pins secured with safety wire.

Bilge Pumps

Boats more than 26 feet in length should have at least two means of pumping bilges; and their bilges must be clean and free of any oil or grease. Wood chips or any other debris that could clog pumps and limber holes must be removed. A manual bilge pump should be carried in every boat irrespective of any electric pump.

Lines

Every boat should have mooring (dock) lines suitable in length and size to that particular craft. These should be of several different lengths for convenience in use. No generalization can be made as to the lengths, but the diameter should correspond roughly to that of storm or working anchor rodes.

A heaving line of light construction is desirable if the craft is large enough to need heavy mooring lines. The use of polypropylene line, or other material that is brightly colored and will float, is recommended for this purpose.

Life Rings

A ring life buoy with a length of light line attached is recommended for rendering assistance to swimmers or accident victims in the water. This can also be used to float a heavier line across to a stranded boat. If of an approved type, this ring buoy may count as the required "throwable" PFD for all boats of Classes 1, 2, and 3. A water light (a device that automatically lights up in contact with the water) makes a ring or horseshoe buoy easier to spot at night.

Operational Equipment

Recommended operational equipment includes fenders in appropriate sizes and numbers for the boat involved. Not only will these be used in normal berthing, but they are also necessary if two boats must make fast to each other while under way or at anchor. A boathook will be found very useful for fending off, placing lines over piles, picking up pennants of mooring buoys, recovering articles dropped over the side, and many other uses.

A searchlight—installed on larger craft, hand-held on smaller boats—serves both as a routine aid in night piloting and as an emergency signaling device. A multicell flashlight or electric lantern can serve these functions, but not as well as a searchlight.

Navigation publications and charts should be carried aboard boats in accordance with their use. A compass is desirable on almost any boat for emergency, if not regular, use.

A hand-held lead line is useful, even as a back-up to the more complicated electronic depth sounder; one is particularly handy when one must probe around a stranded boat in search of deeper water. Also useful is a pole—a boathook will do very well—marked with rings at one-foot intervals; a mark of a different color or size should be added for the draft of the boat.

An emergency supply of drinking water—and perhaps food, too—should be carried on all boats. It may never to used, but when needed it can literally be a lifesaver. Supplies of this nature should be periodically freshened or replaced to ensure acceptable quality when needed. Distilled water should be carried for periodic replenishment of any storage batteries on board; this can, of course, serve as an emergency source of drinking water.

A first-aid kit is an essential item of safety equipment; see the safety section of the *Boatman's Handbook*. The kit should be accompanied by a manual or separate book of instructions.

The list of tools and spare parts to be carried aboard must be developed by each skipper individually for his own boat. The items will be governed by the type of boat, its normal use, and the capabilities of the crew to use them. An item required on USCG Aux Facilities is one or more spare bulbs for the navigation lights. Items for all boats include simple tools, plugs, cloth, screws, nails, wire, tape, and other objects for the execution of emergency repairs at sea. Mechanical and electrical spares will be highly individualized by the particular boat and skipper.

11.

USEFUL TABLES

One way to convey a lot of useful information quickly and easily is through the use of tables. Here are those covering time, speed

Table 11.1

SPEED COMPARISON

km./h	mph	meters/sec.	knots
10	6.22	2.78	5.4
20	12.4	5.56	10.8
30	18.7	8.34	16.2
40	24.9	11.1	21.6
50	31.1	13.9	27.0
60	37.4	16.7	32.4
70	43.6	19.4	37.8
80	49.8	22.2	43.2
90	56.0	25.0	48.6
100	62.2	27.8	54.0
120	74.7	33.3	64.8
140	87.1	38.9	75.6
160	99.5	44.5	86.4
180	112	50.0	97.2
200	124	55.6	108
220	137	61.2	119
240	149	66.7	130
260	162	72.3	140
280	174	77.8	151
300	187	83.4	162

Table 11.2

TIME-SPEED-DISTANCE

	\multicolumn{9}{c}{Time taken to travel 1 nautical mile (or statute mile)}								
Min.	**1**	**2**	**3**	**4**	**5**	**6**	**7**	**8**	**9**
Sec.	\multicolumn{9}{l}{Speed of boat in knots (or statute miles per hour)}								
0	60.00	30.00	20.00	15.00	12.00	10.00	8.57	7.50	6.67
2	58.06	29.51	19.78	14.88	11.92	9.95	8.53	7.47	6.64
4	56.25	29.03	19.56	14.75	11.84	9.89	8.49	7.44	6.62
6	54.55	28.57	19.36	14.63	11.76	9.84	8.45	7.41	6.59
8	52.94	28.13	19.15	14.52	11.69	9.78	8.41	7.38	6.56
10	51.43	27.69	18.95	14.40	11.61	9.73	8.37	7.35	6.54
12	50.00	27.27	18.75	14.29	11.54	9.68	8.33	7.32	6.52
14	48.65	26.87	18.56	14.17	11.47	9.63	8.29	7.29	6.50
16	46.37	26.47	18.37	14.06	11.39	9.57	8.26	7.26	6.48
18	46.15	26.09	18.18	13.95	11.32	9.52	8.22	7.23	6.45
20	45.00	25.71	18.00	13.85	11.25	9.47	8.18	7.20	6.43
22	43.90	25.35	17.82	13.74	11.18	9.42	8.15	7.17	6.41
24	42.86	25.00	17.65	13.64	11.11	9.38	8.11	7.14	6.38
26	41.86	24.66	17.48	13.53	11.04	9.33	8.07	7.12	6.36
28	40.90	24.32	17.31	13.43	10.98	9.28	8.04	7.09	6.34
30	40.00	24.00	17.14	13.33	10.91	9.23	8.00	7.06	6.32
32	39.13	23.68	16.98	13.24	10.84	9.18	7.97	7.03	6.29
34	38.30	23.38	16.82	13.14	10.78	9.14	7.93	7.00	6.27
36	37.50	23.08	16.67	13.04	10.71	9.09	7.90	6.98	6.25
38	36.74	22.79	16.51	12.95	10.65	9.05	7.86	6.95	6.23
40	36.00	22.50	16.36	12.85	10.59	9.00	7.83	6.92	6.21
42	35.29	22.22	16.22	12.77	10.53	8.96	7.79	6.90	6.19
44	34.62	21.95	16.07	12.68	10.47	8.91	7.76	6.87	6.16
46	33.96	21.69	15.93	12.59	10.40	8.87	7.73	6.84	6.14
48	33.33	21.43	15.79	12.50	10.35	8.82	7.69	6.82	6.12
50	32.73	21.18	15.65	12.41	10.29	8.78	7.66	6.79	6.10
52	32.14	20.93	15.52	12.33	10.23	8.74	7.63	6.77	6.08
54	31.58	20.69	15.38	12.25	10.17	8.70	7.60	6.74	6.06
56	31.03	20.45	15.25	12.16	10.11	8.65	7.56	6.72	6.04
58	30.51	20.23	15.13	12.08	10.06	8.61	7.53	6.69	6.02
60	30.00	20.00	15.00	12.00	10.00	8.57	7.50	6.67	6.00

and distance problems; nautical mile-statute mile conversions; propeller selection for inboard and outboard propulsion; cable, rope, and chain strengths and uses; metric conversions; strengths of metals and woods, and weights and measures.

Table 11.3

CONVERSION TABLES—NAUTICAL AND STATUTE MILES

Nautical	Statute	Nautical	Statute	Nautical	Statute	Statute	Nautical	Statute	Nautical	Statute	Nautical
1.00	1.151	8.75	10.075	16.50	18.999	1.00	0.868	9.00	7.815	17.00	14.763
1.25	1.439	9.00	10.363	16.75	19.287	1.25	1.085	9.25	8.032	17.25	14.980
1.50	1.729	9.25	10.651	17.00	19.575	1.50	1.302	9.50	8.249	17.50	15.197
1.75	2.015	9.50	10.939	17.25	19.863	1.75	1.519	9.75	8.467	17.75	15.414
2.00	2.303	9.75	11.227	17.50	20.151	2.00	1.736	10.00	8.684	18.00	15.632
2.25	2.590	10.00	11.515	17.75	20.439	2.25	1.953	10.25	8.901	18.25	15.849
2.50	2.878	10.25	11.803	18.00	20.727	2.50	2.171	10.50	9.118	18.50	16.066
2.75	3.166	10.50	12.090	18.25	21.015	2.75	2.387	10.75	9.335	18.75	16.283
3.00	3.454	10.75	12.378	18.50	21.303	3.00	2.604	11.00	9.552	19.00	16.500
3.25	3.742	11.00	12.666	18.75	21.590	3.25	2.821	11.25	9.769	19.25	16.717
3.50	4.030	11.25	12.954	19.00	21.878	3.50	3.038	11.50	9.986	19.50	16.934
3.75	4.318	11.50	13.242	19.25	22.166	3.75	3.256	11.75	10.203	19.75	17.151
4.00	4.606	11.75	13.530	19.50	22.454	4.00	3.473	12.00	10.420	20.00	17.369
4.25	4.893	12.00	13.818	19.75	22.742	4.25	3.690	12.25	10.638	20.25	17.586
4.50	5.181	12.25	14.106	20.00	23.030	4.50	3.907	12.50	10.855	20.50	17.803
4.75	5.469	12.50	14.393	20.25	23.318	4.75	4.124	12.75	11.072	20.75	18.020
5.00	5.757	12.75	14.681	20.50	23.606	5.00	4.341	13.00	11.289	21.00	18.237
5.25	6.045	13.00	14.969	20.75	23.893	5.25	4.559	13.25	11.507	21.25	18.454
5.50	6.333	13.25	15.257	21.00	24.181	5.50	4.776	13.50	11.724	21.50	18.671
5.75	6.621	13.50	15.545	21.25	24.468	5.75	4.994	13.75	11.941	21.75	18.888
6.00	6.909	13.75	15.833	21.50	24.757	6.00	5.211	14.00	12.158	22.00	19.105
6.25	7.196	14.00	16.121	21.75	25.045	6.25	5.428	14.25	12.376	22.25	19.322
6.50	7.484	14.25	16.409	22.00	25.333	6.50	5.645	14.50	12.593	22.50	19.539
6.75	7.772	14.50	16.696	22.25	25.621	6.75	5.862	14.75	12.810	22.75	19.756
7.00	8.060	14.75	16.984	22.50	25.909	7.00	6.079	15.00	13.027	23.00	19.973
7.25	8.348	15.00	17.272	22.75	26.196	7.25	6.296	15.25	13.244	23.25	20.191
7.50	8.636	15.25	17.560	23.00	26.484	7.50	6.513	15.50	13.461	23.50	20.408
7.75	8.924	15.50	17.848	23.50	27.000	7.75	6.730	15.75	13.678	23.75	20.625
8.00	9.212	15.75	18.136	24.00	27.636	8.00	6.947	16.00	13.895	24.00	20.842
8.25	9.500	16.00	18.424	24.50	28.212	8.25	7.164	16.25	14.112	24.25	21.060
8.50	9.787	16.25	18.712	25.00	28.787	8.50	7.381	16.50	14.329	24.50	21.277
—						8.75	7.598	16.75	14.546	25.00	21.711

1 nautical mile=1.151 statute miles
1 statute mile=0.869 nautical mile

Table 11.4. Inboard Propeller Selection—Diameter

This table, prepared by Columbian Bronze, can be used to determine approximate diameter of normal three-blade propeller that will best match engine horsepower and propeller shaft speed.

Table 11.4

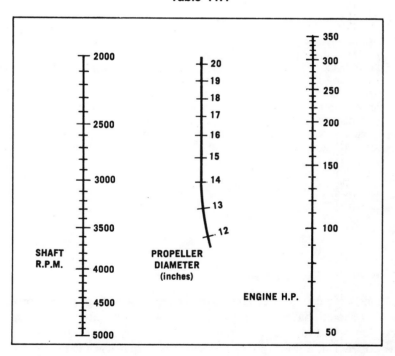

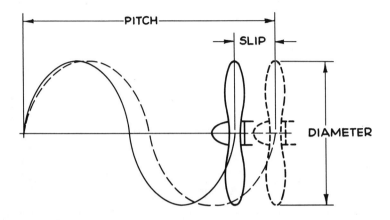

Figure 11.1 Propeller dimensions are diameter and pitch. The diameter is that of a circle described by the outermost point of a propeller blade. Pitch is the distance a propeller would move in one revolution (dotted line) if it operated as a screw being driven through solid material. Actual movement is less than the theoretical pitch distance, and the difference between actual movement (solid line) and pitch distance is the propeller slip. Slip is expressed as a percentage of pitch distance. Depending on the type of boat, slip varies between about 10 percent and 35 percent.

Table 11.5. Inboard Propeller Selection—Pitch

This table can be used to determine the approximate pitch a propeller should have to permit a boat to operate at its optimum cruising speed, or the approximate speed that will result from use of a propeller of a given pitch. Propeller shaft rpm and the boat's slip factor must be known. Light, fast racing boats have a slip of about 10 percent; runabouts, 12 to 20 percent; fast cruisers, 18 to 30 percent; and heavy cruisers, 20 to 35 percent. Shaft speed is engine rpm divided by any reduction gear ratio present.

Table 11.5

INBOARD ENGINE PROPELLER SELECTION

rpm	slip	8 in.	10 in.	PITCH 12 in.	14 in.	16 in.	18 in.
700	10%	4.16	5.18	6.22	7.27	8.31	9.32
	20%	3.68	4.61	5.53	6.45	7.38	8.28
	30%	3.23	4.03	4.83	5.64	6.46	7.27
800	10%	4.76	5.92	7.12	8.32	9.48	10.64
	20%	4.20	5.28	6.32	7.36	8.44	9.48
	30%	3.68	4.60	5.52	6.44	7.40	8.32
900	10%	5.35	6.66	8.00	9.35	10.68	11.98
	20%	4.73	5.93	7.11	8.29	9.49	10.65
	30%	4.15	5.18	6.21	7.49	8.31	9.35
1,000	10%	5.94	7.41	8.88	10.38	11.85	13.32
	20%	5.27	6.58	7.90	9.22	10.55	11.83
	30%	4.62	5.76	6.91	8.06	9.23	10.38
1,200	10%	7.13	8.89	10.65	12.46	14.22	15.98
	20%	6.32	7.90	9.48	11.06	12.66	14.20
	30%	5.54	6.91	8.29	9.67	11.08	12.46
1,400	10%	8.32	10.37	12.43	14.54	16.59	18.64
	20%	7.37	9.22	11.06	12.09	14.77	16.57
	30%	6.46	8.06	9.67	11.52	12.93	14.54
1,600	10%	9.51	11.85	14.21	16.52	18.96	21.30
	20%	8.42	10.54	12.64	14.74	16.98	18.94
	30%	7.38	9.21	11.05	13.13	14.78	16.62
1,800	10%	10.70	13.33	15.99	18.70	21.33	23.96
	20%	9.47	11.86	14.22	16.58	18.99	21.31
	30%	8.30	10.36	12.43	14.74	16.63	18.70
2,000	10%	11.89	14.81	17.77	20.78	23.70	26.62
	20%	10.52	13.18	15.80	18.42	21.10	23.68
	30%	9.22	11.51	13.82	16.12	18.46	20.76
2,200	10%	13.08	16.29	19.55	22.86	26.07	29.28
	20%	11.57	14.50	17.38	20.26	23.21	26.05
	30%	10.14	12.66	15.20	17.73	20.31	22.84
2,400	10%	14.27	17.77	21.33	24.94	28.44	31.94
	20%	12.62	15.87	18.96	22.10	25.32	28.42
	30%	11.06	13.81	16.58	19.34	22.16	24.92
2,600	10%	15.46	19.25	23.11	27.02	30.81	34.60
	20%	13.67	17.19	20.54	23.94	27.43	30.79
	30%	11.98	14.96	17.96	20.95	24.01	27.00
2,800	10%	16.65	20.73	24.89	29.10	33.18	37.26
	20%	14.72	18.51	22.12	25.78	29.54	33.16
	30%	12.90	16.11	19.34	22.56	25.86	29.08
3,000	10%	17.84	22.21	26.67	31.18	35.55	39.92
	20%	15.77	19.83	23.70	27.62	31.65	35.53
	30%	13.82	17.26	20.72	24.17	27.71	31.16

Table 11.6

INBOARD ENGINE PROPELLER SHAFT SELECTION						
SHAFT DIAMETER (inches)			**ENGINE DISPLACEMENT (cu. in.)/ REDUCTION GEAR RATIO**			
Naval or Tobin bronze	Monel, stainless steel, or aluminum bronze	1:1 (direct drive)	1.5:1	2:1	2.5:1	3:1
7/8	3/4	100-175				
1	7/8	175-250	100-175			
1 1/8	1	250-325	175-250	100-175		
1 1/4	1 1/8	325-400	250-325	175-250	100-175	
1 3/8	1 1/4	400-500	325-400	250-325	175-250	100-175
1 1/2	1 3/8		400-500	325-400	250-325	175-250
1 5/8	1 1/2			400-500	325-400	250-325
1 3/4	1 5/8				400-500	325-400
2	1 3/4					400-500

These figures are for gasoline engines. For diesel engines, add 1/8 inches diameter to all shaft size recommendations.

Table 11.7

Weight and Strength—Manila, Nylon, and Chain

	APPROX. WEIGHT OF 100' IN AIR				ROPE—BREAKING STRENGTH		CHAIN—PROOF TEST	
				6 x 19				
DIAMETER	NYLON ROPE	MANILA ROPE	BBB GALV. CHAIN	FIBER-CORE WIRE ROPE	NYLON YACHT ROPE	MANILA YACHT ROPE	BBB GALV. CELL CHAIN	HIGH STRENGTH ALLEY CHAIN
1/4	1.6	1.9	76	100	1,300	650	2,700	6,500
5/16	2.6	3.2	115	160	2,000	1,150	3,700	. . . . .
3/8	3.8	4.0	170	230	2,900	1,550	4,600	13,000
7/16	5.2	5.1	225	310	3,900	1,900	6,200	. . . . .
1/2	6.9	6.5	295	400	5,000	2,900	8,200	22,000
9/16	8.8	8.5	350	510	6,200	3,800	10,200	. . . . .
5/8	10.8	11.2	430	630	7,500	4,800	12,500	33,000
3/4	15.8	13.8	600	900	10,700	5,900	17,700	46,000
7/8	21.8	20.8	810	1230	14,200	8,400	24,000	. . . . .
1	28.5	25.2	1050	1600	18,500	9,900	31,000	. . . . .

Table 11.9

Fiber Cordage—Typical Weights and Minimum Breaking Strengths (pounds)

NOMINAL SIZE (INCHES)		MANILA			NYLON			DACRON			POLYPROPYLENE			DOUBLE NYLON BRAID			DACRON DOUBLE BRAID		
DIA.	CIRC.	NET WT. 100'	FT. PER LB.	BREAKING STRENGTH	NET WT. 100'	FT. PER LB.	BREAKING STRENGTH	NET WT. 100'	FT. PER LB.	BREAKING STRENGTH	NET WT. 100'	FT. PER LB.	BREAKING STRENGTH	NET WT. 100'	FT. PER LB.	BREAKING STRENGTH	NET WT. 100'	FT. PER LB.	BREAKING STRENGTH
¼	¾	1.96	51	600	1.5	66.6	1,700	2.1	47.5	1,700	1.24	80	1,250	1.66	60.3	2,100	1.7	60.2	1,700
⅜	1⅛	4.02	25	1,350	3.6	28	3,650	4.7	21.3	3,500	2.9	34.5	2,600	3.33	30	4,200	3.5	28.5	3,500
½	1½	7.35	13.6	2,650	6.6	15	6,650	8.2	12.2	6,100	4.9	20.4	4,150	6.67	14.9	7,500	6.8	15	6,800
¾	2¼	16.3	6.1	5,400	14.5	6.9	14,600	17.9	5.6	13,200	11.1	9	7,900	15.0	6.7	17,000	15	6.7	15,000
1	3	26.5	3.77	9,000	26	3.84	25,000	30.4	3.3	22,000	18.6	5.4	13,000	25.0	4	28,500	28	3.6	28,000

Table 11.8
Weight and Strength of Wire Rope (Black)

SIZE CIRCUMFERENCE	FLEXIBLE STEEL WIRE ROPE 6 STRANDS, EACH 12 WIRES		DIAMETER OF BARREL OR SHEAVE AROUND WHICH IT MAY BE AT A SLOW SPEED WORKED	EXTRA FLEXIBLE STEEL WIRE ROPE 6 STRANDS, EACH 24 WIRES		SPECIAL EXTRA-FLEXIBLE STEEL WIRE ROPE 6 STRANDS, EACH 37 WIRES		BULLIVANT'S SPECIAL MAKE	SIZE CIRCUMFERENCE
	WEIGHT PER FATHOM APPROX.	GUARANTEED BREAKING STRAIN		WEIGHT PER FATHOM APPROX.	GUARANTEED BREAKING STRAIN	WEIGHT PER FATHOM APPROX.	GUARANTEED BREAKING STRAIN	GUARANTEED BREAKING STRAIN	
INCHES	POUNDS	TONS	INCHES	POUNDS	TONS	POUNDS	TONS	TONS	INCHES
1	.63	1.75	6	.88	2.95	1.0	—	—	1
1-1/4	1.06	2.5	7-1/2	1.31	4.45	1.56	—	—	1-1/4
1-1/2	1.44	4.0	9	1.88	6.7	2.0	7.25	—	1-1/2
1-3/4	2.0	5.5	10-1/2	2.5	8.75	2.88	10.0	—	1-3/4

2	2.44	7.0	12	3.5	11.85	4.0	13.0	—	2
2-1/4	3.37	9.0	13-1/2	4.5	14.6	4.88	15.75	—	2-1/4
2-1/2	4.19	12.0	15	5.44	18.55	5.88	19.75	—	2-1/2
2-3/4	5.25	15.0	16-1/2	6.25	21.95	7.0	24.0	—	2-3/4
3	6.25	18.0	18	7.63	25.7	8.25	29.0	—	3
3-1/4	7.06	22.0	19-1/2	9.37	30.8	10.38	33.5	—	3-1/4
3-1/2	8.25	26.0	21	10.75	35.2	11.5	38.5	—	3-1/2
3-3/4	9.87	29.0	22-1/2	12.19	41.1	13.38	44.5	—	3-3/4
4	11.25	33.0	24	13.62	46.3	15.25	51.0	—	4
4-1/4	12.35	36.0	25-1/2	15.69	52.9	17.12	58.0	—	4-1/4
4-1/2	13.44	39.0	27	17.75	58.6	19.0	63.5	—	4-1/2
4-3/4	—	—	—	19.98	66.4	21.69	71.25	—	4-3/4
5	—	—	—	22.5	74.2	24.38	79.25	—	5
5-1/4	—	—	—	23.25	82.88	27.69	87.75	—	5-1/4
5-1/2	—	—	—	24.5	91.55	31.0	96.75	—	5-1/2
5-3/4	—	—	—	—	—	33.75	103.75	—	5-3/4
6	—	—	—	—	—	36.5	113.75	—	6
6-1/2	—	—	—	—	—	42.5	132.0	—	6-1/2
7	—	—	—	—	—	48.5	154.0	—	7
7-1/2	—	—	—	—	—	55.0	178.5	—	7-1/2
8	—	—	—	—	—	63.0	198.0	202	8
9	—	—	—	—	—	79.0	250.0	257	9
10	—	—	—	—	—	98.5	305.0	318	10
11	—	—	—	—	—	120.0	—	381	11
12	—	—	—	—	—	142.0	—	455	12

Table 11.10

Rope and Fiber Comparison Chart

	MANILA	NYLON	DACRON	POLYOLEFINS
Relative Strength	1	4	3	2
Relative Weight	3	2	4	1
Elongation	1	4	2	3
Relative Resistance to Impact or Shock Loads	1	4	2	3
Mildew and Rot Resistance	Poor	Excellent	Excellent	Excellent
Acid Resistance	Poor	Fair	Fair	Excellent
Alkali Resistance	Poor	Excellent	Excellent	Excellent
Sunlight Resistance	Fair	Fair	Good	Fair
Organic Solvent Resistance	Good	Good	Good	Fair
Melting Point	380° (Burns)	410°F.	410°F.	About 300°F.
Floatability	Only when new	None	None	Indefinite
*Relative Abrasion Resistance	2	3	4	1

(*Depends on many factors—whether wet or dry, etc.)

Key to Ratings: 1 Lowest—4 Highest

Table 11.11

Recommended Rope for Various Uses

	TIE-UP OR MOORING LINES	ANCHOR ROPES OR MOORING PENNANTS	SHEETS AND HALYARDS	FLAG HALYARDS	SEIZING AND WHIPPING	BOLT ROPE SYNTHETIC SAILS	TOWING	WATER SKIING
Nylon	●	●					●	
Dacron	●		●	●		●		
Polyolefin	●						●	●
Braided Dacron			●	●				
Braided Nylon	●	●	●	●	●		●	
Wire (Stainless)		Pennants						
Braided Cotton				●	●			

Table 11.12

Weight and Strength of Metals

METAL	SPECIFIC GRAVITY	POUND IN A CUBIC FOOT	TEARING FORCE	CRUSHING FORCE	MODULUS OF ELASTICITY
			POUNDS ON SQUARE INCH	POUNDS ON SQUARE INCH	POUNDS ON SQUARE INCH
Aluminum, cast	2.560	160.0	—	—	—
Aluminum, sheet	2.670	166.9	—	—	—
Brass, cast	8.396	524.8	18,000	10,300	9,170,000
Brass, sheet	8.525	532.8	31,360	—	—
Brass, wire	8.544	533.0	49,000	—	14,230,000
Bronze	8.222	513.4	—	—	—
Copper, bolts	8.850	531.3	36,000	—	—
Copper, cast	8.607	537.9	19,000	—	—
Copper, sheet	8.785	549.1	30,000	—	—
Copper, wire	8.878	548.6	60,000	—	—
Iron, cast, average	7.125	445.3	16,500	112,000	17,000,000
Iron, wrought, average	7.680	480.0	60,000	36,000	28,000,000
Lead, cast	11.352	709.5	1,792	6,900	—
Lead, sheet	11.400	712.8	3,328	—	720,000
Nickel, cast	7.807	487.9	—	—	—
Steel, hard	7.818	488.6	103,000	—	42,000,000
Steel, soft	7.834	489.6	121,700	—	29,000,000
Zinc, cast	7.028	439.3	8,500	—	13,500,000
Zinc, sheet	7.291	455.7	7,111	—	12,650,000

Table 11.13

Stainless Steel, Monel, and Copper-Nickel in Marine Use

MATERIAL	APPLICATION	YIELD STRENGTH	TENSILE STRENGTH	ELONGATION % IN 2 INCHES
302 S.S.	rails, trim, cable, hardware,	40 KSI	90 KSI	50
304 S.S.	galley equipment	42 KSI	84 KSI	55
305 S.S.	bolts, nuts, screws, fasteners	35 KSI	85 KSI	50
316 S.S.	general use, preferred choice in salt spray	42 KSI	84 KSI	50
316L S.S.	preferred choice for welding	34 KSI	81 KSI	50
17-4 PH S.S.	propeller shafts	175 KSI	205 KSI	15
Monel Alloy 400	pump parts, water boxes, valves, tubing, fasteners	35 KSI	80 KSI	45
Monel Alloy K-500	valves, pump shafts, high-strength applications	130 KSI	160 KSI	22
70/30 Copper-Nickel	pipe, tubing, water boxes, etc.	25 KSI	60 KSI	45
90/10 Copper-Nickel	pipe, tubing, water boxes, etc.	16 KSI	44 KSI	42

Table 11.14

Weight and Strength of Timber

NAME	SPECIFIC GRAVITY	POUNDS IN CUBIC FEET	TEARING FORCE POUNDS ON SQUARE INCH	CRUSHING FORCE POUNDS ON SQUARE INCH	BREAKING FORCE POUNDS ON SQUARE INCH	MODULUS OF ELASTICITY POUNDS ON SQUARE INCH
Acacia	.710	44.4	16,000	—	—	—
Alder	.555	34.6	14,186	6,895	9,540	1,087,000
Apple	.793	49.5	19,500	6,499	—	—
Ash	.753	47.0	17,000	9,000	12,200	1,645,000
Beech	.700	43.8	11,500	9,363	9,336	1,354,000
Birch	.750	46.9	15,000	6,402	11,671	1,645,000
Box	1.000	62.5	20,000	10,299	—	—
Cedar	.486	30.8	11,400	5,800	7,420	486,000
Chestnut	.535	33.4	13,300	—	10,656	1,137,000
Cypress	.655	41.0	6,000	—	—	—
Ebony	1.279	79.4	—	19,000	13,600	1,300,000
Elder	.695	43.4	10,230	8,467	—	—
Elm	.544	33.8	13,489	10,331	6,078	700,000
Fir, larch	.496	31.0	10,220	5,568	5,943	1,363,000
Fir, pitch-pine	.660	41.2	7,818	—	9,792	1,226,000
Fir, red pine	.577	36.1	14,300	5,375	8,844	1,458,000
Fir, spruce	.512	32.0	10,100	6,500	12,346	1,804,000
Fir, yellow pine	.461	28.8	—	5,445	—	1,600,000

Greenheart	1.001	62.5	—	—	16,654	2,656,000
Hawthorn	.910	56.8	10,500	—	—	—
Hazel	.860	53.7	18,000	4,600	—	—
Hornbeam	.760	47.4	20,240	7,289	—	—
Laburnum	.920	57.4	10,500	—	—	—
Lancewood	.675	42.1	—	6,614	17,354	812,000
Lignum-vitae	1.333	83.2	11,800	9,921	11,400	558,000
Lime	.760	47.4	23,500	—	11,202	1,152,000
Mahogany, Australian	.952	59.4	—	9,921	20,238	1,157,000
Mahogany, Honduras	.560	35.0	—	—	11,475	1,593,000
Mahogany, Spanish	.853	53.2	21,800	8,198	7,560	1,255,000
Oak, British	.934	58.3	10,000	10,055	10,032	1,451,000
Oak, Dantzic	.756	47.2	12,780	7,723	8,742	1,191,000
Oak, red	.872	64.4	10,253	5,987	10,596	2,149,000
Oak, Riga	.688	43.0	—	—	12,888	1,610,000
Poplar	.511	31.9	7,200	5,124	10,260	1,134,000
Sycamore	.590	36.8	13,000	—	9,630	1,036,000
Teak, African	.983	61.3	21,000	9,320	14,976 ·	2,305,000
Teak, Indian	.880	55.0	15,000	—	14,600	2,800,000
Walnut	.671	41.8	8,130	6,645	8,000	—
Willow	.405	25.3	—	—	6,570	—
Yew	.807	50.3	8,000	—	—	—

Table 11.15

GALVANIC SERIES OF METALS IN SEA WATER

ANODIC
OR LEAST NOBLE
— ACTIVE

CATHODIC
OR MOST NOBLE
— PASSIVE

Magnesium and magnesium alloys
CB75 aluminum anode alloy
Zinc
B605 aluminum anode alloy
Galvanized steel or galvanized wrought iron
Aluminum 7072 (cladding alloy)
Aluminum 5456, 5086, 5052
Aluminum 3003, 1100, 6061, 356
Cadmium
2117 aluminum rivet alloy
Mild steel
Wrought iron
Cast Iron
Ni-Resist
13% chromium stainless steel, type 410 (active)
50-50 lead tin solder
18-8 stainless steel, type 304 (active)
18-8 3% NO stainless steel, type 316 (active)
Lead
Tin
Muntz metal
Manganese bronze
Naval brass (60% copper—39% zinc)
Nickel (active)
78% Ni.-13.5% Cr.-6% Fe. (Inconel) (Active)
Yellow brass (65% copper—35% zinc)
Admiralty brass
Aluminum bronze
Red brass (85% copper—15% zinc)
Copper
Silicon bronze
  5% Zn.—20% Ni.—75% Cu.
90% Cu.—10% Ni.
70% Cu.—30% Ni.
88% Cu.— 2% Zn.—10% Sn. (composition G-bronze)
88% Cu.— 3% Zn.—6.5% Sn.—1.5% Pb
                              (composition M-bronze)
Nickel (passive)
78% Ni.—13.5% Cr.—6% Fe. (Inconel) (Passive)
70% Ni.—30% Cu.
18-8 stainless steel type 304 (passive)
18-8 3% Mo. stainless steel, type 316 (passive)
Hastelloy C
Titanium
Platinum

Table 11.16

WEIGHT OF WATER

Fresh Water

A cubic foot=.0312 ton=62.39 lb.=998.18 avd. oz.=7.481 gal.
A cubic inch=.0362 lb.=.5776 avd. oz.=.0043 gal.
A gallon=.00417 ton=8.340 lb.=133.44 avd. oz.=.1336 cu. ft.
A ton=32.054 cu. ft.=2000 lb.=239.79 gal.
Weight of fresh water=weight of salt water × .9740.

Salt Water

A cubic foot=.0320 ton=64.05 lb.=1024.80 avd. oz.=7.481 gal.
A cubic inch=.0371 lb.=.5930 avd. oz.=.0043 gal.
A gallon=.00428 ton=8.561 lb.=136.97 avd. oz.=.1336 cu. ft.
A ton=31.225 cu. ft.=2000 lb.=233.59 gal.

Table 11.17
WEIGHT OF LIQUID FUELS

Fuel	Average Pounds Per Gallon
Diesel fuel	7.1
Gasoline	6.0

Table 11.18

Velocity of Sound

In miles for intervals from one to twenty
seconds, at average summer temperature

INTERVAL, SECONDS	DISTANCE, MILES	INTERVALS, SECONDS	DISTANCE, MILES
1	.21	11	2.33
2	.42	12	2.54
3	.63	13	2.75
4	.85	14	2.96
5	1.06	15	3.18
6	1.27	16	3.40
7	1.48	17	3.61
8	1.70	18	3.82
9	1.91	19	4.03
10	2.12	20	4.24

Table 11.19

Visibility at Sea

Approximate distance of sea horizon from height
above sea level

HEIGHT IN FEET	DISTANCE, NAUTICAL MILES	HEIGHT IN FEET	DISTANCE, NAUTICAL MILES
4	2.3	100	11.5
10	3.6	120	12.6
15	4.4	140	13.6
20	5.1	150	14.1
30	6.3	200	16.25
40	7.25	250	18.2
50	8.1	300	19.9
60	8.9	350	21.5
70	9.6	400	23.0
80	10.3	450	24.4
90	10.9	500	25.7

Table 11.20

Metric Conversions

1 mile	1.609 km	1 km	0.621 miles
1 nautical mile	1.852 km	1 m	1.094 yards/3.281 feet
1 yard	0.914 m	1 cm	0.394 inches
1 foot	0.305 m	1 cm²	0.155 sq. in.
1 inch	25.4 mm	1 m²	10.76 sq. ft.
1 square inch	6.452 cm²	1 cm³	0.061 cu. in.
1 square foot	0.836 m²	1 m³	35.315 cu. ft.
1 cubic inch	16.39 cm³	1 m³	1.307 cu.yd.
1 cubic foot	0.283 m³	1 liter	0.264 gallons
1 gallon (U.S.)	3.785 liters	1 liter	2.119 pints
1 pint (U.S.)	0.472 liters	1 kg	35.27 ounces
1 ounce	28.35 grams	1 kg	2.205 pounds
1 pound	0.454 kg	1 kgm	7.233 lb. ft.
1 pound foot	0.138 kgm	1 km/hour	0.621 mph
1 mile per hour	1.609 km/hour	10 liters/100 km	0.042 gpm
1 gallon per mile	235.2 liters/100 km		

Table 11.21

THE DECIMAL EQUIVALENTS OF THE DIVISIONS OF THE FOOT

In.	0	1/16	1/8	3/16	1/4	5/16	3/8	7/16	1/2	9/16	5/8	11/16	3/4	13/16	7/8	15/16
0		.0052	.0104	.0156	.0208	.0260	.0313	.0365	.0417	.0469	.0521	.0573	.0625	.0677	.0729	.0781
1	.0833	.0885	.0937	.0990	.1042	.1094	.1146	.1198	.1250	.1302	.1354	.1406	.1458	.1510	.1563	.1615
2	.1667	.1719	.1771	.1825	.1875	.1927	.1979	.2031	.2083	.2135	.2188	.2240	.2292	.2344	.2396	.2448
3	.2500	.2552	.2604	.2656	.2708	.2760	.2813	.2865	.2917	.2969	.3021	.3073	.3125	.3177	.3229	.3281
4	.3333	.3385	.3437	.3490	.3542	.3594	.3646	.3698	.3750	.3802	.3854	.3906	.3958	.4010	.4063	.4115
5	.4167	.4219	.4271	.4323	.4375	.4427	.4479	.4531	.4583	.4635	.4688	.4740	.4792	.4844	.4896	.4948
6	.5000	.5052	.5104	.5156	.5208	.5260	.5313	.5365	.5417	.5469	.5521	.5573	.5625	.5677	.5729	.5781
7	.5833	.5885	.5937	.5990	.6052	.6094	.6146	.6198	.6250	.6302	.6354	.6406	.6458	.6510	.6563	.6615
8	.6667	.6719	.6771	.6823	.6875	.6927	.6979	.7031	.7083	.7135	.7187	.7240	.7292	.7344	.7396	.7448
9	.7500	.7552	.7604	.7656	.7708	.7760	.7813	.7865	.7917	.7969	.8021	.8073	.8125	.8177	.8229	.8281
10	.8333	.8385	.8437	.8490	.8542	.8594	.8646	.8698	.8750	.8802	.8854	.8906	.8958	.9010	.9063	.9115
11	.9167	.9219	.9271	.9323	.9375	.9427	.9479	.9531	.9583	.9635	.9688	.9740	.9792	.9844	.9896	.9948

Table 11.22

Technical Values and Formulas

1 horsepower = 33,000 foot pounds per minute.

1 atmosphere (technical expression for pressure) = 14.223 lb./sq. in. = 1 kg/cm^2 = water column of 10 meters.

The circumference of a circle = diameter × 3.1416.

The diameter of a circle = circumference × 0.3183.

The area of a circle = radius × radius × 3.1416 (πr^2).

The area of a cylinder = circumference × height + end areas as determined above.

The area of an ellipse = $\dfrac{\text{largest length} \times \text{largest width}}{2}$ × 3.1416

The area of a parallelogram = base × vertical height.

The area of a parallel trapezoid = half the total length of the parallel sides × vertical height.

The volume of a sphere = diameter × diameter × diameter × 0.5236 (or $\dfrac{4\pi r^3}{3}$)

The area of a sphere = diameter × diameter × 3.1416 (or $4\pi r^2$).

The area of a triangle = base × vertical height divided by two.

The volume of a cube = base × side × side. (Also applies to a right-angled parallelepiped.

The volume of a pyramid = side × height divided by three.

The volume of a cone = radius × radius × height × 3.1416 divided by three.

TABLES

Table 11.23

Astronomical Distances

---

1 light-second = 186,000 miles.

1 light-minute = 11 million miles.

1 light-year = 5.88 × 10^{12} miles.

1 parsec = 3.26 light-years.

The distance from the earth to the nearest solar system = 4.3 light-years.

The distance of the sun from the earth = 8.3 light-minutes = approximately 93 million miles = 108 sun diameters.

The distance of the moon from the earth = 1.25 light-seconds = approximately 240,000 miles.

The diameter of the earth = 7,928 miles.

The diameter of the sun = 864,000 miles.

The diameter of the moon = 2158 miles.

The volume of the earth = approximately 259 × 10^9 miles.

The area of the earth = 197 million square miles.

Land area of earth = 29 percent of total area.

Sea area of earth = 71 percent of total area.

The mass of the earth = 6.6 × 10^{21} tons.

The average density of the earth = 5.52.

The mass of the sun = approximately 333,000 times that of the earth.

The mass of the moon = 1/81 of that of the earth.

12.

MAINTENANCE

Some skippers find that half the fun of boating is the work they put into it. Whether it's cleaning, painting, or engine adjustments, they take pride in their ability to do the job; they enjoy using their hands; they have confidence in the results of their efforts.

Whether you find it fun or not, maintenance is as much a part of boat ownership as is the use of the boat. Whether for spring fitting out, or for upkeep of a vessel that's in use all year long, there are jobs that should be part of your yachting routine.

Here is the basic information you need on cleaning and painting, engine maintenance, care of electrical systems, plumbing, trailers, and tool lists. For your convenience, maintenance procedures are presented in check-list form whenever possible.

TOOLS FOR TUNING AND SPRUCING UP

Basic Ashore-and-Afloat Tool Kit

Hammer
Pliers
Screw Driver
Drill and Bits
Knife
Chisel
Adjustable Wrench

Maintenance Tools

Basic Ashore-and-Afloat Kit plus:
Cross-cut Saw
Hack Saw
*Brace with bits up to 1
inch in diameter*
*Set of Screwdrivers with
insulated handles,
large models with square
shafts*
½-inch and 1-inch Chisels
Oval Rasp
Assorted Files
*Set of Open-End
Wrenches*
*Adjustable Plumber's
Wrench*
*Needle and Snub-Nose
Pliers*
Metal Snips
Plane
Plug Cutter
Vise-Grip Pliers
*Yankee Screwdriver with
regular and Phillips head
bits*
Plus your own favorites

Power Tools

Paint-Remover Heaters
Shop Vacuum Cleaners
Soldering Guns and Irons
*Disc, Belt, and Orbital
Sanders*
Circular and Saber Saws
*Hand Drills—with
accessories such as router
and expansion bits,*
*screwdriver, angle and
speed-reduction heads with
slip clutch, drill press,
oversize chucks and bits,
water pump*

Non-Tools for Your Tool Box

Oil can
Fid
Whetstone
Tarpaulin
Magnet
Flashlight
Tape
Whipping Thread
Rags
Plastic Drop Cloth
Monel Wire
Rigger's Apron
Roll of Paper Towel
*Staple Gun and Monel
Staples*
Can of Silicone Lubricant
*Can of Bedding and
Sealing Compound*
Epoxy Putty and Glue
Marline
*Stainless-Steel Cotter
Rings and Pins*
*Stainless Shackles and
Hose Clamps*
*Trouble Lamp and
Extension Cord*
*Current Checker and
Continuity Tester*
Pencils
Pad
Tape Measure

CLUES TO SHIPSHAPE CLEANUP

Basic Cleanup Kit

- Fifty feet of hose
- Soap and scouring cleanser
- Rust remover and old rags
- Large sponge and long-handled mop
- Bilge-cleaner compound
- Metal polish and wax
- Scouring pads, steel or bronze wool
- Wet or dry sandpaper
- Rubber gloves
- Small selected kit of these to also keep aboard

Topsides

With all covers and bracing removed, first hose down to wash off all traces of salt, dust, loose grime. Scrub with a trisodium phosphate-based cleaner, available from paint, hardware, and building-supply outlets. Stubborn spots can be treated with scouring powder, though this may remove gloss. Areas dulled by scouring are buffed to renew gloss.

Bottom

Growth, scum, and waterline weeds along the boot topping that were not removed when the boat was hauled will have hardened and are twice as hard to get off. Marine stores locally may stock compounds particularly suitable for loosening the barnacles or pollutants that attack boats secured afloat all season. As with bottom paints, your most effective mix may vary from harbor to harbor.

- Hose bottom to wash off or soften any growths.
- Attack barnacles with a metal scraper.

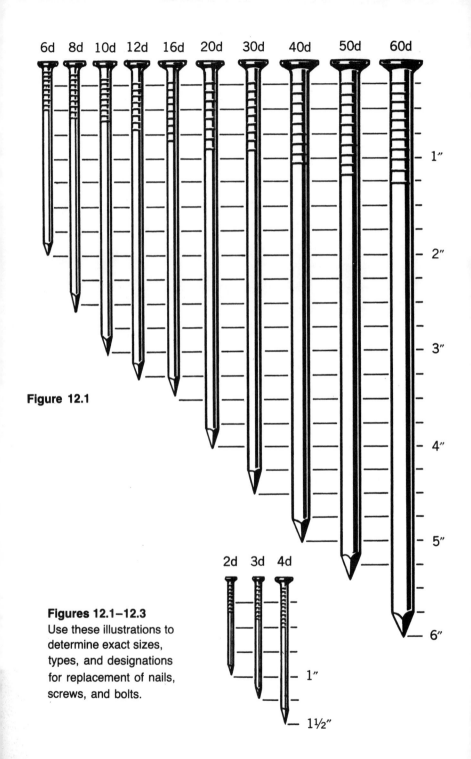

6d 8d 10d 12d 16d 20d 30d 40d 50d 60d

1"

2"

3"

Figure 12.1

4"

5"

2d 3d 4d

Figures 12.1–12.3
Use these illustrations to
determine exact sizes,
types, and designations
for replacement of nails,
screws, and bolts.

1"

1½"

6"

- Use power sander on stubborn spots.
- Keep wetting bottom to avoid breathing toxic dust if anti-fouling paint has been used.
- Note seams or gouges that will require sealant or pointing up before painting.
- Recall and note down, if possible, brand of bottom paint previously used. Application of new type may not bond to old formulation. If in doubt, cleaning down to bare hull may be necessary.

Bilge

Hose out and pump out bilges, checking freedom of limber holes and pumps at same time. Rewash with bilge-cleaner compound or soap concentrate.

If boat normally has some rain water, spray, or leakage collecting in the bilge, consider putting in one of the bilge-cleaner additives that slosh around and maintain clean condition while boat is under way.

Engines

Exterior: Use a marine or automotive cleaner that can degrease and remove any caked dirt from engine so that condition of paint and excessive rusting, chafing hoses, or loose control linkage can be observed.

Interior: Run automotive solvent through carburetor to dissolve any gum formation. Add water inhibitor to gas tank as well.

Lines

Give all cordage freshwater washing while examining for chafes. Switch end for end to equalize wear and replace if in doubt.

Spot check by untwisting lay to examine for interior sand that could be chafing the line. Do not use pressure hose in washing since this also might force in cutting grit.

Interiors

- Wash down bulkheads with soap and water or a cleaner such as Nautabrite.

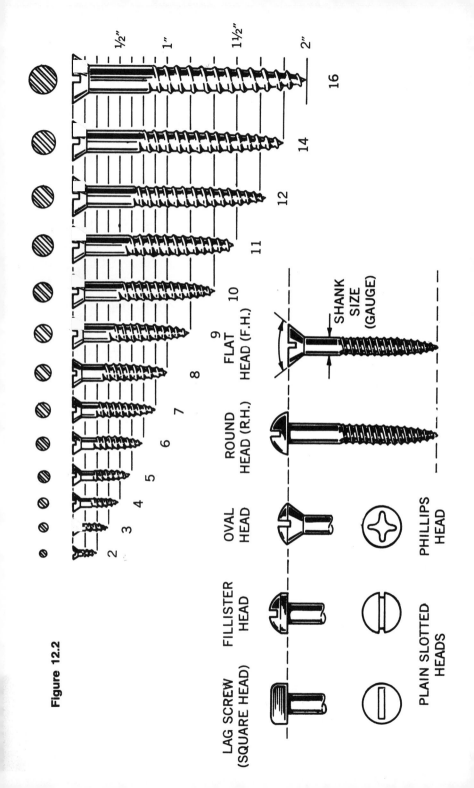

Figure 12.2

LAG SCREW (SQUARE HEAD) FILLISTER HEAD OVAL HEAD ROUND HEAD (R.H.) FLAT HEAD (F.H.)

PLAIN SLOTTED HEADS PHILLIPS HEAD

SHANK SIZE (GAUGE)

2 3 4 5 6 7 8 9 10 11 12 14 16

½" 1" 1½" 2"

- Treat forepeak and cuddy corners that get little ventilation with antidryrot compounds aboard wood boats.

- After washing and airing, use one of the fungus-control treatments like MDR Mildew & Anti-Rot Spray to inhibit must and mold in cabinets and lockers.

Metals

Aluminum: Remove oil and grease with cleaning fluid. A cleaner-wax-polish combination will treat bare aluminum.

For painted aluminum, use mild soap and water or auto-body paint polish-cleaner.

Brass, Bronze, Chrome: Regular metal cleaners and polishes will remove tarnish. Use a heavy-duty compound like ABC Metal Cleanser for tougher corrosion. Spray coatings or waxes will help metals keep shine.

Stainless, Iron, Monel: Scouring pads and powder can remove surface rust. Use products like Rust-Away or Naval Jelly for extensive rust. Polish with wire brush. Rinse down.

Plastics

Fiberglass, Formica, Royalite: Various products are now sold specifically for fiberglass cleaning, or use mild detergent and water.

Gel coat stains can be scoured, though buffing afterward with a product like DuPont White Compound may be necessary to renew gloss plus matching color. Wax for fiberglass can protect surface.

Vinyl: A detergent will remove dirt, and vinyl paint can renew appearance.

Plexiglas: Mild soap and water but no scouring powder. Salt crystals can be washed off with a compound like Travaco's Sea-2 Liquid Concentrate. It also works as wash fluid with windshield wipers.

Scratches can be removed with special Plexiglas buffing compounds.

PVC (Polyvinyl Chloride): Wood alcohol can be used sparingly, but will soften surface if overdone.

Sails

Coastal sailors should wash out salt when sailboat is hauled. Mild

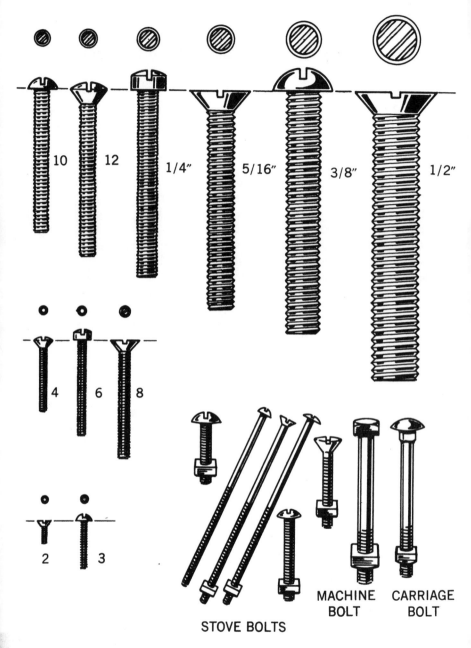

10   12   1/4"   5/16"   3/8"   1/2"

4   6   8

2   3

STOVE BOLTS   MACHINE BOLT   CARRIAGE BOLT

Figure 12.3

sudsing with soap (no detergents) plus freshwater rinse is best spring treatment.

Wood

Painted Surfaces: Washing down with cleaning fluid like Soilax is sufficient. For cabinets, mix in antifungus additive.

Varnished Surfaces: Wash down, though breaks in varnish surface of mahogany may have allowed discoloration to start that will require bleaching before revarnishing.

Teak: Use one of special teak cleaners. Then restore color with compound like Kuhls Teak Oil.

MARINE PAINTS

Painting Principles

- Read the instructions on the can.
- Clean and prepare surface carefully.
- Remove loose flakes of previous coat, and all of it if in doubt about its compatibility with new paint.
- Use same brands, if possible, for each coat.
- Observe specified temperature and humidity requirements.
- Note if boat should be launched while bottom paint is still wet.
- Clean brushes before they dry.

Aluminum

Your boatbuilder can probably recommend the proper paints and tell you which brands were previously used. Vinyl-based paints are usually satisfactory. Prepare previously unpainted aluminum by washing with an etching cleaner. Then rinse and let dry before applying vinyl-base primer.

Before applying antifouling bottom paint, start with vinyl primer-undercoater. Final coats should be vinyl base with Tributyl-Tin Oxide as the active toxic agent and called TBTO or Bio-Met. Use of copper or red lead paints is not recommended.

Canvas

Paint coats year after year on canvas decks can build up layers that accelerate cracking. One answer is to use low-cost house paint that chalks and wears off during the season. Synthetic resin paints are also suitable, and sand or grit compound can be added to final coat for nonskid surface.

Treat flexible canvas tops and covers with primer and one of the new liquid vinyl coatings.

Engines

Paints that resist high heat are used, and fire-retardant paints or additives can be employed to paint engine compartment.

Fiberglass

Unpainted surface should first be washed with solvent to remove any wax or mold-release substance. Cracks, dents, or orange-peel hairlines can be filled with surfacing compound recommended by paint manufacturer. For use on fiberglass, Alkyd, Alkyd Acrilic, Alkyd Polyurethane, Polyurethane, Polyester Silicone, Epoxy, and Vinyl paints are all satisfactory.

Tinted epoxy and polyester resins are now available with pigments to match breaks in the gel coat or areas that have weathered and changed color so that molded-in hue can be matched.

Boats that are hauled out after every use may need no bottom paint, but could use a hard gloss containing no antifouling properties for speed.

For antifouling treatment, no primer may be needed after the solvent wash to remove any wax. Copper, lead, or tin-bearing antifouling paints may be used with any base except the alkyds.

Lower Drive Units

Stern drive and outboard motor shafts that stick down into the water may be treated with anticorrosive enamels and, in some cases, antifouling compounds. Engine builders and paint manufacturers can make recommendations. Original colors can usually be matched.

Steel

Once the metal has been properly prepared, paints used on wood, fiberglass, or aluminum, as well as those with special rust inhibitors, can be employed. First sand blast or use an etching-type wash. Prime with zinc chromate, red lead, or other rust inhibitor.

Before applying antifouling on the bottom, two coats of barrier nonmetallic paint should go over the primer beneath the final antifouling. Galvanic corrosion could result if copper-bearing paint came in contact with the steel. Some paint producers provide a system of compatible paints for steel hull use.

Vinyl

Cushions, seat covers, and curtains, as well as tops and cockpit covers of vinyl, can be renewed with liquid vinyl coatings available in many colors.

Wood

Suitable for application on wood are Alkyd, Alkyd Acrilic, Alkyd Polyurethane, Polyurethane, Polyester Silicone, Epoxy, Latex Liquid Rubber, and Vinyl. Success, however, will depend on how well the wood surface has been cleaned, sanded, and prepared. Priming and fillers should usually be of the nonoily type and perferably of the same brand as the final paint. A wood bottom may be treated with any of the antifouling paints or with a hard nontoxic racing surface if the boat will not be left in the water.

Varnishes, whether tung oil and phenolic resin types or the newer synthetics and two-part epoxy systems, require careful application. Follow instructions as to surface sanding and bleaching if brightwork has weathered. Then, on a nearly windless day with the right temperature, apply the needed number of coats.

HOW MUCH PAINT DO YOU NEED?

From the Woolsey booklet *How to Paint Your Boat,* copyright 1967 by Woolsey Marine Industries, Inc. Reprinted by permission.

In estimating the amount of material needed for a specific job, you may assume that one gallon of paint or enamel will cover 500 square feet for one coat on the average painted surface. Over new wood, use the figure of 325 square feet per gallon. One gallon of varnish will cover 750 square feet average on recoat work, and 500 square feet on new wood. Paint and varnish remover may take several applications and consequently can be expected to soften only about 200 to 250 square feet per gallon.

Some Useful Formulas

Here are some formulas based on practical experience. They should help you in determining how much paint you will need. The results are stated in gallons.

Spars (Varnished)

Multiply the greatest diameter (in feet) by the length (in feet) and multiply the result by 2.5. For new wood, divide the result by 500 and for previously finished wood divide by 750 to obtain the gallonage required.

For example, suppose you have a new spar 8″ in diameter and 40′ long. Then $\frac{8/12 \times 40 \times 2.5}{500} = \frac{67}{500}$ or approximately ⅛ gallon (1 pint) for the priming coat. For refinishing work, a pint is enough for about 1½ coats. To determine the requirements for painted spars, change the coverage factor to 325 for new work and to 500 for previously painted wood.

Cabins or Deck Houses. Multiply the height of the deck house (in feet) by the girth (in feet). Deduct the area of any large areas such as windows and doors. If the deck house is to be painted, divide the result by 325 for the priming coat and 500 for each finishing coat. If it is to be varnished, divide by 500 for the first coat and 750 for the following coats.

Figure 12.4	**PAINT LOG for ...** 19___		19___		19___		19___	
Surface	**Color**	**Product Used**	Amount	Cost	Amount	Cost	Amount	Cost
Spars								
Decks								
Brightwork								
Cabins								
Interior								
Topsides								
Boot topping								
Bottom								
Engine								
Dinghy								
Seams								

Decks. Multiply the length of the boat (in feet) by its greatest beam (in feet) and then multiply the result by 0.75. From this deduct the area of cabin houses, hatches, etc. Divide the remainder by 325 to obtain gallons required for priming coat and by 500 for each finishing coat of color.

If the deck is to be coated with Cawspar Varnish, divide the figure by 500 and 750, respectively.

Topsides. Multiply the length over all (in feet) by the greatest freeboard (in feet). Multiply the result by 1.5. Divide by 325 for new work and by 500 for old work to obtain the gallonage.

The Bottom. Multiply the waterline length (in feet) by the draft (in feet). For a keel boat, multiply by 3.5 and for a centerboard boat multiply by 3.0. Divide the result by 300 for priming new work, and by 400 for subsequent coats, to give the required gallonage.

SEALANTS AND BEDDING COMPOUNDS

Spring used to be the time of year when seams were caulked and then the boat launched and watched carefully to see if the seams would swell shut before the boat took on too much water and started to sink. Fortunately, raking out old dried compound and refilling the seams of wooden boats is no longer a major part of fitting-out. But keeping water outside the boat where it belongs is still the job of a variety of sealants.

The old oil-base putty type of seam compounds are still available, but when used in wood-boat seams, the seams should be primed first to prevent absorption of the oil from the compound into the wood so quickly that the caulking promply dries up. Deep seams were first filled with cotton and sometimes packed so tightly by amateurs that fastenings and planking let go as the wood tried to expand once in the water.

Bedding compound used under deck fittings to keep water from leaking through the bolt holes and moisture from starting rot in the wood would also dry out and harden in a year or so. It is still used, however, to bed through-hull fittings below the waterline when a toxic mixture is needed to repel barnacles. But now most bedding and sealing chores are handled by the rubber-type products that keep their elasticity indefinitely, do not dry out or harden, and do not use an oil that keeps paint from bonding. Only in the bilge around the engine, where gasoline and oil can get at them, are the rubber-base types less than ideal.

These new compounds can be divided into polysulfide (Thiokol), polyurethane, and silicone compounds. These synthetic rubbers are available in two-part systems that combine the sealant with a catalyst to cure it, or one-part products that take moisture from the air to cause the curing and are usually slower acting.

All are available in a variety of colors and are suitable for bonding a fitting that is being bolted to the deck, repairing a leak around a windshield gasket, or stopping the dribble of water seeping from a through-hull fitting. Seams, of course, are usually sealed once and for all if the wood is first carefully primed, since the material has great adhesion plus stretch and sheer strength.

Treatment of electrical connections to provide insulation and protection from corrosion is also easy with some of the silicones. GE's new RTV (room temperature vulcanizing) Silicone Rubber Adhesive Sealant can be applied directly to electrical junction-box connections. In its transparent form, terminals and wiring can be seen right through it but are protected from vibration and corrosion. No premixing is required with RTV, and it air cures with minimum shrinkage.

Fortunately, boatbuilders are using these same new sealants in quantity as well so that a new boat is less likely to require much corrective treatment at fitting-out time. But when a new fitting or locker is installed, a through-hull fitting added, or a leak noted around an engine connection, chances are one of the new polysulfide, polyurethane, or silicone compounds, under a variety of trade names, can cure the problem quickly and permanently with the squeeze of a tube. Read the directions on each to make the most suitable choice.

OUTBOARD MOTOR MAINTENANCE

Spark plugs: Replace with fresh, correctly gapped ones.

Ignition wiring: Inspect. Replace tired-looking high-voltage wires. Tighten all connections.

Distributor or magneto cap: Remove, clean, inspect for chips or cracks. Replace unless perfect. Wipe with dielectric moisture-fighting spray.

Distributor or magneto rotor: Remove and inspect for cracks or burning. Replace unless perfect. Wipe with dielectric spray.

Ignition points: Inspect. Replace if pitted. Adjust to specs. Readjust after ten hours of operation.

Ignition timing: Adjust "by the book" after points are set.

Condenser: Check connections and mounting hardware.

Fuel tank: Empty out stale gas. Flush.

Fuel line: Inspect for tightness.

Fuel filter: Drain. Clean. Replace element.

Carburetor: Send it to the shop if it gave trouble last season. Otherwise, tighten hold-down nuts; check control linkages and lubricate them.

Oil cups: Inspect the motor and its accessories, looking for oil cups. Put a few drops of oil in any that are found.

Lower unit: Drain all oil from the lower unit. Refill with fresh lubricant of specified grade and viscosity.

Cooling system: Flush out the cooling system with clean fresh water. Alternately, run the motor in a tank or barrel of fresh water to purge it and allow you to watch the water pump operate.

Propeller: Inspect the propeller critically. If it's nicked or dented, replace it. Keep it for a spare.

Anticorrosion: Install new sacrificial anodes on the lower unit. Sometimes these are combined with a trim tab.

Oil film: Wipe down the entire power head and lower unit with an oily cloth. Alternately, spray with rust-proofing compound.

TABLE 12.1

Inboard Gasoline Engines

Three series of crankcase lubricants are being marketed which are recommended for inboard gasoline engines, Havoline Supreme and Havoline Super Premium motor oils in the wide-range, multi-viscosity grades and Havoline Motor Oils in the single viscosity grades. These series exceed engine manufacturers' requirements and are primarily intended for API Engine Service Classifications SF and SE. Both series provide excellent wear protection, resistance to high temperature oxidative thickening, rust and corrosion protection, and deposit control.

NAME AND MODEL	HAVOLINE SAE GRADE (NORMAL OPERATION)
ALLIS-CHALMERS (All Models)............	30 or 10W-40
ARNOLT Sea Mite (All Models)	30
BARR (All Models)	30
BERKELEY JET DRIVE....................	40
CHRIS CRAFT (All Models)	30 or 10W-40
CHRYSLER (All Models)...................	30 or 10W-40
COMMANDER (All Models)	10W-40 or 20W-50
CRUSADER (All Models)..................	30
DAYTONA (All Models)	20-20W
DEARBORN (All Models) (See Eaton)	
EATON (All Models)......................	30
EVINRUDE (See OMC)	
FEDERAL (All Models)....................	30 or 10W-40
FLAGSHIP (All Models)	30 or 40
GRAYMARINE	
1964 Fireball V-8, 1965 Fireball V8CH-280 .	20-20W
All V-8 Models from 1971 to date..........	30 or 10W-40
All 6 cyl. Models from 1971 to date	30 or 10W-40
All flat head 4 and 6 cyl..................	30
HOLMAN AND MOODY (All Models)	10W-40
INTERNATIONAL HARVESTER (All Models)	
Above 20°F.............................	30
10°F-90°F	20-20W
−10°F-90°F	10W-40

NAME AND MODEL	HAVOLINE SAE GRADE (NORMAL OPERATION)
INTERNATIONAL PALMER (All Models)	30
JOHNSON (See OMC)	
MARINE ENGINE CENTER	
ECON-O-POWER........................	30 or 10W-40
MERCURY MARINE	
Mercruiser Above 50°F..................	40
32°F-50°F....................	30
Below 32°F...................	20-20W
OMC (Outboard Marine)	
2-Cycle stern drive only 1971 and prior	
models.............................	50-1 Outboard and Two-Cycle Engine Oil
4-Cycle stern drive and inboard models,	
1983 and prior.......................	30
ONAN	
MAJ, MCCK, MJC Generator Sets.........	30
PALMER	
PA-220, PA-255.......................	30
PA-350..............................	40
TURBO MARINE (Cummins Northwest Industrial).................................	10W-40
UNIVERSAL	
Atomic Four...........................	30 or 10W-40
V-8 Engines...........................	30
Super Sabre V-6.......................	10W-40
Utility Four Above 90°F.................	40
32°F-90°F...................	30
Below 32°F...................	20-20W
All Others Above 32°F.................	30
Below 32°F...................	20-20W
VOLVO PENTA (All Models)...............	10W-40 or 30
WHITE ENGINES (Hercules) (All Models) ·	30

Table 12.2

Inboard Diesel Engines

Havoline Motor Oils (single-viscosity grades) are intended for API Engine Service Classification CC as well as SF and SE and meet MIL-L-2104B requirements. This series is recommended for marine diesel engines which require a CC or SF/CC lubricant. Ursa Super Plus is a versatile motor oil recommended for most gasoline and diesel engines in all types of service. It is intended for API Service CD, CC, SF and SE, and meets the requirements of MIL- L-2104C, MIL-L-46152, and the obsolete specifications MIL-L-45199B, MIL-L-2104B, and Caterpillar Series 3. It also meets Caterpillar's TO-2 friction specifications and is an approved Allison C-3 fluid. Ursa Oil Extra Duty exceeds the requirements of MIL-L-2104B and is intended for API Services CC, CB and SB.

NAME AND MODEL	TEXACO OIL RECOMMENDED (NORMAL OPERATION)
ALLIS-CHALMERS (All Models)	Ursa Super Plus SAE 30 or Ursa Super Plus SAE 15W-40
BARR (All Models)	Havoline Motor Oil SAE 30
CATERPILLAR	
300, 3300 and 3400 Series. .	Ursa Super Plus SAE 30 or Ursa Super Plus SAE 15W-40
(Preferred for 3200 Series) . .	Ursa Super Plus 15W-40 or Havoline Supreme 10W-30
CRUSADER (All Models except	
9 Liter engine)	Ursa Super Plus SAE 40
(9 Liter Engine)	Ursa Super Plus SAE 30
CUMMINS (All Models)	Ursa Super Plus SAE 15W-40
DAYTONA	Havoline Motor Oil SAE 30
DETROIT DIESEL ALLISON	
(All Models)	Ursa Oil Extra Duty SAE 40 Ursa Super Plus SAE 40
GRAYMARINE (All Models) . . .	Havoline Motor Oil SAE 30
HOLMAN AND MOODY	Ursa Super Plus SAE 30
INTERNATIONAL PALMER	
(All Models)	Ursa Super Plus SAE 40

NAME AND MODEL	TEXACO OIL RECOMMENDED (NORMAL OPERATION)
JOHNSON & TOWERS (See Detroit Diesel Allison)	
LEHMAN ECON-O-POWER	
Naturally Aspirated.........	Havoline Motor Oil
10°F-60°F...............	SAE 20-20W
32°F-90°F...............	SAE 30
Over 90°F..............	SAE 40
Turbocharged Models	Ursa Super Plus
10°F-60°F..............	SAE 20-20W
32°F-90°F..............	SAE 30
Over 90°F..............	SAE 40
ONAN MDJA, MDJB, MDJC, MDJE, MDJF Generator Sets....................	Ursa Super Plus SAE 30
OSCO (All Models)	Havoline Motor Oil SAE 30
PERKINS	
Naturally Aspirated Engines .	Havoline Series
Naturally Aspirated Engines . (High Load Factor, older engines)	Ursa Super Plus
Turbocharged Engines	Ursa Super Plus
30°F and above..........	SAE 20W-50
30°F-81°F...............	SAE 20-20W
0°F and above...........	SAE 10W-30
0°F-45°F	SAE 10W
14°F and above..........	SAE 15W-40
81°F and above..........	SAE 30
PETTER AC1WM Mini Seven and AC2WM Mini Twin	Havoline Supreme SAE 10W-30
UNIVERSAL (All Models)	Ursa Super Plus SAE 30, Ursa Super Plus SAE 15W-40
VOLVO PENTA (All Models) ..	Ursa Super Plus SAE 15W-40, Ursa Super Plus SAE 30

NAME AND MODEL	TEXACO OIL RECOMMENDED (NORMAL OPERATION)
WESTERBEKE	
Model 10Two (3KW); W-13 (4.4KW); W-21(7.7KW); W-27 (11KW); W-33(12.5KW)	
Above 68°F	Havoline Motor Oil SAE 30 or Havoline Supreme SAE 10W-30
41°F-68°F.	Havoline Motor Oil 20-20W or Havoline Supreme SAE 10W-30
Below 41°F.	Havoline Supreme SAE 10W-30
Model W-51(15KW); W-58(20KW); W-70 (25KW); W-100 (32KW); W-80 (30KW); W-120(45KW)	
Above 80°F	Havoline Motor Oil SAE 30
30°F-80°F.	Havoline Motor Oil SAE 20-20W
Below 30°F.	Havoline Motor Oil SAE 10
NOTE: The use of lubricating oils designated for diesel turbo-charge service is prohibited.	
YANMAR	
32°F and above.	Ursa Super Plus SAE 15W-40 or Havoline Super Premium 20W-50
32°F-10°F.	Havoline Supreme SAE 10W-30
WHITE ENGINES	
(Hercules)(All Models)	Ursa Super Plus SAE 30 or Ursa Super Plus SAE 15W-40

Table 12.3

Inboard Reduction and Reverse Gears

Separately Lubricated

A variety of Texaco products is available to meet the recommendations of the individual manufacturers of separately lubricated gears. Outboard Gear Oil EP 90 may be added as makeup to gear cases containing other EP 90 lubricants.

NAME AND MODEL	TEXACO LUBRICANT RECOMMENDED (NORMAL OPERATION)
BARR (See Warner Gear)	
BORG-WARNER (See Warner Gear)	
CAPITOL (All Models).............	Havoline Motor Oil SAE 30
CATERPILLAR	
(3192, 3181, 7200 Series)	Ursa Super Plus SAE 30
CHRIS CRAFT (Hydraulic).........	Texamatic Fluid
CHRYSLER	
Hydraulic pump and	
transmissions	Texamatic Fluid
COMMANDER	
Borg-Warner Transmissions	Texamatic Fluid
CRUSADER	
V-Drive......................	Outboard Gear Oil EP 90
Warner Gear..................	Texamatic Fluid
DAYTONA (See Warner Gear)	
DEARBORN	
Dearborn and Warner Transmissions,	
Paragon V-Drive	Texamatic Fluid
FALK	
MR, MRV, M, MV and MB (Diesel Driven).....................	Meropa 320 or
Inlet oil temp, up to 150°F........	Regal Oil R&O 320
FEDERAL	Texamatic Fluid
FLAGSHIP	Texamatic Fluid

NAME AND MODEL	TEXACO LUBRICANT RECOMMENDED (NORMAL OPERATION)
GRAYMARINE	
Vee-Drive	Thuban 140
INTERNATIONAL PALMER	
XLHS, YCHS	Havoline Motor Oil SAE 30
OXKB (Paragon)	Texamatic Fluid
MARINE ENGINE CENTER	
ECON-O-POWER	Texamatic Fluid
OMC (Outboard Marine)	
Inboard Transmission	Texamatic Fluid
PARAGON POWER	
All Units.....................	Texamatic Fluid or
Mechanical and V-Drive Units....	Ursa Super Plus SAE 30
TWIN DISC	
Models MG-502, MG-506, MG-507, MG-509 MG-510A, MG-512, MG-514, MG-514C, MG-514-M	

Start Up	Steady Operation	
32°F Min	150°F-185°F	Ursa Super Plus SAE 30 or Havoline Motor Oil SAE 30
32°F Min	175°F-210°F	Ursa Super Plus SAE 40 or Havoline Motor Oil SAE 40

Models MG-518, MG-520, MG-521, MG-527, MG-530, MG-530-M, MG-540

Start Up	Steady Operation	
32°F Min	150°F-185°F	Ursa Super Plus SAE 40 or Havoline Motor Oil SAE 40
32°F Min	175°F-210°F	Ursa Super Plus SAE 50 or Havoline Motor Oil SAE 50

NAME AND MODEL	TEXACO LUBRICANT RECOMMENDED
UNIVERSAL	
V-Drive.....................	Havoline Motor Oil SAE 30
Diesel with ZF Trans.	Ursa Super Plus SAE 30
Diesel with Hurth Trans......	Texamatic Fluid
WALTER V-Drive.............	Havoline Motor Oil SAE 30

MAINTENANCE

NAME AND MODEL	TEXACO LUBRICANT RECOMMENDED (NORMAL OPERATION)
WARNER GEAR (Borg-Warner)	
Velvet-Drive (All Models)	Texamatic Fluid
Where transmission input speed does not exceed 3000 rpm	Ursa Super Plus SAE 30 or Havoline Motor Oil SAE 30
NOTE: SAE 40 is acceptable if high operating temperatures are encountered.	
YANMAR	
Model YP/KM	Same oil as engine
Model KBW/KH.	Texamatic Fluid

Table 12.4

Outboard Motors

Use Texaco 50-1 and Two-Cycle Engine Oil with Royal Guard for all engines in which the oil is mixed with the fuel. This product has been engine tested and Certified for Service TC-W and is specifically formulated to meet the requirements of all two-cycle outboard motors and other two-cycle engines. It contains a light petroleum diluent to facilitate mixing. This predilution does not affect amount of oil used to obtain desired fuel/oil ratio. Royal Guard imparts a reddish-purple tint to the gasoline mixture indicating oil has been added. The quantity of oil required is shown in the following table. Make sure that oil and gasoline are thoroughly mixed. The quantity of oil shown below is based on the manufacturers' recommendations for engines which are broken in. Some engine manufacturers specify more oil for break-in and their recommendations should be strictly followed.

NAME AND MODEL	PRODUCT	OUNCES OF OIL PER GALLON OF GASOLINE	PINTS PER 6-GALLON TANK
BEARCAT			
55 and 85 hp (Separately Lubri-cated)	Havoline SAE 40	(Do not mix oil & gasoline)	(Do not mix oil & gasoline)
BRITISH SEAGULL	OBEO	12 (Pre-1979) 5 (1979-81)	(Integral tank)
CHRYSLER			
1966-76 3.5, 3.6 hp			
1966-67 9.2 hp	OBEO	5½	2
All Others	OBEO	2½	1
CLINTON			
2, 3.5, 4hp Models	OBEO	8	3
All Other Models	OBEO	3	1⅛
ELGIN (See Sears, Roebuck)			

NAME AND MODEL	PRODUCT	OUNCES OF OIL PER GALLON OF GASOLINE	PINTS PER 6-GALLON TANK
ESKA			
1980-83 3.5 hp	OBEO	2½	1
1977-83 4 thru 15 hp	OBEO	2½	1
1977-80 1.2, 2.5, 3 hp	OBEO	4	1½
1975-76 3, 4.5, 5.5 hp	OBEO	4	1½
1975-76 9.9, 15 hp	OBEO	2½	1
1974-76 7.5 hp	OBEO	4	1½
1974 3.5, 5, 7 hp	OBEO	4	1½
1974 9.5, 14 hp	OBEO	2½	1
EVINRUDE			
All models	OBEO	2½	1
HONDA			
7.5 and 10 hp (Separately Lubricated)	Havoline SP 10W-30	(Do not mix oil & gasoline)	(Do not mix oil & gasoline)
JOHNSON			
All Models	OBEO	2½	1
McCULLOCH			
1960-62 3.5 hp	OBEO	6½	2½
Model 590/630	OBEO	8	3
All Other Models	OBEO	2½	1
MERCURY			
1962 and earlier	OBEO	5½	2
1963-83	OBEO	2½	1
MONTGOMERY WARD (Sea King)			
1956-63 All Models	OBEO	8	3
1964-69 3.5 hp	OBEO	8	3

NAME AND MODEL	PRODUCT	OUNCES OF OIL PER GALLON OF GASOLINE	PINTS PER 6-GALLON TANK
1964-66 6 and 9 hp	OBEO	8	3
1967-69 6 and 9.2 hp	OBEO	5½	2
1964-69 20 thru 80 hp	OBEO	2½	1
All Others (Water Cooled)	OBEO	2½	1
1980–81 Models (Air Cooled)	OBEO	2½	1
NEPTUNE (Mighty Mite)			
All Models	OBEO	5	2
SEA KING (See Montgomery Ward)			
SEARS, ROEBUCK (ELGIN)			
1982-83 1.75, 3 hp	OBEO	4	1½
1977-83 1.2 hp	OBEO	4	1½
1977-83 5, 7 hp	OBEO	2½	1
1974-83 9.9, 15 hp	OBEO	2½	1
1980-81 3.5 hp	OBEO	2½	1
1977-79 3.5 hp	OBEO	4	1½
1977 4 hp	OBEO	2½	1
1974-76 3 thru 7.5 hp	OBEO	4	1½
1974 10.5 hp	OBEO	2½	1
1973 10.5 hp	OBEO	4	1½
1971-73 3, 3.5, 4, 4.5, 5, 7, 7.5 hp	OBEO	5½	2
1970 3, 3.5 3.6, 4, 5, 7 hp	OBEO	6½	2½

NAME AND MODEL	PRODUCT	OUNCES OF OIL PER GALLON OF GASOLINE	PINTS PER 6-GALLON TANK
SUZUKI			
DT2-DT65,			
DT85TEL (Normal Operation)	OBEO	2½	1
(Break-in)	OBEO	4	1½
DT40 O/I, DT50 O/I, DT60 O/I			
DT75 O/I, DT85 O/I, DT115 O/I			
DT140 O/I			
(O/I Models have oil injection)	OBEO	(Do not mix oil and gasoline	(Do not mix oil and gasoline)
TECUMSEH			
Single cycle, air-cooled			
1977-78 3, 3.5 hp	OBEO	4	1½
1977-81 4-7.5 hp	OBEO	2½	1
1974-76 3-7.5 hp	OBEO	4	1½
Twin cyl. water-cooled			
1974-81 9.5-15.0 hp	OBEO	2½	1
1971-73 Models	OBEO	5½	2
WEST BEND			
1956-65 2 thru 9 hp	OBEO	8	3
1956-64 10 thru 80 hp	OBEO	5½	2
1965 20 thru 80 hp	OBEO	2½	1
WESTERN AUTO (See Wizard)			

NAME AND MODEL	PRODUCT	OUNCES OF OIL PER GALLON OF GASOLINE	PINTS PER 6-GALLON TANK
WIZARD			
1977-81 5, 7.5, 15 hp	OBEO	2½	1
1975-76 4.5, 5.5, 7.5 hp	OBEO	4	1½
1974-76 6, 9, 9.2, 9.9 hp	OBEO	2½	1
1974 3.5, 5, 7, 7.5 hp	OBEO	4	1½
1970-73 5, 7 hp	OBEO	5½	2
1969 5, 7 hp Special	OBEO	8	3
1966-71 3.5 hp	OBEO	8	3
1966-71 6, 9.2, 20 hp	OBEO	2½	1
1965 3.5, 6, 9 hp	OBEO	8	3
1965 20hp	OBEO	2½	1
1963-64 All Models	OBEO	5½	2
YAMAHA			
1968-70 3.5, 5, 7.5 hp	OBEO	6½	2½

OUTBOARD GEAR LUBRICATION

OUTBOARD MOTOR GEARS—Use Texaco Outboard Gear Oil EP 90 for clutch and shift models when an SAE 90 EP gear oil is specified by the manufacturer. Special products are supplied by outboard manufacturers for electric shift models. When an SAE 30 or 40 oil is recommended, use Havoline or Texaco Motor Oil in the prescribed viscosity grade.

Table 12.5

Stern and Outboard Drives

NAME AND MODEL	TEXACO LUBRICANT RECOMMENDED (NORMAL OPERATION)
CHRIS CRAFT	
Volvo 280	Havoline Super Premium 10W-40
CHRYSLER	
Volvo 250 and 270	Havoline Super Premium 10W-40
Model 300	Multigear Lubricant EP 80W-90
COMMANDER	
Volvo 280	Havoline Super Premium 10W-40
EATON	
Powernaut	No Texaco Product
HOLMAN AND MOODY	Havoline Super Premium 10W-40
HONDA	
Transmission Gear Case	Multigear Lubricant EP 80W-90
MARINE DRIVE SYSTEMS	
STERN-POWR Models 60, 80, 81, 82, 83, 91, 101, 103, 105, 107	Multigear Lubricant EP 80W-90
Dana/MDS Models 60, 80, 81, 91	Multigear Lubricant EP 80W-90
Extra Performance Models 84SP, 84SSP, 85SP, 85SSP	Multigear Lubricant EP 80W-90
RANGER Models 66A, 70A	Multigear Lubricant EP 80W-90
DIESELDRIVE, RENAULT, FLAGSHIP, HARMAN, (includes CEDKON and other private label models)	Multigear Lubricant EP 80W-90
MERCURY MARINE* MERCRUISER	Outboard Gear Oil EP 90
MUNCIE (Flexidrive)	No Texaco Product

NAME AND MODEL	TEXACO LUBRICANT RECOMMENDED (NORMAL OPERATION)
OMC (Outboard Marine)	
1977 and prior models	
Electric shift gearcase	
Upper gear housing only	Meropa 150
Lower gear case only	Texamatic Fluid
1978 and later models	
Mechanical shift gear case	
Upper gear housing and lower gear case	Meropa 150
PERKINS Z Drive	Multigear Lubricant EP 80W-90
RANGER (See Marine Drive Systems)	
SHARK-O-MATIC (West Bend)	Outboard Gear Oil EP 90
TURBO MARINE (Cummins Northwest Industrial)	Texamatic Fluid
UNIVERSAL (Sabre V-6 and Super V-6)	Multigear Lubricant EP 80W-90
VOLVO PENTA	
Mod. 100A	Multigear Lubricant EP 80W-90
Mod. 100B, 100S	Havoline Super Premium 10W-40
Mod. 200 up to Ser. 219752	Multigear Lubricant EP 80W-90
Mod. 200 after Ser. 219752	Havoline Super Premium 10W-40
Mod. 250, 270, 280	Havoline Super Premium 10W-40
Mod. 270T, 280T, (Hyd. System)	Texamatic Fluid
Mod. 750 (Dr. & Hyd. System)	Ursa Super Plus
Below 14°F	SAE 10W
14°F-68°F	SAE 20-20W
Above 68°F	SAE 30
Mod. MS, MSB	Same oil as engine

*During warranty period follow manufacturer's recommendations.

Table 12.6

Oil-Fuel Mixtures—Mixing Procedure

Correct mixture ratios for engines using oil-fuel blends are very important to assure proper engine operation and protection along with maximum economy of both fuel and oil. The ratios of oil to gasoline shown in the accompanying table are those recommended by the various manufacturers for their individual makes and models. They are for average conditions of use, and it is recommended for special situations (racing, for example) that the engineering department of the outboard engine manufacturer be consulted.

Outboard engine manufacturers caution against adding any special chemicals or compounds to gasoline in an attempt to secure greater power output.

Correct mixture ratios also depend on thorough blending of the oil and gasoline portions. First, measure the ingredients accurately; next, put a small amount of the fuel in the mixing can or tank, and then add the lubricating oil and the remainder of the gasoline. Shake well, or otherwise agitate to assure thorough mixing.

Gasoline-to-Oil Ratio Table

		PINTS WHEN APPLIED TO				
PINTS OF OIL PER GAL.	ACTUAL RATIO	2 GALLON	3 GALLON	4 GALLON	5 GALLON	6 GALLON
$1/12$	96:1	$1/6$	$1/4$	$1/3$	$5/12$	$1/2$
$1/6$	48:1	$1/3$	$1/2$	$2/3$	$5/6$	1
$1/5$	40:1	$2/5$	$3/5$	$4/5$	1	$1\frac{1}{5}$
$1/3$	24:1	$2/3$	1	$1\frac{1}{3}$	$1\frac{2}{3}$	2
$3/8$	21:1	$3/4$	$1\frac{1}{8}$	$1\frac{1}{2}$	$1\frac{7}{8}$	$2\frac{1}{4}$
$1/2$	16:1	1	$1\frac{1}{2}$	2	$2\frac{1}{2}$	3
$3/4$	11:1	$1\frac{1}{2}$	$2\frac{1}{4}$	3	$3\frac{3}{4}$	$4\frac{1}{2}$

NOTE: In some cases, it may be more convenient to mix by the ounce rather than by the pint. Graduations on the container are given in both pints and ounces. There are sixteen fluid ounces to the pint.

INBOARD ENGINE MAINTENANCE

Spark plugs: Remove. Crank engine to clear cylinders of excess oil. Clean and gap plugs or, preferably, replace them.

Ignition wiring: Inspect. Replace if insulation is cracked or chafed. Tighten all connections. Wipe with antimoisture dielectric spray.

Distributor Cap: Remove, clean, inspect for chips or cracks. Replace unless perfect, unblemished. Wipe with dielectric spray.

Distributor rotor: Remove and inspect for cracks or burning. Replace unless perfect. Wipe with dielectric spray.

Distributor points: Inspect. Replace if pitted. Adjust to specification using a dwell meter if possible. Readjust after first ten hours.

Ignition timing: Adjust to spec after points are properly set. Use a timing light if possible.

Coil: Snug up mounting hardware and connections. Wipe down with dielectric spray.

Ignition switch: Test all connections. Looseness here is a frequent cause of unexplained engine miss.

Condenser: Check connections and mounting hardware.

Fuel tank: Inspect mountings for security. Pour in several cans of gum-dissolving solvent to fight tar, which may have formed.

Vents: Uncover and blow clear. Inspect for integrity to tank and that vent spills overboard.

Fuel valves: Open all.

Fuel lines: Inspect all connections for leaks. Be sure lines are secure and tight.

Fuel pump: Snug up mounting-cap screws. Drain and clean filter if pump has one. Replace the pump (or rebuild) if it's four seasons old or older.

Filter: Drain. Replace the element.

Flame arrester: Remove and clean thoroughly.

Carburetor: Send it to the shop for rebuild if it gave trouble last season. Otherwise, tighten hold-down nuts, check connections, and, if possible, pour a few ounces of gasoline into the float bowl vent tube as a prestart prime. Careful with the gas!

Distributor: Put a few drops of oil on the felt under the rotor. If there's an oil cup on the distributor body, squirt in a few drops of engine oil.

Generator: Look for oil cups. Put several drops of oil in cups that are found.

Crankcase: Warm the engine, change the oil.

Oil filter: Replace with fresh element.

Transmission: Warm the engine. Change the transmission lubricant.

Block and Head: Wipe the entire engine down with rust-proofing oil.

Drain plugs, cocks: Replace those removed for lay-up. Close all cocks.

Hoses: Carefully inspect. Replace cracked and rotten-looking hoses.

Clamps: Look for rusty clamps. Replace "tired" ones with good stainless-steel ones. Tighten all.

Water pump: Install a new drive V-belt. Readjust this belt after first hour or two of operation. If possible, hand prime pump before first start-up.

Sea cocks: Test for functioning. Lubricate if applicable. Test hose connections.

Transom pipe: Remove plugs or tape from outlet.

Fittings: Replace rusted clamps, preferably using double clamps. Inspect entire system for gas-tight integrity.

Cooling: Immediately after the first start-up, see that the cooling water pump is functioning.

Instruments: Watch the "pins" to see that there is oil pressure, that the generator is charging, and that engine temperature settles at the correct point.

POWER TRAIN MAINTENANCE

Transmission: Warm the transmission by running the engine; then change the lubricant. Follow manufacturer's specs as to grade of oil.

Alignment: Align the engine/transmission assembly exactly with the propeller shaft *after* the boat has been afloat several days.

Outdrive: Service and lubricate the outdrive lower unit according to specs.

Propeller: Inspect the prop minutely. If it is even slightly nicked or dented, send it to the shop for rework and balancing.

Prop shaft: Inspect the shaft, looking for bends or scoring.

Struts: Physically shake the prop-shaft struts, making sure they are secure and tight to the hull.

Strut bearings: Shake the prop shaft in the strut bearings, seeking excess looseness. Some clearance is OK. If you're in doubt, get expert opinion.

Prop replacement: Mount prop hub on taper snugly; don't let it ride up on the key and get off center.

Shaft log: Be sure the shaft log is well bedded to the hull and secured to the boat's bottom. Tighten the fastenings; they often loosen as the bedding compresses.

Stuffing Box: If the box dribbles, tighten the gland nuts slightly. Don't overdo.

Zincs: Install fresh new protective zinc anodes on the struts and prop shaft.

CONTROLS MAINTENANCE

Steering gear: Test the control for full starboard and port rudder (or outboard swing). Clear possible obstructions.

Steering lubrication: Oil or grease all working parts of the steering mechanism.

Throttle adjustment: Definitely see that when the hand lever is closed (idle) the throttle stop is against the adjusting screw on the carburetor. Also see that the throttle opens wide as required for full-bore operation.

Throttle lubrication: Work oil or thin grease through the throttle linkage and cable until action is smooth and free.

Throttle friction: Adjust the friction device in the throttle quadrant, if necessary, to prevent the throttle from creeping.

Choke: Lubricate the choke control and adjust as described for the throttle. Be *sure* choke opens wide.

Clutch: Disconnect from clutch lever on transmission. Work the control, making sure there is adequate travel for forward and reverse. Lubricate.

Trim: If the boat has trim tabs, lubricate and adjust the controls according to specs.

Zinc: Install a fresh new zinc protective anode on the rudder, outdrive, or outboard, as applicable.

Table 12.7

INBOARD ENGINE MAINTENANCE LOG

☐ STARBOARD ENGINE ☐ PORT ENGINE

DATE
ENGINE HOURS

Column headers (repeated groups): Inspect | Adjust | Lubricate | Replace

IGNITION SYSTEM	Spark Plugs
	H. T. Wiring
	Distributor Cap
	Points / Rotor
	Condenser
	Coil
	Switch(s)
	Alternator / Gen.
FUEL SYSTEM	Filler Pipes & Cap
	Fuel Tank(s)
	Shut-off Valve(s)
	Lines
	Pump(s)
	Filter(s)
	Carburetor
	Flame Arrestors
COOLING SYSTEM	Water Pump (Fresh)
	Water Pump (Sea)
	Hoses and Clamps
	V Belt(s)
	Water Jackets
	Expansion Tank
	Heat Exchanger
	Fresh Water Coolant
	Thermostat Control
	Temperature Gauge
LUBRICATION	Engine Oil Level
	Oil Pressure Gauge
	Transmission Fluid
	Oil Filter(s)
	Oil Cooler
STARTER	Battery
	Switches
	Solenoid
	Cables
	Connectors
CONTROLS	

Table 12.8

Inboard Engine Troubleshooting

How to use this chart: (1) find below situation matching trouble; (2) note treatment key; (3) refer to treatment in Table 12.9 in order of key.

BREAKDOWN	TREATMENT
Motor stops suddenly after period of proper operation.	A, E, B, C, D, K, F
Motor stops suddenly, no spark to spark plugs.	A, E, G
Motor stops, has good spark, won't restart.	A, D, J, K, S
Motor stops, restarts when cool, stops again when hot.	F
Motor stops suddenly, will not turn through full revolution. (Do not restart until after inspection and repair.)	Q
Motor stops "frying hot," won't turn over when cool.	OVERHAUL
Motor stops after period of rough, uneven operation.	A, B, C, D, E, G, H, I, S
Motor overheats before stopping, coolant OK. (Restart only when it has cooled.)	H, L, I
Motor stops hot, low coolant or no coolant flow. (Restart only when it has cooled.)	A, C, LL, L, M
Motor runs by spurts, stops, fuel filters clean.	D, E, H, I, J
Motor runs by spurts, stops, water in fuel filters.	S, R
*Motor stops with heavy black smoke from exhaust pipe.	O
*Motor stops with loud clatter.	A, Z, ZZ, P, Q

MALFUNCTIONS	TREATMENT
Motor misses, gallops, spits, backfires, loses power.	A, R, E, I, S, J
Motor runs rough, idles poorly, overheats. (Do not run at full power until overheating is corrected.)	L, H, I, J
Motor starts hard, especially in cold weather.	G, I, E, Y, GG
Motor "pops" and "pings" in exhaust pipe at all speeds, loss of power and compression, hard starting.	Y, Z
**Lube oil level rises, oil looks and feels gummy.	M
**Lube oil level rises, oil feels very thin.	N
Motor idles poorly, indicates ice in carburetor throat, loses top rpm's after a change in brand or type of fuel.	V
Motor "pings" at full load, starts hard.	H, V
Starter motor spins without engaging flywheel gear.	T
Starter motor turns engine, engine won't operate.	D, E, F, H, I, K
Starter motor jams against flywheel gear, won't turn.	U
Solenoid clicks when starter button is pushed. Battery up.	
**Motor runs rough, noisy, one or more cylinders not giving power as shown by shorting spark plugs with insulated screwdriver.	P
**Motor runs rough, loses power, water on spark plug electrodes.	W

MALFUNCTIONS	TREATMENT
**Hot water in the bilges.	X
Motor "eats" lube oil, low compression and power.	Z, B
**Motor runs with thumping or knocking noise.	ZZ

---

*Restart and operate motor before prescribed repairs only in an emergency.

**Continue to operate motor at low power only in emergency before correcting condition.

IMPORTANT! Always check your engine manual for proper repair and adjustment procedures!

DANGER! Always mop up spilled fuel and ventilate engine compartment before restarting a marine engine!

SAFETY FIRST! Disconnect and cover batteries before working on starter, generator, or where tools can fall on terminals, causing electrical short!

Table 12.9

Inboard Engine Treatment

KEY

A   Inspect motor for obvious damage, excessive heat, leaking fuel, oil or coolant, loose or disconnected wires, control parts, fuel and water lines.

B   Check lube oil level and quality on dip stick, add oil if needed, if level too high, refer to treatments M and N.

C   Check for leaks in coolant system, leaky pump shaft seal, defective circulating pump. Check exhaust cooling water.

KEY

D   Check to see if fuel tank is empty or shut off.

E   Check ignition system for: loose, broken or disconnected wires; cracked distributor cap; broken breaker-point spring; shorted condenser, disconnected battery "hot" line; broken rotor; ignition switch "off."

F   Replace defective ignition coil that shorts out when hot.

G   Battery voltage low. Bad cell, generator not charging,

generator not big enough to carry electrical load, poor battery hot and ground connections.

GG Change to lighter lubrication oil for cold weather operation.

H *Spark timing incorrect; have readjusted with timing light.

I *Ignition points burned and/or spark plug electrodes eroded. Replace, adjust. Inspect high-tension ignition wires for insulation breaks.

J *Look for and repair break or leak in fuel line.

K *Replace fuel pump and/or pump diaphragm.

L *Replace worn or broken circulating pump impellers, check thermostat.

LL Raw (sea) water suction plugged or shut off. Remove obstruction.

M *Coolant leaking into lube oil in base. Check for internal gasket leaks, cracked head or block; do not operate until overhauled.

N *Fuel leaking into oil in crank case. Use treatment K.

O Carburetor needle valve stuck open. STOP MOTOR INSTANTLY if still running. Drain raw gas from carburetor throat, mop up spilled fuel. Ventilate motor compartment thoroughly. Reseat valve by tapping carburetor lightly on side with hammer. Have mechanic replace valve as soon as possible.

P *Valve springs broken, motor probably running too cold. Overhaul.

Q *Broken-off valve head is on top of piston, hits cylinder head at top of piston stroke. Remove cylinder head, replace broken valve, look for further internal damage.

R *Dirt or water in carburetor jets and bowl. Remove, clean, readjust.

S Clean fuel filter more often. Remove water and dirt from fuel tank.

T *Disconnect battery, remove starter, clean drive shaft with kerosene and steel wool, look for and replace broken Bendix spring.

---

*Should be done by a competent mechanic familiar with your model of motor.

u   Starter gear is jammed against flywheel gear teeth. Disconnect battery, loosen starter holding bolts until starter is free from block, turn motor over in reverse rotation with wrench applied to V-belt wheel or shaft at front end to unjam gears. Tighten starter bolts, reconnect battery.

v   Fuel octane rating wrong for your motor. Change to proper fuel.

w   *Coolant is leaking into intake manifold or cylinders.

Remove head, look for leaky gasket or crack in head or motor block. Have repaired before operating.

x   Exhaust pipe or hot raw water discharge is leaking into bilges. Repair.

Y   *Exhaust valves burned. Motor needs overhaul.

z   *Worn or broken piston rings and/or worn valve guides. Overhaul.

zz *Burned main or connecting rod bearings. Overhaul.

Basic Repair Tools

Ignition	Mechanical	Special
Ignition wrench set	Combination box,	Oil squirt gun
Ignition point file	end wrenches	Hand oil-pan pump
Feeler gauge	Stillson and monkey	Hydrometer
Low-voltage test bulb	wrenches	Flashlight, troublelight
Neon test bulb	Set of Allen	
Spark plug wrench	wrenches	
Timing light	Vise grip and regular	
	pliers	
	Machinist's hammer	
	Hack saw and blades	
	Screwdriver set	
	Jackknife	
	Ratchet sockets, extension bar	

MAINTENANCE

Basic Spare Parts

Ignition	Mechanical	Fluid, etc.
2 sets breaker points	Pump impellers, shaft seals	Extra lubricating oil
2 sets point condensers	Fuel pump or diaphragm	Pump and gear grease
1 set of spark plugs	Head valve cover gaskets	Hydraulic clutch fluid
Distributor cap, rotor	Thermostat	Penetrating oil
Ignition coil	V-belts to fit	Gasket shellac
	Flexible hose to fit	
	Assorted hose clamps	
	Mixed bolts, nuts, washers	
	Plastic and common tape	
	Sheet gasket material	
	Fuel and lube filter elements	

ELECTRICAL SYSTEM

Wiring: Inspect all visible wires. Watch for frayed insulation, poor connections. Repair or replace as required.

Main switchboard: Check every connection for tightness. Do same for distribution panels.

Bonding: Make sure that tanks, engine, all electrical accessories are bonded together with heavy wire.

Battery: Charge the battery(s) fully. Clean the posts and terminals. *Observe* polarity and connect securely.

Battery mounting: Fasten the battery tightly so pitching and rolling will not move it.

Battery cables: Provide the heaviest possible gauge battery cables to assure minimum voltage drop. Replace worn, acid-eaten cables. Replace weak clamps.

Alternator: Install a fresh V-belt and retighten this belt after an hour of operation. Check electrical connections.

Starter: Tighten cable connection and mounting-cap screws or bolts.

Lights: Test every light on the boat. Lay in a stock of replacement bulbs.

Fuses: Test every fuse on the boat. Lay in a stock of replacement fuses.

Bilge pump: Test. Be sure switch and fuse are in "hot" ungrounded side of the line.

Windshield wiper: Test. Lubricate if required. Install new blade. Check wiring. Clean commutator.

Ground plate: Trace through and be sure the ground plate is electrically tied to the bonding system and lightning protective system.

Voltage: Measure voltage drop at the terminals of accessories such as blowers. When motor is energized, voltage must not drop more than 10 percent (only 3 percent for electronic gear).

Auxiliary AC generator: Give engine same check as inboard engine. Tighten all connections.

AC system: As far as practical, inspect the wiring. See that all white wires tie to other whites, blacks to blacks, and green to green.

Electronics: Perform voltage drop checks as cited under "voltage." Increase wire conductor size where voltage sags.

MARINE PROPULSION SYSTEM LUBRICATION

The following tables for marine engine and gear system lubrication were supplied by Texaco. The products listed are for normal operating temperatures. It should be remembered that SAE numbers are viscosity limits only, and for cold-weather operation, the next lower viscosity grade should be used. In cases of very high temperatures and loads, it may be necessary to use the next higher viscosity grade.

Recommendations are also based on the assumption that engine speeds and loads are normal and that engines are in good mechanical condition. Mechanical faults, such as worn pistons and bearings, cannot be corrected with oil, although frequently the use of a heavier grade will offer temporary relief. In all instances, equipment manufacturer's recommendations supplied at the time of purchase, or up-dated by manufacturers' bulletins, should be followed.

Equivalent products of other reputable oil companies are equally suitable for each indicated application.

SAILS AND RIGGING

Sails: Sails should be washed in mild detergent and cool water by hand—and scrubbing brush.

After washing they should be inspected thoroughly for rips or tears. Stitching in Dacron sails is the point of most weakness so inspect each seam with care. Most experienced sailors make a practice of having their sailmaker examine and restitch each sail as needed every year. It is cheap and worth every penny. Home repairs are possible but usually not as satisfactory.

Spars: Anodized spars can be merely washed. Nonanodized spars should be cleaned up with an abrasive (scouring powder, scouring pads, or fine wet sandpaper) and then coated with one of the clear coatings formulated for this purpose. If you want a really shiny spar, buff with rubbing compound before coating. While you're cleaning, check spars for straightness, check fittings for looseness and defects (cracks in castings), and oil all sheaves.

Lights and Instruments: Test all circuits and replace components as needed. Better, summarily replace all bulbs.

Noise Abatement: Aluminum spars are noisy, particularly with internal halyards and wiring. Wiring can be enclosed in a plastic tube(s) or it can be seized to the after side of the spar. To do this, lay the spar aft side down, drill pairs of holes about six feet apart each side of the sail track, and seize the wires through the holes with stainless seizing wire. Finish holes with epoxy.

Standing Rigging: All standing rigging should be examined with great care. Particular attention should be paid to all swage fittings. Examine these with a magnifying device that will show any hairline cracks present. Cracked swage fittings are unreliable and should be discarded.

All hardware should be examined with a jaundiced eye. Clevis pins in particular should be replaced if they show wear, and all cotter pins should be replaced as a matter of course. Lock nuts aloft should be drilled and pinned if they haven't been already.

Running Rigging: Check for wear and chafe. Replace as indicated. Sometimes sheet life can be extended by shifting them end for end. Additionally, a long sheet with one worn section may be useful in another function requiring a shorter length. Finally, fenders always need lines.

Wire running rigging should also be examined for wear, indicated by short barbs sticking out at the point of chafe or wear. Remove damaged section, end for end the wire or replace entire wire as indicated. If flexible wire running rigging is fitted with swage fittings pay particular attention to junctions that are points of particular sensitivity. Consider replacing swage fittings with more flexible splices or Nicopress fittings.

Oil: Be liberal with the oil can throughout the rig. Shackles should snap, pole fittings should open easily, sheaves should revolve without strain, and track cars should move without having to be forced.

Tape: White rigging tape is a rigger's best friend. Everything that can possibly get near a sail should be taped to eliminate tearing. Additionally, when a wire is to be seized to another wire or to a piece of hardware (spreaders), tape the wire first, then seize it and follow with more tape. The first taping will effectively prevent slipping.

PLUMBING

Fuel System

Filler. Make sure cap assembly is secure to deck. Inspect hose, ground wire from filler cap to tank. Tighten or replace hose clamps as necessary.

Tank vent. Inspect and clean.

Tank. Inspect for leaks. Make sure hold-downs or straps are tight and secure. Check operation to tank shut-off valve. Drain, refill with fresh gasoline or diesel fuel.

Fuel lines. Inspect for cracks, abrasions, leaks at fittings.

Cooling System

Intakes. Check, tighten, replace clamshell fastenings as required. Clean clamshells, sediment screens.

Through-hull fittings, valves. Check operation. These should open and close with hand pressure alone. Clean, lubricate, replace units as necessary. Check bedding blocks and caulking.

Pumps. Clean, check packing and washers.

Hoses. Inspect; replace any that are worn, abraded, or weak. Tighten, replace clamps as necessary.

Raw (sea) water cooling. Drain and flush. Inspect for leaks.

Freshwater cooling. Drain and flush raw water side of system. Drain, flush, and refill freshwater side. Use rust inhibitor, other additives as specified by engine or cooling system manufacturer. Check intake, screens of keel coolers; disassemble if necessary to clear obstructions in keel cooler unit.

Exhaust System

Transom flanges. Inspect fastenings; replace as necessary.

Hoses, piping. Inspect, replace if necessary. Tighten or replace clamps.

Standpipe. Inspect, clean expansion chamber.

Manifold water jackets. Inspect for leaks. Drain and flush.

Wet mufflers. Check thermostat operation, if one is present, at engine side of feed to muffler. Clean, inspect muffler. Paint with heat-resistant finish, if necessary.

Potable (Freshwater) System

Tanks. Drain, refill. Add purifying tablets as required. Check and adjust tanks hold-downs.

Hoses. Inspect, replace as required. Tighten or replace clamps as needed.

Pumps. Inspect packing, washers. Clean screens. Check float valves, polarity of connections to electrical pumps. Switches must be in "hot" wire from battery.

Heater. Clean, check operation, thermostat settings.

Vents, drains. Clean, inspect. Check through-hull fittings, valves. Seacocks and valves should open and close by hand pressure alone. Lubricate or replace units as necessary.

Toilets

Pumps. Inspect and clear joker or check valves of hand pumps. Check connections, operation of electrical units.

Hoses. Clean inside and out. Inspect, replace as necessary. Tighten or replace hose clamps as required.

Bowl. Clean. Inspect for cracks, chips. Check hold-down fastenings. Lubricate lid hinges.

Chlorinators, other chemical units. Clean, inspect; replace chlorine or other chemical according to manufacturer's specifications.

Holding tanks. Should be drained when boat is hauled. Clean and inspect for cracks, leaks, including hoses and pump-out fittings.

Through-hull fittings, seacocks, valves. Check bedding blocks and caulking. Seacocks and valves should open and close with hand pressure alone. Lubricate, replace units as required.

Miscellaneous

Clear dirt and debris from scuppers, self-bailing ducts, limber holes, and similar passages through which water must pass.

TRAILER MAINTENANCE

A well-built boat trailer should remain in excellent condition indefinitely with a minimum of maintenance. In addition to periodic inspections and lubrication, the most important ingredient is a thorough wash down after each use. Wash with soap and water, just as for your car, to remove road tars and soil.

Trailer Frame

Use a stiff wire brush to remove rust scale. Paint as necessary with a rust-inhibiting coating. Inspect and lubricate tilt lock and hinge mechanism, if trailer is so equipped. Lubricate rollers several times each season and use strips of old carpeting to replace torn or rotted bunker covers.

Winch

Inspect and lubricate winch gears, handle and lock mechanism.

Table 12.10

Load Capacity of Trailer Tires

TIRE SIZE	PLY RATING	POUNDS OF TIRE PRESSURE (MEASURED COLD)											
		30	35	40	45	50	55	60	65	70	75	80	85
4.80/4.00 × 8	2	**380**											
4.80/4.00 × 8	4	380	420	450	485	515	545	575	**600**				
5.70/5.00 × 8	4		575	625	665	**710**							
6.90/6.00 × 9	6		785	850	915	970	1030	**1080**					
6.90/6.00 × 9	8		785	850	915	970	1030	1080	1125	1175	1225	**1270**	
20 × 8.00–10	4	825	**900**										
20 × 8.00–10	6	825	900	965	1030	**1100**							
20 × 8.00–10	8	825	900	965	1030	1100	1155	1210	1270	**1325**			
20 × 8.00–10	10	825	900	965	1030	1100	1155	1210	1270	1325	1370	1420	**1475**
4.80/4.00 × 12	4	545	550	595	635	680	715	755	**790**				
5.30/4.50 × 12	4	640	700	760	810	865	**915**						
5.30/4.50 × 12	6	640	700	760	810	865	915	960	1005	1045	1090	**1135**	
6.00 × 12	4	855	935	**1010**									
6.00 × 12	6	855	935	1010	1090	1160	1230	**1290**					
6.50 × 13	6	895	980	1060	1130	1200	**1275**						

NOTE: Figures in bold face represent maximum permissible pressure.

Wipe metal cable with an oily rag to prevent rust; if cable is worn or frayed, replace with new cable. If fiber winch line is used, inspect and replace if necessary.

Springs

Wash well after each trip. Use a paint brush to coat springs with motor oil, or spray on a commercial rust preventive.

Wheel Bearings

Remove hub and grease seals and wipe axle spindle clean. Inspect bearings and bearing cups for pitting, then check grease seals for undue wear. Coat inside bearing with grease and put it in position. Press on the grease seal. Put additional grease on the open area of the hub and install the hub on the spindle. Grease the outer bearing and install it. Replace the nut on the spindle and tighten as far as it will go. Then back it off until the wheel spins freely. Replace the cotter pin to hold the nut in place. Replace hub caps.

Lights and Wiring

If lights have been submerged accidentally, remove glass or plastic cover, drain water, and dry insides with cloth or paper towels. If you can't remove lights and it's necessary to submerge them, cover the entire light housing with a plastic bag secured with rubber bands. It's better than no protection. Check wiring for cracks and breaks; replace as necessary. Be sure connectors are clean.

STOWAGE PLAN

Sketch location of lockers and cabinets. Label "A," "B," "C," etc., and list
contents below.

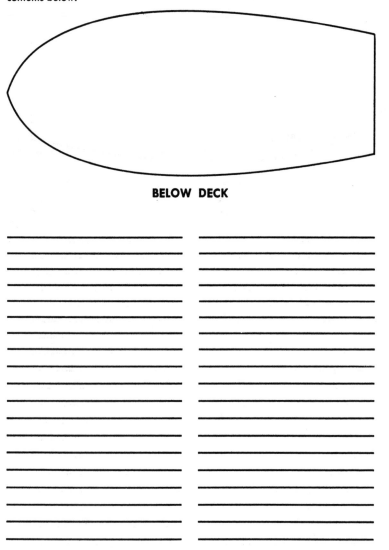

BELOW DECK

Figure 12.5

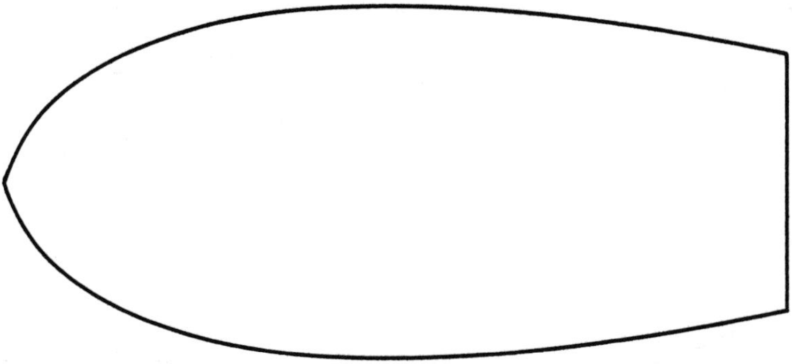

ABOVE DECK

Figure 12.6

WIRING DIAGRAMS

Sketch in location of battery, running lights, other electrical accessories, and the run of the wiring to each. Note wiring color code, and other distinguishing characteristics.

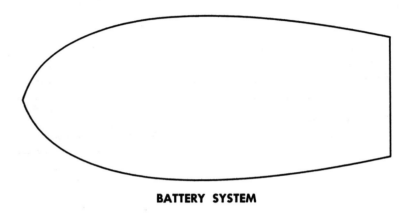

BATTERY SYSTEM

Sketch location of items served by the 110 volt AC system, location of generator, service panel, shore connectors, and run of the wiring.

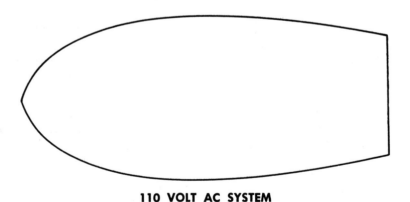

110 VOLT AC SYSTEM

Figure 12.7

Table 12.11

General Information

Boat Name_____ Manufacturer_____
Year Built_____Designer_____
Length Overall_____Waterline Length_____Beam_____
Draft_____Sail Area_____Displacement_____
State Registration Number_____
Engine(s) Make_____Horsepower_____Year_____

INSURANCE
Firm Name_____Agent Name_____
Address_____Address_____

Phone_____Phone, Office_____Home_____

BOATYARD   MECHANIC
Name_____Name_____
Address_____Address_____

Phone_____Phone, Office_____Home_____
Manager's Home Phone_____

Licensed Radio Technician   Radio Call Sign_____
Name_____Frequencies_____
Address_____ _____
Phone, Office_____Home_____ _____

NUMBERS AND SIZES
Engine(s) Make_____Serial Number(s)_____
Spark Plug Size_____Gap_____Firing Order_____
Distributor Point Gap_____
Timing Mark Location_____Setting_____
Oil Grade_____Oil Capacity_____
Transmission Lube Grade_____Capacity_____

MAINTENANCE

Table 12.12

ELECTRONIC EQUIPMENT
Radiotelephone Make_____Serial Number_____
Radio Direction Finder Make_____Serial Number_____
Depth Indicator Make_____Serial Number_____
Other Electronic Gear
    Make—Item_____Serial Number_____
    Make—Item_____Serial Number_____
    Make—Item_____Serial Number_____
FRESHWATER COOLING SYSTEM CAPACITY_____

SAIL INVENTORY

SAIL	MAKER	YEAR	REMARKS

BULB SIZES
Running Lights_____Masthead_____
    Starboard*_____Stern_____
    Port_____Others_____
Cabin Light(s)_____ _____
_____ _____
Searchlight_____
Instrument Panel_____
Others_____
FUSES, CIRCUIT BREAKER SIZES (Amps)
Main_____ Radiotelephone_____
Running Lights_____ Appliances_____
General Lighting_____ _____
Receptacle Outlets_____ _____
Bilge Pump_____ Other Electronic Gear_____
_____
_____

*Starboard light usually requires brighter bulb than port light to meet United States Coast Guard visibility requirements.